'Well worth reading and full of valuable insights that will make this volume of use to students and scholars alike.' – **Michele Stepto**, *Yale University, USA*

'An authoritative collection of essays which together offer a wide range of critical approaches to a substantial proportion of Dahl's work.' – **Elizabeth Thiel**, *Roehampton University, UK*

Roald Dahl is one of the world's best-loved authors. More than twenty years after his death, his books are still highly popular with children and have inspired numerous feature films – yet he remains a controversial figure.

This volume, the first collection of academic essays ever to be devoted to Dahl's work, brings together a team of well-known scholars of children's literature to explore the man, his books for children and his complex attitudes towards various key subjects. Including essays on education, crime, Dahl's humour, his long-term collaboration with the artist Quentin Blake, and film adaptations, this fascinating collection offers a unique insight into the writer and his world.

Introduction by Catherine Butler. Essays by: Ann Alston, Peter Hunt, Beverley Pennell, Pat Pinsent, June Pulliam, David Rudd, Carole Scott, Jackie E. Stallcup, Deborah Thacker, Heather Worthington.

Ann Alston and Catherine Butler are both Senior Lecturers in English at the University of the West of England, Bristol, UK, where they specialise in children's literature.

This latest series of *New Casebooks* consists of brand new critical essays specially commissioned to provide students with fresh thinking about key texts and writers. Like the original series, the volumes embrace a range of approaches designed to illuminate the rich interchange between critical theory and critical practice.

New Casebooks
Collections of all new critical essays

CHILDREN'S LITERATURE

ROBERT CORMIER
Edited by Adrienne E. Gavin

ROALD DAHL
Edited by Ann Alston & Catherine Butler

C. S. LEWIS: *THE CHRONICLES OF NARNIA*
Edited by Michelle Ann Abate & Lance Weldy

J. K. ROWLING: *HARRY POTTER*
Edited by Cynthia J. Hallett & Peggy J. Huey

FURTHER TITLES ARE CURRENTLY IN PREPARATION

For a full list of published titles in the past format of the New Casebooks
series, visit the series page at www.palgrave.com

New Casebooks Series

Series Standing Order
ISBN 978–0–333–71702–8 hardcover
ISBN 978–0–333–69345–2 paperback
(Outside North America only)

You can receive future titles in this series as they are published by placing a
standing order. Please contact your bookseller or, in case of difficulty, write
to us at the address below with your name and address, the title of the series
and the ISBN quoted above.

Customer Services Department, Macmillan Distribution Ltd Houndmills,
Basingstoke, Hampshire RG21 6XS, England

New Casebooks

ROALD DAHL

Edited by

ANN ALSTON & CATHERINE BUTLER

palgrave
macmillan

First published 2012 by
PALGRAVE MACMILLAN

Palgrave Macmillan in the UK is an imprint of Macmillan Publishers Limited, registered in England, company number 785998, of Houndmills, Basingstoke, Hampshire RG21 6XS.

Palgrave Macmillan in the US is a division of St Martin's Press LLC, 175 Fifth Avenue, New York, NY 10010.

Palgrave Macmillan is the global academic imprint of the above companies and has companies and representatives throughout the world.

Palgrave® and Macmillan® are registered trademarks in the United States, the United Kingdom, Europe and other countries.

ISBN 978–0–230–28360–2   hardback
ISBN 978–0–230–28361–9   paperback

This book is printed on paper suitable for recycling and made from fully managed and sustained forest sources. Logging, pulping and manufacturing processes are expected to conform to the environmental regulations of the country of origin.

A catalogue record for this book is available from the British Library.

A catalog record for this book is available from the Library of Congress.

10 9 8 7 6 5 4 3 2 1
21 20 19 18 17 16 15 14 13 12

Printed and bound in China

Contents

Contents

Series Editor's Preface

Welcome to the latest series of New Casebooks.

Each volume now presents brand new essays specially written for university and other students. Like the original series, the new-look New Casebooks embrace a range of recent critical approaches to the debates and issues that characterize the current discussion of literature.

Each editor has been asked to commission a sequence of original essays which will introduce the reader to the innovative critical approaches to the text or texts being discussed in the collection. The intention is to illuminate the rich interchange between critical theory and critical practice that today underpins so much writing about literature.

Editors have also been asked to supply an introduction to each volume that sets the scene for the essays that follow, together with a list of further reading which will enable readers to follow up issues raised by the essays in the collection.

The purpose of this new-look series, then, is to provide students with fresh thinking about key texts and writers while encouraging them to extend their own ideas and responses to the texts they are studying.

Martin Coyle

Notes on Contributors

Ann Alston lectures at the University of the West of England, Bristol, where she specialises in children's literature. Her work covers nineteenth- and twentieth-century children's literature and has, to date, focused more specifically on the construction of the family. Ann Alston is the author of *The History of the Family in English Children's Literature* (Routledge, 2008), and has written articles on food, spaces and the family which have been published in various collections of essays and journals. Alongside a continued interest in nineteenth-century concepts of the family with regard to authors such as Charlotte Yonge she is currently researching aspects of Welsh children's literature.

Catherine Butler is Associate Professor of English at the University of the West of England. Her critical work has appeared in, amongst other places, *Children's Literature in Education* and *Children's Literature Association Quarterly*, and has been honored with a ChLA Article Honor Award, and a Mythopoeic Scholarship Award (for *Four British Fantasists* (Scarecrow/ChLA, 2006)). Catherine was the editor of *Teaching Children's Fiction* (Palgrave, 2006), and is the author with Hallie O'Donovan of *Reading History in Children's Books* (Palgrave, 2012). Catherine has so far produced six novels for children and teenagers, as well as some shorter works. The latest of these, *Hand of Blood*, was published by Barrington Stoke in 2009.

Peter Hunt was the first specialist in Children's Literature to be appointed Professor of English in a British University (Cardiff). He has written or edited 24 books (and over 130 articles) on the subject, including *Children's Literature: Critical Concepts in Literary and Cultural Studies* (Routledge, 2006), the *York Notes Companion to Children's Literature* (with Lucy Pearson, Penguin, 2011), and editions of *Alice's Adventures in Wonderland, The Wind in the Willows, Treasure Island* and *The Secret Garden* (Oxford University Press's World's Classics). In 2003 he was awarded the Brothers Grimm Award for services to children's literature from the International Institute for Children's Literature, Osaka. He is currently Visiting Professor at Newcastle University.

Beverley Pennell lectures in English Curriculum and Children's Literature and Film, Charles Sturt University, Australia. Her publications include scholarly articles and academic book chapters mainly in the field of children's literature, particularly Australian children's literature. Beverley was a contributor to, and assistant editor of, John Stephens's *Ways of Being Male* (Routledge, 2002), which was awarded the Honour Book Award by the International Research Society for Children's Literature in 2003. Beverley's current research interests in children's literature concern colonial and post-colonial representations of nature and the environment in Australian children's novels. In English Curriculum, she is researching the problems and possibilities of the Education for Sustainability initiative in pre-service teacher education.

Pat Pinsent is Senior Research Fellow in the National Centre for Research in Children's Literature at Roehampton University London. Her 15 published books include *The Power of the Page: Children's Books and Their Readers* (David Fulton Publishers, 1993), *Children's Literature and the Politics of Equality* (David Fulton Publishers, 1997), and edited compilations concerning children's literature. She has published numerous articles both on children's literature and on seventeenth-century poetry. Her current research investigates the relationship between children's literature and spirituality/religion. She edits *The Journal of Children's Literature Studies*, *IBBYLink*, the journal of the British Section of the International Board on Books for Young People, and *Network*, a journal for women interested in spirituality, theology, ministry and liturgy.

June Pulliam teaches courses in Young Adult literature and horror fiction at Louisiana State University. Her previous publications include articles about Dahl's *Charlie and the Chocolate Factory* (2007), Stephenie Meyer's Twilight Saga (2011), George A. Romero's *Land of the Dead* (2010), and the figure of the female werewolf in Young Adult fiction (2012). She is the co-author (with Anthony Fonseca) of *Hooked on Horror: A Guide to Reading Interests in the Genre*, Volumes 1–3 (Libraries Unlimited, 1999, 2003, 2009) and *Read On … A Guide to Horror Fiction* (Libraries Unlimited, 2006) and of the journal *Dead Reckonings: A Review Magazine for the Horror Field*.

David Rudd is Professor of Children's Literature at the University of Bolton, where he runs an MA in Children's Literature and Culture. He has published two monographs on children's literature – one an analysis of Roald Dahl's *The Twits* and children's responses to it (*A Communication Studies Approach to Children's Literature*, Perpetuity Press, 1992), the second, a similar look at the enduring popularity of Enid Blyton (*Enid Blyton and the Mystery of Children's Literature*, xii Notes on Contributors

Palgrave Macmillan, 2000) – plus about a hundred articles (most recently on Neil Gaiman, Shaun Tan and Diana Wynne Jones). In 2010 he edited *The Routledge Companion to Children's Literature* (Routledge, 2010). He is also an editor of the international journal, *Children's Literature in Education*.

Carole Scott is Professor Emeritus of English and former Dean of Undergraduate Studies at San Diego State University, California, and is a founding member of its National Center for the Study of Children's Literature. She has served on the boards of the Children's Literature Association (ChLA) International Research Society for Children's Literature (IRSCL), and as Senior Scholar for the Nordic Children's Literature Network (NorChiLNet). She is co-author with Maria Nikolajeva of *How Picturebooks Work* (Garland, 2001), has shared editorial responsibility with Muriel Lenz for *His Dark Materials Illuminated* (Wayne State University Press, 2005), and writes and reviews for a variety of children's literature journals, essay collections and books.

Jackie E. Stallcup is Chair of the Department of English at California State University, Northridge, where she teaches graduate and undergraduate courses in children's and adolescent literature. She has published essays on a variety of topics, including child-rearing theory in L. M. Montgomery's novels; the politics of adapting *Gulliver's Travels* for children; and economic issues in the Elsie Dinsmore series. Two of her essays won the Children's Literature Association Article of the Year award: 'Power, Fear, and Children's Books' in 2002 and '"The Feast of Misrule": *Captain Underpants*, Satire, and the Literary Establishment' in 2008. She is currently working on a book-length project on child-rearing experts and female novelists.

Deborah Cogan Thacker is Deputy Head of Department (Humanities) at the University of Gloucestershire and Course Leader for the interdisciplinary MA The Child: Literature, Language and History. She is co-author (with Professor Jean Webb) of *Introducing Children's Literature: From Romanticism to Postmodernism* (Routledge, 2002) in addition to a range of articles and chapters on theoretical approaches to children's literature and the representation of child language in literature. Two of her articles, originally published in *The Lion and the Unicorn*, have been reprinted in *Children's Literature: Critical Concepts in Literary and Cultural Studies*, edited by Peter Hunt (Routledge, 2006). She is a member of IRSCL and ChLA.

Heather Worthington is Senior Lecturer in English Literature at Cardiff University, where she teaches nineteenth- and twentieth-century crime fiction and children's literature. She is the author of *The Rise of the Detective in Early Nineteenth-Century Popular Fiction* (Palgrave, 2005) and *Key Concepts in Crime Fiction* (Palgrave, 2011) and has published articles on the work of T. H. White, Edward Bulwer Lytton and G. K. Chesterton and on forensics in early crime narratives. She has contributed entries to *A Companion to Crime Fiction* (Wiley-Blackwell, 2010) and *The Oxford History of the Novel in English, Vol. 3: The Nineteenth-Century Novel 1820–1880* (Oxford University Press, 2011).

Introduction

Catherine Butler

When Roald Dahl died in 1990 he was indisputably the most popular and best-known British children's writer of his day. In a purely quantitative sense, his dominance is easy to demonstrate: in a survey of favourite books carried by the *Young Telegraph* section of the *Telegraph* newspaper in October 1993, for example, '8 of the top 10 titles, including all of the top 5', were written by Dahl. Three years later, the National Centre for Research in Children's Literature (NCRCL) at Roehampton surveyed 9,000 school pupils about their reading habits: Dahl accounted for the top six titles for 7- to 11-year-olds, and six out of the top ten for those aged 11 to 16.[1] Nor was his popularity confined to Britain. He broke into the American market even before the UK one, and his first books for children were originally published in the USA. It was in the United States, too, that he found early big-screen success, with Mel Stuart's *Willy Wonka and the Chocolate Factory* (1971).

Since those surveys of the 1990s J. K. Rowling's success has dwarfed even that of Dahl, although as late as 2000 Dahl still topped a World Book Day survey to find Britain's favourite author (polling 4.5% of the votes to Rowling's 3.5%),[2] and today he maintains sales that would by any other measure be spectacular. At the last count, Dahl's books were available in 54 languages, from Afrikaans to Welsh, with combined sales of approximately 100 million worldwide.[3] When the NCRCL conducted a second study in 2005, he remained as one of the top three authors for children in both the Key Stage 2 (aged 7–11) and Key Stages 3–4 (aged 11–16) groups, alongside Rowling and Jacqueline Wilson.[4] The Roald Dahl Museum and Story Centre, an institution with no parallel in Britain, continues to thrive, and Dahl remains a staple of classrooms and of children's bookshelves in Britain and across the world.

Dahl was not only popular and prolific: he was (and remains) controversial. His books have been widely praised, but they have also been criticised as vulgar, meretricious, racist, misogynistic, and as lacking in nutrition as the sugary confections that figure so large within their covers. His defenders have answered these criticisms in

various ways. They point to his wordplay as a mark of technical innovation; or defend his characterisation and plots as drawing on such
stylised forms as cartoons or on folk tale traditions that have always
dealt vividly in violence and moral extremes. At the very least, they
argue, he has got children reading, with reluctant male readers in
particular finding that Dahl's humour and plot-driven stories satisfy
them as relatively little other fiction does.

Considering Dahl's importance and enduring international popularity as a writer, and the size and controversial nature of his output,
probably the most striking thing about academic criticism of his
work is that there is so little of it. His life is better served: there are
two full-length biographies, by Jeremy Treglown (1994) and Donald
Sturrock (2010), with a third by Michael Rosen due out in 2012.[5]
However, since Mark West's short critical study published two years
after Dahl's death there has been no monograph or collection of critical essays devoted to him.[6] Even the haul of individual articles and
book chapters is relatively light, certainly by comparison with authors
of comparable status; and although some of the existing criticism is
excellent it has tended to cluster around a relatively small number of
subjects, with Dahl's suitability as a writer for children, the relationship between his life and work, and his status as a 'phenomenon' all
being familiar topics. Dahl is a writer who tends to polarise opinion,
dividing critics into detractors and defenders. It seems that the tools
developed for the literary criticism of children's fiction have had relatively little traction on his books, and in their place discussions tend
to collapse into binary questions about whether he is a good writer
or a bad one, honest or dishonest, authoritarian or subversive, moral
or immoral. The present volume is in part an attempt to redress this
situation, and to seed what we hope will be renewed critical discussion of Dahl in the future.

The question of controversy cannot, of course, be sidestepped.
Dahl is perhaps unique in terms of the concentrated dislike displayed
by his critics. Eleanor Cameron, David Rees and Michele Landsberg,
amongst others, have seen in Dahl's books a celebration of vulgarity, racism, sexism and violence, and these criticisms often appear to
extend beyond the texts into ad hominem attacks on Dahl's own
character and motives. Dahl was equally forthright in his own defence,
calling Cameron's criticisms 'insensitive and monstrous' in their famous
Horn Book exchange of the early 1970s.[7] Many of the criticisms of
Dahl are discussed at greater length elsewhere in this volume – for
example, in Beverley Pennell's essay on Dahl and feminism, and Heather
Worthington's discussion of violence in his novels. Here it may, however,

be appropriate to broach the question of Dahl's treatment of race, since it finds a parallel in many other areas of controversy.

There is little doubt that Dahl shared the casual racism of many of his generation and background. Notoriously, his depiction of the Oompa-Loompas in *Charlie and the Chocolate Factory* (1964) (as African pygmies delighted to be taken from their home and set to work in Willy Wonka's factory in exchange for cacao beans) was altered after complaints from the NAACP (National Association for the Advancement of Colored People) about the early editions of that book. Obviously insulting as Dahl's portrayal appears today, however, it is significant that until those complaints its offensiveness seems to have escaped not only Dahl and his publishers but all the book's (white) reviewers – an indication not that racism was absent but that it was so ubiquitous as to be effectively invisible. Donald Sturrock reports that Dahl had originally intended the book's hero, Charlie Bucket, to be a black child,[8] and it seems unlikely that Dahl's depiction was the result of a conscious intent to demean black people, but his easy resort to stereotype is still telling.

More insidious perhaps than any specific slur is Dahl's habitual adoption of a kind of saloon-bar rhetoric which works to put readers in an affective arm lock, conscripting them to the views of the narrator in a way that can feel coercive. Jonathon Culley has convincingly analysed *The Twits* (1980) in these terms. That text begins with a passage that inculcates suspicion against men with beards:

> *What* a lot of hairy-faced men there are around nowadays.
> When a man grows hair all over his face it is impossible to tell what he really looks like.
> Perhaps that's why he does it. He'd rather you didn't know.
> Then there's the problem of washing.
> When the very hairy ones wash their faces, it must be as big a job as when you or I wash the hair on our heads.
> So what I want to know is this. How often do all these hairy-faced men wash their faces? […]
> I don't know. But next time you see a man with a hairy face (which will probably be as soon as you step out on to the street) maybe you will look at him more closely and start wondering about some of these things.[9]

As Culley notes, the structure of Dahl's text uncannily echoes that of some racist and other prejudiced discourses:

> Dahl idly muses on the frequency of men with facial hair. Why do they have facial hair? Is it a cover-up? Then he introduces one almost as an

example, as though this example will answer our musings. He elaborates
on Mr. Twit, on his eating habits, the state of his beard, and ends with a
statement of personality. There is no explicit connection. We are never
told he is horrid because he is hairy. It is, however, heavily implied by the
structure of the narrative.[10]

To this analysis there is an obvious riposte, which is that, however
much Dahl may in fact have disliked beards (and he seems to have
done so quite intensely),[11] he is here parodying his own intoler-
ance by presenting it in absurdly inflated terms rather than seriously trying to incite childhood mistrust of the hirsute. Similarly,
when he mischievously suggests in *The Witches* that 'even ... your
lovely school-teacher who is reading these words to you at this very
moment' may be a witch,[12] it is in the service of humour and the
ephemeral 'making-strange' of an everyday school situation, rather
than misogyny. However, the 'I'm only joking' defence is also the
familiar redoubt of challenged prejudice, and can even constitute a
kind of counter-attack on critics reluctant to be thought lacking in
humour. As so often with Dahl, pinning the text down (or the author
through the text) is no easy task.

Dahl's first two children's books, *James and the Giant Peach* (1961) and
Charlie and the Chocolate Factory, are in some ways atypical of his work
as a whole, which usually centres on situations in which the powerless
and oppressed defeat their oppressors (although that is an overly-simple
formula, to which we shall return). This is not the case in either of
these early books, at least once the atrocious Aunts Sponge and Spiker
are killed by the giant peach, which happens quite early in *James*. Both
nevertheless present us with familiar story types: *James* is a bizarre quest
novel, featuring a cast of ill-assorted companions (mostly human-sized
arthropods) all of whom are given the chance to prove themselves as
they make the perilous journey from England to New York. *Charlie
and the Chocolate Factory* is a cautionary tale, and, as that label implies,
it comes with a very explicit moral apparatus, including admonitory
verses, punishments and warnings about greed, gum chewing, over-
indulgent parents and addiction to television. More specifically, it is a
parable of the strait gate, a secular *Pilgrim's Progress* in which many are
called but only one – Charlie – is chosen.

The apparent surrealism of Dahl's settings may seem designed
to disguise the conventional forms of these two books, but from
Hoffmann and Belloc through to Edward Gorey, the cautionary
tale has always been a semi-subversive genre in which didacticism is
balanced finely against self-parody. *Charlie,* in particular, is a book that

is deceptive in its apparent simplicity of approach. As well as being a type of *Pilgrim's Progress*, it is also a *Divine Comedy*, but one in which the roles of Virgil, God and Satan are combined in one overdetermined figure, Willy Wonka. Wonka moves in mysterious ways: he both tempts the children and punishes them for their infractions, while in the book's prehistory he appears as vindictive as any Old Testament Nobodaddy, sacking all his workers because of rival chocolate makers' industrial espionage. Yet the text absolves him: this is a being beyond blame, a magical dispenser of rewards whose final promise to make Charlie his heir is a blessing to the whole Bucket tribe.

The factory itself seems to invite allegorical reading, particularly in terms of the human body. Wonka's industrial-age Castle of Alma is clearly not a place of emaciated asceticism, but neither is it bloated through excess nor warped through addiction: instead, it is a paradoxically superabundant, lurid and extravagant temple to the principles of temperance and moderation. The Oompa-Loompas act as the factory's immune system, rejecting naughty children like viruses or expelling them like waste products. As if to underscore this reading one of the children is even named Veruca, while another (Mike Teavee) was Herpes Trout in an early draft of the story.[13] The shared physicality of food and of those who consume it is emphasised as children are pushed down chutes, digested in juicing rooms or excreted via a chocolate-flavoured alimentary canal.

If the factory offers rich pickings for those who wish to see in it a parable about consumption, it also forms the second half of a Freudian diptych devoted to childhood sexuality. Where James's peach offers a retreat from the cruelties and vicissitudes of the world in the form of a giant, edible womb, the chocolate factory leads Charlie on a bewildering voyage of polymorphous perversity that encompasses Augustus Gloop's cloacal desires, Veruca Salt's metamorphosis into a swollen purple berry, the oral fixation of gum-chewing Violet Beauregarde and Mike Teavee's narcissism. All these contrast with Charlie's own normatively healthy appetites, which culminate in his being propelled with orgasmic vigour through the very roof of the factory by Willy Wonka (a name one solitary vowel from obscenity), thence to continue the confectioner's work into the next generation.

Whether Dahl would have endorsed these readings is debatable, but he was well aware of the power of double entendre in names (something in which he may have been encouraged by the example of his friend and role model Ian Fleming, creator of Pussy Galore), and in this book particularly he seems often to be taking pleasure in staying just on the right side of a line that has adult awareness and

lubricity one side, and candy and chaos on the other. Before becoming a children's author Dahl had been a successful commercial writer
for adults and, as Laura Viñas Valle has shown, in moving between those
markets he made relatively little attempt to modify his narrative voice.[14]
Not only did he recycle plots from his adult stories for use as children's
books, but the cynical and even sadistic elements within his adult fiction
sometimes find disguised expression in his books for children. Dahl
once described his writing as a tightrope act,[15] and in that remark lies a
clue as to where much of its abiding fascination lies – in the sense that
his control of his material is precarious, and that at any moment we
may witness a disastrous fall.

Dahl was ambivalent about many things – authority, modern life,
education, violence, growing up – and his writing is often at its most
successful when it is poised on the fulcrum of that ambivalence. Eleanor
Cameron, in excoriating *Charlie and the Chocolate Factory*, complained of
'its hypocrisy which is epitomized in its moral stuck like a marshmallow
in a lump of fudge – that TV is horrible and hateful and time-wasting
and that children should read good books instead, when in fact the
book itself is like nothing so much as one of the more specious television shows'.[16]

Cameron is right to spot a tension here, but hasty in identifying it as
hypocrisy. Dahl was unrepentant in his wish to make a popular appeal
to children and to do so on their terms, without needing to look for
approval from parents or teachers, let alone critics. He was, however,
equally driven by an instinctive dislike of modernity and automated
mass culture. The difficulty lay in keeping these attitudes distinct.
Similarly, Dahl's attitude to formal education combined rebelliousness
towards authority (and a particular loathing of corporal punishment)
with an impatience of anything that smacked of the trendy or politi-
cally correct. The advent of new educational orthodoxies in the 1960s
placed him in a particular dilemma. The 1967 Plowden Report, for
example, not only recommended the banning of corporal punishment in primary schools, but also stressed the centrality of children in
the education process.[17] Peter Hunt notes in this volume that Dahl
claimed a special affinity with children, based on his ability to see the
world from their point of view: 'If you want to remember what it's
like to live in a child's world, you've got to get down on your hands
and knees and live like that for a week. You find you have to look up
at all these bloody giants around you who are always telling you what
to do and what not to do.'[18]

As of 1967 Dahl was no longer the only person on all fours attempting to look at the world from a child's viewpoint: rather, the nursery

floor was cluttered with psychologists, sociologists and educationalists, all representative of a left-leaning intelligentsia Dahl himself despised. His reaction was to distinguish himself from this group by stressing his belief in old-fashioned forms of learning and knowledge – 'proper parsing and proper grammar'.[19]

Versions of this tension showed itself in other ways. Although desirous of establishment recognition, Dahl remained essentially unclubbable, lasting only one meeting when co-opted onto Professor Brian Cox's 1988 government working party on English teaching.[20] Instead, he cultivated a public persona as a curmudgeonly, plain-speaking, not-quite-respectable uncle who was nevertheless unambiguously on children's *side* in a world of arbitrary adult restrictions, and who shared their enjoyment of the ridiculous and the scatological. (Matilda's *enfant terrible* observation that her mother picks her nose is, whatever its value as humour, an effective Swiftian levelling tactic aimed squarely at adult pretensions.)[21] Through interviews, audio recordings of his own books, narratorial digressions, and above all through his two autobiographical volumes, *Boy* (1984) and *Going Solo* (1986), Dahl made a direct and personal appeal to children, designed to fly below the radar of parental disapproval.

Despite this, in the opening pages of *Matilda* (1988) Dahl's narrator fantasises about being a truculent teacher writing 'scorchers' of reports on his unsatisfactory charges. The ostensible targets of his indignation are the deluded, doting parents of these pupils rather than the children themselves (pp. 2–3), but the terms he uses – 'total wash-out', 'grub', 'stinkers' – are not far from the abusive language of Miss Trunchbull, the book's child-hating head teacher. Matilda's literary education, as described in the book's early chapters, is highly traditional, consisting entirely of canonical or semi-canonical texts for adults (Dickens being especially prominent), only one of which was published in the second half of the twentieth century,[22] while the librarian Mrs Phelps, whose judgement is implied to be trustworthy, omits more recent literature written for teenagers when considering her recommendations (p. 9). Even the saintly Miss Honey expects her charges to have memorised their multiplication tables up to 12 within a year of arriving at school, although this is primarily to protect them from punishment at Trunchbull's hands (p. 63).

In *Matilda* Dahl accommodates this ambivalence by surreptitiously splicing two independent sets of generic rules. On the one hand, the book reads as a realist novel subject to real-world constraints, in which (for example) Miss Trunchbull is aware that corporal punishment is no longer permitted (p. 83), and Miss Honey is careful to obtain parental consent from the Wormwoods for Matilda to move in with her. In this mode Dahl is able to indulge his conservative beliefs by including such items as Mrs Phelps's reading list – which is presumably also intended as a realistic (if aspirational) set of recommendations for his own readers. However, *Matilda* also presents us with a stylised world of cartoon violence, in which the same Miss Trunchbull feels no difficulty about swinging a girl around by her pigtails, or locking children in a home-made iron maiden lined with broken glass.

Dahl does not feel obliged to address the lack of fit between these two versions of *Matilda* consistently, although he implicitly acknowledges it at selected points. 'Thank goodness we don't meet many people like her in this world,' the narrator says of Miss Trunchbull, half-admitting that she is a creature of storybook nightmare, only to take it immediately back: 'although they do exist and all of us are likely to come across at least one of them in a lifetime' (p. 61). A little later, Matilda's friend Lavender asks how Miss Trunchbull's regime survives: why don't the children simply tell their parents? Matilda's reply uses the incompatibility of the book's two modes to advantage, pointing out that Miss Trunchbull's continuance is due to the very fact that the parents think they are living in a world of realism: 'No parent is going to believe this pigtail story, not in a million years' (p. 111). Then there is the impoverished Miss Honey, who lives in a fairy-tale cottage (p. 180) on the obviously impossible sum of one pound per week, but who proceeds to give an *almost* plausible account of how this might actually be managed. The result of this generic soldering is that the reader is able simultaneously to hiss the tyranny of the caricature villain, while maintaining a more considered and indeed conservative view of the realistic issues raised by the story.

Matilda is perhaps the book in which Dahl negotiates the tension between his authoritarian and subversive sides with the greatest success, but his work is frequently at its most interesting when he creates characters who do not quite fit the narrative roles that seem to have been prepared for them. Mr Fox is (literally) an underdog; but he is also a predator, killing chickens without compunction. Danny's father in *Danny, the Champion of the World* (1975) is a hero to his son, but a thief in the eyes of the law. The grandmother in *The Witches* is both an elderly invalid and a virile, cigar-smoking heroine. The BFG is at the same time a giant *and* a seven-stone weakling. The Twits are vile human beings, but the physical and spiritual squalor in which they live lends them a bleak pathos. Almost all of Dahl's books after *Charlie and the Chocolate Factory* involve pitting the small against the large, the powerless against the powerful or the young against the old, but these are categories that do not always coincide exactly or straightforwardly, and in general this is much to the advantage of the resulting books.

Dahl's sense of what would engross, amuse and delight children – or at least a large proportion of them – was an unusually assured one. He created a new realm within children's fiction, the influence of which can be seen in books as diverse as *Harry Potter and the Philosopher's Stone* and Andy Stanton's *Mr Gum* series. 'Dahlesque' instantly conveys a recognisable style and approach, but Dahl was also a writer who worked at reinventing himself, who experimented with many different genres, and who was unafraid of taking artistic risks, often in the teeth of prevailing tradition within children's writing. For example, in one of his early stories, *The Magic Finger* (1966), the unnamed narrator uses her magical gift to turn her teacher, Mrs Winter, into a cat, adding with relish: 'if any of you are wondering whether Mrs Winter is quite all right again now, the answer is No. And she never will be.'[23] This gleeful gesture of defiance against the perceived obligation of children's fiction to provide a reset button for the restoration of all losses and the righting of all wrongs is daring, but almost 20 years later in *The Witches* (1983) a similar move provides a moment unique in the risks it takes with customary assumptions about the plots of children's books. At the end of that story, the narrator (again unnamed) has been turned into a mouse by the Grand High Witch. Conventional story logic would dictate that by the end of the book he must be made 'quite all right again' – and, indeed, when Nicholas Roeg came to film *The Witches* the studio insisted on just such a restoration.[24] Not only does Dahl's protagonist remain a mouse but he is not even destined to live out his natural human span: as a boy-mouse he can expect only about nine more years of life at the end of the story. His calm acceptance of this fact, and his contentment at the prospect of dying at around the same time as his own grandmother, ought to be a disaster for the book. Indeed, there are many possible objections to it: that it is morbid, that it is cruel, that it is sentimental, that it idealises an unhealthy and static model of mutual dependency between young and old. However, it is also an image of love that speaks powerfully to many children, for whom the prospect of outliving their parents may indeed be as frightening as that of their own death. Perhaps only C. S. Lewis, in bringing his grown-up Pevensie siblings back from Narnia at the end of *The Lion, the Witch and the Wardrobe* (1950) and forcing them into the minds and bodies of young children again without any acknowledgement that this might be a traumatic experience, has shown so little regard for the conventions of psychological realism as understood by adults, and at the same time so sure an instinct for what might make perfect psychological and emotional sense to a child.

The centrality of conflict and of resistance to oppression in Dahl's work gave way only at the end of his career to a different pattern, in the benign whimsy of *Esio Trot* (1990) and *The Vicar of Nibbleswicke* (1991), children's books notable amongst other things for the absence of children, and hence of child–adult antagonism. Instead, Dahl here gives pride of place to two of his other abiding interests: wordplay (an aspect of his work discussed elsewhere in this volume by David Rudd) and the detailed construction and execution of elaborate, implausibly successful solutions to formidable practical difficulties. Mr Hoppy's wooing of Mrs Silver by means of a dangled tortoise harks all the way back to James's elaborate plan to conscript seagulls to carry the giant peach across the Atlantic almost three decades earlier, or to the grandmother of *The Witches* lowering her grandson over her hotel balcony into the room of the Grand High Witch. The outwitting of Farmers Boggis, Bunce and Bean by Mr Fox; the upside-down room trick used by the animals against the Twits; the business model of the giraffe, monkey and pelican; Matilda's scheme to bring down Miss Trunchbull using telekinesis, chalk and a fake ghost – all are described with an obvious and lingering satisfaction in ingenious detail. Diana Wynne Jones once remarked: 'My feeling about most fantasy stories is that what they're really doing is echoing the way your brain works, and your brain likes to come out with the solution – you like to jump out of your bath and run into the road shouting "Eureka!"'[25] Dissimilar as Jones and Dahl were in almost every way, a love of finding solutions, and an exuberant joy in their execution, are things that they have very much in common. Significantly, it a pleasure that is equally available to all generations, from toddlers building towers of bricks to retired stockbrokers finishing the *Times* crossword over breakfast. It is certainly a pleasure that Dahl shared with his readers.

The essays that follow explore a variety of aspects of Dahl's writing. Some are devoted to the traditions within which his work is situated and his practice as an author: thus, Deborah Thacker considers his debt to folk tale, while Jackie E. Stallcup examines his use of humour and David Rudd his linguistic innovation. Drawing on the work of scholars such as Jack Zipes and Maria Tatar, Thacker's essay places Dahl's work at the interface between the mutable tradition of oral storytelling, and the more regulated form of the printed tale for children, which has often been fashioned so as to highlight a didactic point. Stallcup considers Dahl's deployment of different styles of humour, based on incongruity, on the breaking of taboos and on 'derision', analysing the ways in which these may model and enforce systems of values and behaviour, but also subvert them. Rudd's essay complements this project, providing a tour of the various kinds of linguistic innovation employed by Dahl – lexical, phonological, typographical, syntactical and semantic – and arguing that his inventiveness functions as more than context-free 'playfulness', offering instead an exposure of and intervention in the power structures embodied in language.

Other essays address more overtly ideological aspects of Dahl's writing, in its representations of education (Pat Pinsent), the family (Ann Alston), women and girls (Beverley Pennell) and crime (Heather Worthington). Pinsent's essay explores in greater depth some of the issues raised in this Introduction, setting Dahl's views on education in the context of his personal experience of school, which was deeply formative and is repeatedly represented in his fiction and non-fiction. In her essay on Dahl and family Ann Alston places the child–adult relationships that lie at the heart of Dahl's books within the larger structure of the family unit, arguing that there is no straightforward correlation between conventional family structures and functional family dynamics in his books. Pennell, in her assessment of Dahl's treatment of girls and women, takes a more positive view of his achievement than many of his critics, and challenges those who would dismiss him as anti-feminist in his writing. Worthington, for her part, takes on another common criticism – that Dahl tends to glorify violence and even criminality – and contends that Dahl's provision of escapist and cathartic fantasy meets an emotional need in child readers to which few other writers are prepared to cater.

Dahl's associations with other media are explored in different ways by June Pulliam, in her discussion of the film adaptations of his work, and Carole Scott, who analyses his long-term collaboration with the artist Quentin Blake. Dahl's association with the screen (both large and small) is of long standing, and Pulliam considers how the various adaptations of his work reshape it both aesthetically and ideologically. Whereas most of the film adaptations of Dahl's books took place without the author's own involvement, Dahl's relationship with Blake was a close and symbiotic one, in which both men were careful to play to each other's strengths and tastes, as Scott's analyses of the inter-relation of word and picture in several key texts demonstrate.

Finally, Peter Hunt looks critically at Dahl as a writer who was able to exploit a moment of cultural change in order to establish a pivotal position within British children's literature, arguing that Dahl took advantage of 'a perfect storm' to create a product that simultaneously flattered and manipulated its child readers. Although there are many areas of common concern within the essays contained in this book, Hunt's more sceptical perspective is indicative of the fact that there is far from being a critical consensus as to the position of Dahl's work within children's literature. The argument is set to continue for some time to come.

Of course, there are other topics that deserve to be addressed: Dahl's poetry, the relationship between his work for adults and for children, the uses he made of autobiography, and his power as a rhetorician being just a few examples. As noted above, the field of Dahl studies is an underpopulated one, and a single volume of essays can only begin the task of remedying that state of affairs. But we hope that it is a task well begun.

Notes

1. Sally Maynard and Cliff McKnight, 'Author Popularity: An Exploratory Study Based on Roald Dahl', *New Review of Children's Literature and Librarianship* 8(1) (2002): 153–75, at 2.
2. Maynard and McKnight: 3.
3. The Roald Dahl Museum and Story Centre (personal correspondence, 17 May 2011).
4. National Centre for Research in Children's Literature (NCRCL): www.roehampton.ac.uk/Research-Centres/National-Centre-for-Research-in-Childrens-Literature/Publications/ (accessed 14 May 2012).
5. Jeremy Treglown, *Roald Dahl: A Biography* (London: Faber, 1994); Donald Sturrock, *Storyteller: The Life of Roald Dahl* (London: Harper Press, 2010); Michael Rosen, *Fantastic Mr Dahl* (London: Puffin, forthcoming in 2012).
6. Mark I. West, *Roald Dahl* (New York: Twayne, 1992).
7. Roald Dahl, '"Charlie and the Chocolate Factory:" A Reply', *The Horn Book* (Feb. 1973): www.hbook.com/magazine/articles/1970s/feb73_dahl.asp. Links to the whole *Horn Book* exchange can be found here: www.hbook.com/history/magazine/camerondahl.asp (accessed 13 May 2011).
8. Sturrock: 493.
9. Roald Dahl, *The Twits* [1980] (London: Puffin, 2007): 1.
10. Jonathon Culley, 'Roald Dahl – "It's About Children and It's for Children" – But Is It Suitable?' *Children's Literature in Education* 22(1) (1991): 59–73, at 61.
11. Treglown: 211–12.
12. Roald Dahl, *The Witches* [1983] (London: Puffin, 2001): 4.
13. 'The Story in the Early Drafts of Charlie and the Chocolate Factory': www.roalddahlmuseum.org/uploads/Charlie%20and%20the%20Chocolate%20fact.pdf (accessed 11 May 2011).

14. Laura Viñas Valle, 'The Narrative Voice in Roald Dahl's Children's and Adult Books', *Didáctica. Lengua y Literatura* 20 (2008): 291–308.
15. Cited Treglown: 249.
16. Eleanor Cameron, 'McLuhan, Youth, and Literature: Part I', *The Horn Book* (October 1972): www.hbook.com/magazine/articles/1970s/oct72_cameron.asp (accessed 17 May 2011).
17. *Children and Their Primary Schools*, Central Advisory Council for Education (England): www.educationengland.org.uk/documents/plowden/ (accessed 5 May 2011).
18. Christopher Sykes, 'In the Lair of the BFG', *Harpers and Queen* (October 1991): 80–5, at 82.
19. *Daily Mail*, 16 November 1988; cited in Treglown: 249.
20. Treglown: 248.
21. Roald Dahl, *Matilda* [1988] (London: Puffin, 2001): 29.
22. *Matilda*: 12. The exception – by a whisker – is Hemingway's *The Old Man and the Sea* (1951).
23. Roald Dahl, *The Magic Finger* [1966] (London: Puffin, 2008): 7.
24. Sturrock: 536.
25. Charles Butler, 'Interview with Diana Wynne Jones', in Teya Roseberg et al. (eds), *Diana Wynne Jones: An Exciting and Exacting Wisdom* (New York: Peter Lang, 2002): 163–72, at 168.

1

Fairy Tale and Anti-Fairy Tale: Roald Dahl and the Telling Power of Stories

Deborah Cogan Thacker

Towards the beginning of *Matilda*, Roald Dahl portrays his epony-mous heroine as someone who is knowledgeable about the power of story to have a controlling effect on a listener.[1] Matilda has put superglue on her father's hat and it is stuck to his head. She tells her traumatised father about a boy who got superglue on his finger without knowing it and then got it stuck up his nose.

> Mr Wormwood jumped. 'What happened to him?' he spluttered.
> 'The finger got stuck inside his nose,' Matilda said, 'and he had to go around like that for a week. … He looked an awful fool.'[2]

Matilda is both knowing and subversive in her use of a cautionary story to teach lessons, and she neatly reverses the relationship of power in the father–daughter relationship through the telling of the tale. Mr Wormwood is unkind to Matilda – but the lesson itself does not change his behaviour. However, Matilda, the ignored and powerless child, attains a fleeting position of authority and control as the 'teller', deepening her father's foolishness. In this way, she exacts some vestige of satisfaction through her power as a 'storyteller'. While at no point does Matilda exact a lasting revenge on her father for her mistreat-ment, this sense of power over him reaches its culmination when Matilda leaves her family altogether at the end of the book, to start a new life with Miss Honey. According to Maria Tatar, '[t]he economy of the cautionary tale operated in such a way as to provide maximum advantage to the teller',[3] and Dahl, by giving Matilda a role usually taken by adults, celebrates the power of stories over and above the valorisation of literature elsewhere in the book.

By embedding the telling of this 'cautionary' tale within his fictional narrative, Dahl demonstrates his tendency to put his child characters in powerful positions. The complex awareness of the nature of traditional tales that he displays throughout his novels for children is a distinctive feature of his work and goes some way to explain not only why he is often reviled by adult readers, but also why he continues to be so popular with children. The familiar tropes of folk and fairy tales, such as the orphaned child triumphing over adversity in order to attain selfhood, the predominance of fantastical violence as a method of retribution, and a fascination with eating and being eaten, provide allusive richness to his stories. His ability to call attention to the use of such tales to indoctrinate and suppress children can be seen to characterise the particular quality that defines his distinctiveness. By reversing the roles of teller and recipient of the tale, as he does in *Matilda*, Dahl is able not only to show his debt to folk and fairy tales, but also to undermine their controlling force by playing with 'the scaffolding'.

Even Dahl's own autobiographical writing, according to Catriona Nicholson, is built on a fairy tale framework, blurring the lines between the struggles and tragedies of his own life and his fictions:

> The themes and conflicts made manifest in Dahl's *Tales of Childhood* prefigure the forces for good and evil in his tales of fantasy. Characterised by brave children, malevolent adults, and magical possibilities, they replicate the structure of fairy tales where fortunes are reversed, the ordinary becomes fabulous, and native cunning outwits pompous stupidity.[4]

The connection between Dahl's own life and his approach to children's fiction, as well as his bizarre and disturbing adult fiction, is marked by a declared mistrust and resentment of the adult world and the mistreatment of children, himself among them. Peter Hollindale claims that knowledge of Dahl's own life struggles informs the reading of his fiction, and finds consistency in 'a pattern widely discernible in Dahl's work, of adult authority falling contemptibly short of the good and necessary reasons why authority exists'.[5] This position inflects all of his work with a subversive flavour, as he appears to reject the power relationships inherent in adult–child story interactions. Similarly, although it is admittedly impossible to erase or entirely reverse the normative author–reader relationship, Dahl's ability to destabilise it is distinctive and, through metafictive play, he is able to show irreverence for the expected authorial presence.

Throughout his fiction for children, Dahl uses and abuses folk and fairy tale conventions, entering into a conspiratorial relationship with his child readers 'against adults',[6] whose need to control and improve is considered by contemporary critics to have motivated the translation of folk tales into print form. Though his humorous rewritings of familiar fairy tales in *Revolting Rhymes* (1982), for instance, more deliberately reverse and, thus, undermine the moral emphasis of the stories, his adoption of the formal aspects of narrative relationships offered by such tales challenges the use that adults have made of them in the transition from folk culture to children's literature.[7]

Dahl expressed the view that stories are a part of a process, driven by 'the relentless need to civilize "this thing that when it is born is an animal with no manners, no moral sense at all"'.[8] Through his novels for children, he at once performs the process and undermines it in a way that offers children, as readers, a dimension of authority, or at least, a sense of collusion in the process of storytelling. What is more significant is that Dahl's own recognition of the power of fairy tales to indoctrinate, control and encourage conformity anticipates the examination of power structures in the author–reader relationship by contemporary critics. Recent criticism has re-evaluated the history of folk and fairy tales, demonstrating the need to look beyond the tales themselves to the circumstances of their telling. By doing so, critics such as Maria Tatar and Jack Zipes provide a revisionary analysis of the genre that brings a new perspective to Dahl's particular approach. According to Tatar: 'Foucault's point is … that the entire project of childrearing, including the telling of tales, is invested in a metaphysic of power and is therefore never really in the best interest of the child. Any attempt to pass on stories becomes a disciplinary tactic aimed at control.'[9]

Contemporary criticism of fairy tales, which re-examines and often challenges the previously dominant psychoanalytic and structuralist studies, draws on cultural theory to explain both the cultural construction of traditional tales and the importance of their use and reception. Fairy tale theory since the 1980s has developed approaches that at once emphasise the change in ideological force implicit in the transition from oral roots to written children's stories, and provide an understanding of children's literature in terms of the power relations embedded in adult–child encounters, as Tatar claims: 'Whenever a book is written by adults for children, there is a way in which it becomes relentlessly educational, in part because the condition of its existence opens up a chasm between the child reader and the older, wiser adult who has produced the book.'[10]

It is this quality, and the shift away from the carnivalesque tendencies of folk tales – which, with their excessive and playful retributive violence and a fascination with bodily appetites, momentarily reverse the prevalent power structures of society – into improving texts for children that Roald Dahl appears to subvert. Both through subject matter and unconventional use of language, Dahl returns to the grotesque, the fantastical violence, and the undermining of authoritative power structures of folklore. These factors work to enhance the 'conspiratorial' engagement with children as his readers, interrupting the educational and improving qualities of much contemporary children's literature. Paradoxically, it is Dahl's attention to storytelling that does most to suggest a return to the complicit nature of the folk tale. By continually reminding his readers of the act of storytelling and representing that act in his fiction, Dahl returns to the dialogic circumstances of the folk tale, and thereby challenges the power relationships that surround most adult author–child reader encounters.

Although it is a common assumption that children choose to read Dahl's books for themselves *against* the wishes of disapproving adults, it is adults who often read his books aloud to children. The role that adults take in these reading situations provides a further layer of transgressive complicity, since they, as readers, must give voice to Dahl's narrative approach. If Dahl sees himself as an ally to children in a world of foolish adults exercising arbitrary power, then the shared reading experience brings complex power relationships into play. Whether it is a teacher reading in *The Witches* that a child's teacher might be a witch,[11] or a parent who earlier in the evening has insisted on table manners reading about 'whizzpoppers' in *The BFG*,[12] Dahl's playful use of the narrative contract provides a deep pleasure in the power of stories to challenge compliance, similar to the original circumstances of the transmission of folk tales. As Tatar remarks: '[i]n cultures that consistently play adult authority and privilege against childish impotence and inadequacy, these stories have a liberating power that should not be underestimated'.[13]

Fairy tale theory and the instability of the text

While many critics point to Dahl's anarchic humour, often denigrating it,[14] a more considered view can be gained if his work is viewed through the lens of fairy tale theorists such as Zipes and Tatar. The recognition that children's literature derives from a folk tradition that rests on the playful transgression of normative power structures has a particular significance to the work of Roald Dahl, whose reputation might be summed up in Tatar's definition of childhood and its difference from adulthood:

Exuberance, energy, mobility, irrepressibility, irreverence, curiosity, audacity – these are traits that we are right to envy of youth. But they are also the very characteristics that make the child intractable – resistant to the civilizing powers of the adult world. The boundless transgressive energy of children will forever confound and vex adults as they set about the task of socializing the young.[15]

This is precisely the attitude that Dahl has expressed in his remarks about the 'relentless' need of adults to civilise children.

Tatar, in *Off With Their Heads: Fairy Tales and the Culture of Childhood*, rejects the notion upon which previous commentators have relied that fairy tales are stable texts. Rather, her emphasis is on the fact that the text that we readily accept as the 'ideal text', 'is nothing more than one of many constructs created by adults'.[16] Jack Zipes, similarly, in *Fairy Tales and the Art of Subversion*, relies on a predominantly Marxist approach to reconceptualise fairy tales as 'part of a social process, as a kind of intervention in the continuous discourse, debate, and conflict about power and social relations'.[17] This view emphasises the use of fairy tales to indoctrinate and control, but also draws attention to the instability of any particular text. While we often expect fairy tales to offer moral direction, or at least a means by which the child can work through struggles towards autonomy, both Zipes and Tatar place more importance on the circumstances of the transmission of the tale and the construction that takes place in the author–reader exchange. Thus, the instability of the tale itself relies on the power of the teller to use the circumstances of the telling, of the relationship to the audience, to construct the tale.

Collectors of folk tales, like the Grimm brothers, were able to transform the tales they collected and to construct stories that served the purpose of socialisation.[18] By writing tales down, authors, particularly in the nineteenth century, were able to embed ideologically freighted messages, in order to 'mould behaviour', 'to deter children from being too inquisitive about the world they inhabit and deviating in any way from behavioural norms. Using intimidation, cautionary tales persuade children to obey the laws set down by parental authority, celebrating docility and conformity while discouraging curiosity and wilfulness.'[19]

This shift towards docility and conformity represents a loss. In the transition from the oral folk tradition to the literary, from an unstable text to a stable one, and from a participatory relationship to one of receiving an 'authorised' version, the transmission of story from reader to hearer became a didactic one, 'no longer responsive to an active audience, but seeking to manipulate it according to the vested interests of the state'.[20] It is the narrative relationship of the folk tale that Dahl seeks to restore, by undermining the 'improving' quality of literature, and demonstrating the deep pleasure to be had in colluding in a work of the imagination. Dahl does not ignore the fact, either, that adults are part of the transmission process of children's literature and many of his allusions are meant for those who may happen to be reading to their children, further enhancing the notion of performance.

While Dahl is able to defamiliarise the fairy tale by calling attention to the constructedness of his stories – both James and the BFG, for instance, are revealed as the authors of the stories that 'you have just been reading'[21] – he also relies on many of the tropes familiar to readers of 'Cinderella' or 'Little Red Riding Hood'. Not only does he provide playful retellings of such classic tales, but he also echoes the retributive violence and the related concerns with eating and being eaten familiar to such stories. In her discussion of the use of violence in children's literature, Tatar offers Dahl as an example of a writer who understood the 'cathartic' power of violence, but also recognised that 'surreal comic effects' were an important part of the 'delicate weave that constitutes the appeal of violence for children'.[22] The adoption of fairy tales as literature has removed us from 'the festive violence' of the original folk tales and, thus, their cathartic function, in order to allow adults to 'instrumentalize violence in order to discipline and socialize children in the name of guiding and healing them'[23]. It is this cathartic and playful violence that Dahl returns us to. The retribution played out on the oppressors of both children and other victims in his books is not intended as discipline, but as 'surreal excess',[24] characteristic of 'the narrative excesses of folk raconteurs', complete with 'comic exaggerations, burlesque humour and a form of earthy realism'.[25]

When, for example, Sophie rams a pin into the Fleshlumpeater's ankle, the violence perpetrated is made more comical and surreal by the fact that the BFG tells him that he has been bitten by a snake.[26] The terror and pain experienced by the giant does not serve an improving purpose, but forms a satisfying retribution for the bullying that the BFG has experienced throughout his life. So, too, the punishment of having to eat nothing but snozzcumbers represents an apt revenge on the other giants for all of the child eating, reversing a typical fairy tale ending of the reward of food.

Food, or lack of it, is also a common theme in Dahl's novels and provides another significant debt to the fairy tale tradition. While a Freudian mapping or its Kleinian reinterpretation of eating/being eaten[27] as a projection of child–parent antagonism can be read into Dahl's work, the withholding of food can no longer be seen to be associated with the poverty that informed original folk tales. However, the mistreatment of children by adults or, more broadly, modern capitalist society, can be seen in Dahl's depiction of, for example, the starving Miss Honey and the Bucket family. The use of food as a signifier for power is effective in Dahl's work, precisely because he is aware of this psychoanalytic mapping and gives it a performative function, so that the consequences of eating are overemphasised. James's heroic behaviour includes feeding his companions with the peach, with all the sensuous pleasure that implies: 'the Centipede, with his mouth full of peach and the juice running down all over his chin'.[28] The eating of the peach by the children of New York, and the eating of chocolate, whether a Wonka bar or the giant chocolate cake in *Matilda*, give food an exaggerated importance and celebrate excessive appetites.

In *Charlie and the Chocolate Factory*, the punishment and condemnation of greed are directed not at the children, but at their parents. Though children might find an uncomfortable mix of humour and danger in the fate of Augustus Gloop, as Tatar suggests, the pain and pleasure of comeuppance is due in part to Dahl's playful dependence on fairy tale tropes to undermine a more conventional lesson about eating too much.[29] Rather, it is the adults who are the main target of Dahl's humour and the parents who are made to seem foolish:

> 'Mr. Wonka doesn't seem to think so!' cried Mrs. Gloop. 'Just look at him! He's laughing his head off! How *dare* you laugh like that when my boy's just gone up the pipe! You monster!' she shrieked, pointing her umbrella at Mr. Wonka as though she were going to run him through. 'You think it's a joke, do you? You think that sucking my boy up into your Fudge Room like that is just one great big colossal joke?'
>   'He'll be perfectly safe,' said Mr. Wonka, giggling slightly.
>   'He'll be chocolate fudge!' shrieked Mrs. Gloop.
>   …
>   'I wouldn't allow it!' cried Mr. Wonka.
>   'And why not?' shrieked Mrs. Gloop.
>   'Because the taste would be terrible', said Mr. Wonka.[30]

While it is a child who suffers, Dahl here undermines the cautionary force of the tale by characterising Wonka as not only a naughty, 'giggling' child, but one with power. By celebrating Wonka's interpretation of events through the irreverence of the joke, Dahl returns to a narrative relationship with his readers that includes, but then immediately disrupts, both psychoanalytical and moral readings. The catharsis comes through the 'festive' violence of the text, with the knowledge that stories for children often attempt to regulate behaviour around eating.

Most significantly, Dahl's distinctive ability is to rely on fairy tales while also transforming them, by undermining the authority of the storytelling persona. Recent reconceptualisations of fairy tales, which describe the consequences of translating an oral, dialogic relationship to an ideological act of control, deconstruct the process in order to suggest alternatives that might be more liberating for the child as a reader. Both Tatar and Zipes call for retellings of familiar tales that can 'interrogate and take the measure of their own participation'[31] through a disruption of the narrative, and although Zipes uses Dahl's retelling of 'Little Red Riding Hood', neither critic points to Dahl as an exemplar of the return to the relationship of teller to told found in oral encounters. While it can be claimed, as Tatar does, that 'private oral exchanges between parent and child'[32] offer a vestige of the more democratic relationship of oral storytelling events, it is in Dahl's narrative method that precisely a kind of liberating disruption occurs.

Playing with the scaffolding: the development of Dahl's approach

Dahl's transgressive approach does change over time and must be considered in relation to a growing confidence in his ability to challenge and subvert. While his first two novels for children, written in the 1960s, present fairly straightforward mappings of fairy tale structures and make frequent allusions to folk and fairy tales, his later work, such as *The BFG*, *Matilda* and, in particular, *The Witches*, does more to subvert such conventions. Both James, in *James and the Giant Peach*, first published in 1961 and Charlie, in *Charlie and the Chocolate Factory*, published in 1964, follow the typical 'Romance' trajectory so familiar to folk and fairy tales. As Nicholson points out, Freud's parallel between 'wishful fantasies' and popular fiction in 'Creative Writers and Daydreaming'[33] is significant to Dahl's pervasive use of the heroic figure: 'regeneration through endurance and suffering is a persistent motif in mythology, traditional tale, and legend'.[34]

Though James is an orphan and both a Jack (of the Beanstalk) and a Cinderella figure in the house of Aunts Sponge and Spiker, themselves a combination of the wicked stepmother and ugly sisters, Charlie is more reminiscent of the third son in numerous folk tales and fairy tales. While Dahl makes him one of five instead of the more familiar pattern of three found in tales of this type, Charlie is characterised from the beginning as the least likely to succeed. He is weak and meek, but honest. The other four children are dispatched and physically undermined due to their greed and selfishness, in much the same way that the 'Black Brothers' Hans and Schwartz are punished by being turned to stone in John Ruskin's *The King of the Golden River*, thereby leaving their meeker and kinder brother Gluck to succeed.[35] Both James and Charlie are rewarded for their goodness and intelligence and both rewards, as in many folk and fairy tales, are equated with food and a display of generosity, as in 'Hansel and Gretel'. James shares his peach with the children of New York City and Charlie is able to feed his starving family. Both attain new homes and new, typically adult functions: Charlie as the owner of a chocolate factory and a future 'inventor' like Willy Wonka, and James as an author, entertaining other children (including those reading the book) with his stories.

All of this indicates an allegiance to fairy tale conventions and points to Dahl as a descendant of writers such as Ruskin, who saw in fairy tales both an improving and entertaining function, and the potential to awaken the creative imagination, claiming 'the most instructive histories you can compile for [a child] will never conquer the interest of the tale which a clever child can tell itself'.[36] In these early novels, Dahl appropriates expected fairy tale trajectories and power relationships, whether reflecting the child's struggle for selfhood in the face of devouring parents or through a moral testing ground. Both novels, however, do provide examples of Dahl's subversive humour and dry acceptance of violence and tragedy. James's parents are dispatched early by an 'enormous angry rhinoceros' in 'full daylight',[37] while Charlie's companions are punished in shocking ways.

The later novels, however, published in the 1980s, appear to be more thoroughly influenced by the *Zeitgeist* of the 1970s and the commensurate interest in post-structuralist and postmodern cultural theory, which have given rise to new approaches to the study of culture. Significantly, the re-examination of folk and fairy tales, influenced by these theoretical discourses and challenging both structuralist and psychoanalytic paradigms, were published in that decade: Zipes's groundbreaking work, *Breaking the Magic Spell: Radical Theories of Folk and Fairy Tales*, was first published in 1979, and Maria Tatar's work, *The Hard Facts of the Grimms' Fairy Tales*, in 1987.[38] Both offer a revisionist approach that throws light on the distinctive character of Dahl's reworking of the fairy tale.

Although the shift in alignment is perhaps subtle, it is significant in terms of both the burgeoning popularity of Dahl, and the charges against him as subversive, a situation described by Peter Hollindale as his 'dubious public status and ambivalent reception as a children's writer'.[39] It is still possible to read both *The BFG*, published in 1982 and *Matilda*, published in 1988, as fairy tales in the conventional sense, yet Dahl appears to find a new way of expressing his interest in discourses of power in his portrayals of his adult and child characters and their status in fairy tale terms. Dahl may still offer a message that is true to Bruno Bettelheim's dictum that fairy tales show 'that a struggle against severe difficulties in life is unavoidable, is an intrinsic part of human existence'.[40] However, he also shows, through the use of metafictive structures and a ludic approach, an awareness of the process by which fairy tales indoctrinate and control, and thereby challenges interpretations, such as Bettelheim's, which have done as much to construct notions of children as the stories themselves.[41]

Sophie in *The BFG* is an orphan and Matilda, like a changeling child, is clearly in the wrong family. Both novels can be seen as tales of constructing new, and happier, families and a journey towards selfhood. Yet the function of these characters goes beyond the familiar child's role and further than that of James and Charlie. Both Sophie and Matilda can be mapped more persuasively as the 'fairy godmother' figure, providing solutions to the problems of, and 'rescuing', the admittedly childlike adult figures: the Big Friendly Giant and Miss Honey. Both of these 'adults' are closer to Charlie and James than they are to Sophie and Matilda. They are abused by their families (or step-families) and their plights are signified by lack of food. Sophie is able to find the BFG relief from an exclusive diet of 'filthsome' snozzcumbers, and after witnessing the near starvation of Miss Honey, Matilda is moved to act to save her.

Of course, like James and Charlie, both Sophie and Matilda are typical fairy tale heroes, but they also perform the fairy tale function of 'magical figure' – Sophie through her strength, bravery and storytelling ability, and Matilda, through channelling her anger and frustration into energy that moves objects, in order to avenge the wrongs done to Miss Honey. In fact, Dahl deliberately alludes to fairy tales on a number of occasions in both *The BFG* – the opening states that '[t]he houses look bent and crooked like houses in a fairy tale'[42] – and in *Matilda*, making Miss Honey's character not only a religious figure with her 'pale oval Madonna face' in relation to Miss Trunchbull as the 'Prince of Darkness, the Foul Serpent, the Fiery Dragon',[43] but a character out of fairy tales. Her own reference to her favourite poem – Dylan Thomas's poem 'In Country Sleep', which itself alludes to Little Red Riding Hood and other tales – allows us to see her own sense of herself as a child in a fairy tale.[44] Though Matilda never comments on this connection, it triggers her own reaction to Miss Honey's cottage. She relies on her knowledge of fairy tales to forewarn the reader of Miss Honey's threatened situation. The house, described in the third person, but focalised through Matilda's point of view 'was like an illustration in Grimm or Hans Andersen. It was the house where the poor woodcutter lived with Hansel and Gretel and where Red Riding Hood's grandmother lived and it was also the house of the Seven Dwarfs and the Three Bears and all the rest of them'.[45] As discussed above, Matilda herself has a strong relationship to fairy tales, and she recognises and uses the power of cautionary tales to strengthen her moral power over her father, so that the allusions have a dual purpose: they demonstrate Matilda's imagination and they offer the reader of the story a sense of collusion with the narrator.

Allusion and collusion: the power of the storyteller

Alluding to specific fairy tales is one of the ways in which Dahl calls attention to them as a distinct form with a relationship to his own stories. At times, these allusions perform an ironic function and thus undermine the moral purpose behind the original tale. The much-quoted example from *Revolting Rhymes*, for instance, is used to emphasise Dahl's anarchic transformation of 'Little Red Riding Hood' in which Red 'whips a pistol from her knickers'.[46] However, what is more significant in his attitude towards fairy tales is the way in which he draws attention to the metanarrative. When Red Riding Hood compliments her grandmother on her fur coat, the Wolf corrects her:

> 'That's wrong!' cried Wolf. 'Have you forgot
> To tell me what BIG TEETH I've got?'[47]

Not only does Dahl transform the tale in a humorous way; not only does he undermine the moral force of the story, put into a folk tale for a heterogeneous audience by adults wanting to teach children a lesson, but he is also able to point out that stories are told in different ways and that it is the storyteller who makes that choice.[48]

Similarly, Dahl demonstrates his awareness that stories are put to use, as Zipes has made clear, for particular purposes and that the stories typically read to children are de-fanged. In the opening poem, a retelling of 'Cinderella', Dahl places himself on the side of the original tellers of folk tales, rather than those who have, since the nineteenth century, constructed stories in order to encourage conformity. Dahl's work represents a return to the subversive approach to storytelling, one that embraces violence in what Tatar might call 'a festive register':

> I guess you think you know this story.
> You don't. The real one's much more gory.[49]

Directed as much to the adult 'voicing' the poem, the rhyme playfully prevents a seriousness of purpose. The motivation to return to the original celebratory and carnivalesque function of the tale is also marked by Dahl's method, repeated in many of his books, of *performing* the storytelling event. These episodes, which act out a dialogue reminiscent of storytelling in action, in which the child listener questions the teller and thereby influences the outcome of the tale, derive from the early history of the folk tale, and the opportunity for active engagement. This is a return to the tradition that Zipes describes, in which '[g]ifted narrators told the tales to audiences who actively participated in their transmission by posing questions, suggesting changes and circulating tales among themselves'.[50] In addition, and perhaps as an indication of the recognition due to Dahl's work as a challenge to much that is insipid in a great deal of modern children's literature, this narrative method invites a chance, as Tatar suggests, 'to engage in a joint interpretive effort that acknowledges the child's power to read the events, and, finally, to collaborate once again with the child in creating a new story based on the old'.[51] When Cedric Cullingford claims that '[t]he style is the personality', it is likely that he is referring to this aspect of Dahl's work: 'told with all the self-belief of the storyteller, with a sense of spontaneity and pleasure in the telling'.[52] Although false, the sense of spontaneity evident in these later novels must be considered as a key factor linking Dahl's work with the folk and fairy tale tradition.

It is possible to find many examples of this kind of dialogue: Charlie's quizzing of Grandpa Joe about the history of the mysterious Willy Wonka, Matilda's questioning of Miss Honey as she tells her story, Sophie's lengthy conversations with the BFG (which seem to take up a large proportion of the book) during which he informs her about the predilections of the various giants. The most significant use of this method is in *The Witches*. Not only is the unnamed boy the narrator and a storyteller himself, but he also destabilises the narrative by informing his readers about the 'true' nature of witches, displacing the whole notion of fairy tales. After finding out that witches have no toes, the boy asks:

> 'Are those the only differences then, Grandmamma?'
> 'There's one more,' my grandmother said. 'Just one more.'
> 'What is it, Grandmamma?'

'Their spit is blue.'

'Blue!' I cried. 'Not blue! Their spit can't be *blue*!'

'Blue as a bilberry,' she said.

'You don't mean it, Grandmamma! Nobody can have blue spit!'

'Witches can,' she said.

'Is it like ink?' I asked.

'Exactly,' she said. 'They even use it to write with. They use those old-fashioned pens that have nibs and they simply lick the bib.'

'Can you *notice* the blue spit, Grandmamma? If a witch was talking to me, would I be able to notice it?'

'Only if you looked carefully,' my grandmother said.

'If you looked very carefully you would probably see a slight bluish tinge on her teeth. But it doesn't show much.'

'It would if she spat,' I said.

'Witches never spit,' my grandmother said. 'They daren't.'[53]

It is worth reproducing this passage at length to draw attention to the performance of a particular kind of storytelling, one that mimics possible adult–child interactions. Although it is possible to claim that this kind of writing is lazy and repetitive, it is in such passages that Dahl is at his most playful and irreverent; in which he most effectively conspires with children against adults. This exchange comes at the end of an eight-page dialogue between the boy and his grandmother. The reading child (or the child being read to) thus learns about witches at the same time as the boy, and is presented with a very different reading experience (as is the adult reader) from a straightforward narrative conveying the same information. By reproducing the storytelling *act*, Dahl makes us aware of the process by which a story is made, and it is not by the author alone. There is give and take, and there are shared ideas. What is more, the boy, upon hearing the facts, repeatedly considers his grandmother's role as a teller – is she lying or is she telling the truth? These are questions that the reader must decide. Whereas our expectations are often founded on the assumption that the author tells and the reader receives that knowledge, Dahl's revealing of the scaffolding of the story is playful and imbues the reading experience with power.

What Dahl demonstrates in his work is that taking possession of the story – inviting 'the reader in on the conspiracy of power an author has over his victims'[54] – becoming the teller rather than merely the told, is the most significant way to overcome powerlessness, and perhaps the only way. The mouse-boy at the end of *The Witches* does not return to his normal state, but he does tell the story and is able to 'tell' the poisoning of the witches to his grandmother, as well as to his readers. The positive mood of the book, although it appears to prefigure the death of both the grandmother and the boy, is signified by his sense of power and satisfaction, as though the telling of this 'true' story – his testimony – is the most important result.

This attitude towards storytelling as power suggests a position familiar to those of many postmodern and post-structural theorists of the late twentieth century, and although there is no evidence to claim that Roald Dahl was deliberately calling upon such ideas, the implications of his subversion of the normative role of the author in the tradition of children's literature touch on challenges offered by thinkers influenced by cultural theory. His awareness that adults have a 'relentless need to civilize'[55] suggests the recognition that childhood is embedded in Ideological State Apparatuses,[56] which include the education system and, thus, children's literature. Sharon Royer's claim that 'Dahl's societal view, characterized by the belief that authorities and social institutions, such as government and schools, should not be trusted',[57] implies his suspicion of that impulse to control, as well as his sensitivity to the extent to which power relations between adults and children are embedded in the relationship between author and reader.

The idea of the play of power in these relationships is closely allied to any theoretical position which focuses on the importance of the role of language in shaping subjectivity. While the sense of pleasure in the shared premise of storytelling may be only momentary, these fleeting effects can lead to an awareness of the extent to which a sense of self relies upon an active engagement with language. The interplay of both socio-political and psychoanalytical lines of thought can be seen in the extent to which the subject can be considered as a construction of both social forces and of the symbolic order. Where Dahl can claim to collude with the child is through a challenge to the expected function of children's literature and the unequal relationship between the adult author and child reader – that is, through a return to the folk tale paradigm. As both Zipes and Tatar suggest, the transformation of the folk tale into fairy tales for children represented a shift in the power structure of storytelling, away from a shared act in which the teller and the told could, if only momentarily, become 'the producers as well as the product of meaning'.[58]

The tellers of Dahl's stories – James, the BFG and the mouse-boy hero of *The Witches* – achieve their selfhood through telling their own 'folk' stories. Matilda, too, uses her 'writing' skills to reshape the fairy tale of Miss Honey's past. It could even be said that Matilda removes Miss Honey from the 'fairy-tale' entirely and positions her in a new story – one in which the magical powers that made Matilda her fairy godmother have disappeared. Dahl also invites a return to the 'folk' tradition by presenting, in dialogue form, the act of telling the story. His method of 'performing' the storytelling event – allowing his child characters to ask questions that his child readers might ask – shows the pleasure of the experience of mutual engagement in the making of a story. The pleasure of this experience, for both teller and told, is at once subversive and liberating, but it is in the *act* of telling that the power resides.

The recognition of the power of the teller may be the most vital aspect of Dahl's distinctive style, as both Hollindale and Nicholson suggest. Dahl's own sense of himself is delivered by his own writing acts. The strength of his memories of being a child, reported in *Boy*, both as a victim of powerful adult authority and in his love of chocolate, is continually communicated through the energy of expression – his 'inventive joy of language'.[59]

While Dahl appears, to his more stringent critics, to eschew the moralising function of children's literature, he embraces and invites the strongest moral position: to 'write' one's own story and refuse to be subjected to others. This is surely the truth that folk tales offer us and it is a truth that continues to challenge, if only during the process of reading, the power structures that define and subject us.

Notes

1. Roald Dahl, *Matilda* (London: Jonathan Cape, 1988).
2. *Matilda*: 34.
3. Maria Tatar, *Off With Their Heads: Fairy Tale and the Culture of Childhood* (Princeton: Princeton University Press, 1992): 25.
4. Catriona Nicholson, 'Dahl, The Marvellous Boy', in Dudley Jones and Tony Watkins (eds), *A Necessary Fantasy? The Heroic Figure in Children's Popular Culture* (New York: Garland, 2000): 309–26, at 319–20.
5. Peter Hollindale, '"And Children Swarmed to Him Like Settlers. He Became a Land": The Outrageous Success of Roald Dahl', in Julia Briggs, Dennis Butts and M. O. Grenby (eds), *Popular Children's Literature in Britain* (London: Ashgate, 2008): 271–86, at 280.
6. William Honan, 'Roald Dahl, Writer, 74, is Dead; Bestsellers Enchanted Children', *New York Times*, 24 November 1990.
7. Roald Dahl, *Revolting Rhymes* (London: Puffin, 1982).
8. Tatar (1992): xvi (citing Honan).
9. *Ibid.*: 236.
10. *Ibid.*: 92.
11. Roald Dahl, *The Witches* (London: Puffin, 1983): 10.

12. Roald Dahl, *The BFG* (London: Jonathan Cape, 1982): 70.
13. Tatar (1992): 228.
14. See Hollindale.
15. Maria Tatar, '"Violent Delights" in Children's Literature', in Jeffrey H. Goldstein, *Why We Watch: The Attractions of Violent Entertainment* (Oxford: Oxford University Press, 1998): 69–87, at 85.
16. Tatar (1992): 77.
17. Jack Zipes, *Fairy Tales and the Art of Subversion* (New York: Routledge, 1991): 3.
18. *Ibid.*: 7.
19. Tatar (1992): 30.
20. *Ibid.*: 20.
21. In *The BFG*, the last sentence reads: 'You've just finished reading it' (224). In *James and the Giant Peach* (New York: Knopf, 1961), the last sentence reads: 'And *that* is what you have just finished reading' (119).
22. Tatar (1998): 81.
23. *Ibid.*: 71.
24. *Ibid.*: 72.
25. *Ibid.*: 71.
26. *BFG*: 206–8.
27. Melanie Klein was a Freudian psychoanalyst whose work with children gave rise to object relations theory. Eating – or, more fundamentally, the breast – is the source, for Kleinians, of both pleasure (when given) and anger (when denied). These 'split' feelings can be seen in fairy tale tropes of stepmothers who want to starve their children or witches who want to eat them, as well as in the use of food as a reward or punishment.
28. *James and the Giant Peach*: 52.
29. Roald Dahl, *Charlie and the Chocolate Factory* (New York: Knopf, 1964).
30. *Charlie and the Chocolate Factory*: 81–2.
31. Tatar (1992): 237.
32. *Ibid.*
33. Sigmund Freud, 'Creative Writers and Daydreaming', in David Lodge (ed.), *20th Century Literary Criticism* (London: Longman, 1972): 36–43, at 41.
34. Nicholson: 314.
35. John Ruskin, *The King of the Golden River* [1841] (London: George Allen, 1892).
36. John Ruskin, 'Fairyland', in *The Art of England* (Kent: Elibron, 2006): 117–60, at 121.
37. *James and the Giant Peach*: 1.
38. Jack Zipes, *Breaking the Magic Spell* (Lexington: University Press of Kentucky, 2002); Maria Tatar, *The Hard Facts of Grimms' Fairy Tales* (Princeton: Princeton University Press, 1987).
39. Hollindale: 271.
40. Bruno Bettleheim, *The Uses of Enchantment* (New York: Knopf, 1977): 8.

41. Tatar (1992): 78.
42. *The BFG*: 11.
43. *Matilda*: 66, 109.
44. *Ibid.*: 184.
45. *Matilda*: 186.
46. *Revolting Rhymes*: 39.
47. *Ibid.*: 5.
48. Dahl does this, too, in *The Witches*, when he starts off by claiming that, unlike fairy tales, 'This is about REAL WITCHES' (7).
49. *Revolting Rhymes*: 5.
50. Zipes: 7.
51. Tatar (1992): 236.
52. Cedric Cullingford, *Children's Literature and Its Effects: The Formative years* (London: Cassell, 1998): 154.
53. *The Witches*: 31–2.
54. Cullingford: 157.
55. Tatar (1992): xvi.
56. Louis Althusser, 'Ideology and Ideological State Apparatuses', in *Lenin and Philosophy and other Essays* (1970), translated by Ben Brewster (New York: Monthly Review Press, 1972): 121–76.
57. Sharon E. Royer, 'Roald Dahl and Sociology 101', *The ALAN Review* 26(1) (Fall 1998): http://scholar.lib.vt.edu/ejournals/ALAN/fall98/royer.html#. howard (cited 11 August 2010).
58. Robert Lapsley and Michael Westlake, *Film Theory: An Introduction* (Manchester: Manchester University Press, 1988), cited in Paula Murphy, 'Psychoanaylsis and Film Theory Part I, "A New Kind of Mirror"', *Kritikos* 2 (Feb. 2005): 6.
59. Hollindale: 274. Roald Dahl, *Boy: Tales of Childhood* (London: Cape, 1984).

2

Discomfort and Delight: The Role of Humour in Roald Dahl's Works for Children

Jackie E. Stallcup

Many of the literary techniques used to create humour parallel those involved in triggering disgust, and both disgust and humour can be used in multiple ways to trace and traverse our social boundaries. What we find humorous and what we find disgusting signal the limits of the acceptable and unacceptable, telling us what behaviour will allow us to maintain our in-group status and what behaviour will cause us to become outcasts. For this reason, humour and disgust can be used conservatively: not only to define acceptable behaviour but also to urge us to adopt it. But both can also be used subversively, to trace the boundaries of the acceptable in order to call attention to their arbitrariness or even to encourage their demolition. In this chapter, I explore how Dahl intertwines the oddly related pleasures of humour and disgust in order to create slyly satirical commentary.

Of course, it has long been acknowledged that Dahl's books are very funny.[1] We need look no further for confirmation of this than the Roald Dahl Funny Prize, established in Britain in 2008 by Children's Laureate Michael Rosen to honour the funniest children's books published each year. But Dahl's humour is often seen as low-brow and unsophisticated, or as catering to the basest impulses of children. Adult readers in particular have not always appreciated how Dahl gleefully makes fun of many things that we piously teach children that they should not even notice, let alone laugh at, such as gender, appearance, weight, disability, and so on. In fact, some critics of Dahl's work seem unable to confine themselves to a dispassionate discussion of his work, but instead plunge into diatribes laden with visceral distaste. For such readers, the fine balancing act that teeters

31

between laughter and revulsion comes tumbling down decisively on the side of disgust.[2] Much of Dahl's humour, as we will see, turns upon cruelty or situations of disgust or debasement and abuse, and (like many a good satire) may make readers laugh out loud and cringe simultaneously.

Humour in literature serves a number of purposes. It can allow us to deal effectively and in a socially acceptable manner with the problems and anxieties of being human. It can help to establish and maintain social taboos (for example, we confirm incest taboos when we make mocking 'redneck' jokes about marrying one's close relatives). Or it can be used to blow social *mores* sky high, as with George Carlin's riff on the 'Seven Words You Can Never Say on Television'.[3] For children in particular, humour can – among other functions – help them to work through anxieties about impending maturity.[4] The grotesque transformations of Violet Beauregarde and Mike Teavee in *Charlie and the Chocolate Factory* are two of many possible examples that suggest how Dahl encourages young readers to laugh at issues related to their own expanding, developing bodies. Dahl himself recognised the importance of humour for young readers.[5] In *Matilda*, when Matilda discusses with Miss Honey the kind of literature that she enjoys, we might almost think of her commentary as Dahl's manifesto:

> 'Do you think that all children's books ought to have funny bits in them?' Miss Honey asked.
> 'I do,' Matilda said. 'Children are not so serious as grown-ups and they love to laugh.'[6]

Throughout his career as a writer for children, Dahl astutely recognised and sought to assuage the anxieties that young readers might be wrestling with, offering them explosive forms of release through laughter.

From the time of Aristotle to the present, theorists in fields as diverse as philosophy, psychology, biology, sociology, anthropology and literary studies have weighed in on the seemingly simple question, 'What does it mean to be funny?'[7] Up through the twentieth century, theorists sought a kind of 'grand unified theory' that could account, simply and succinctly, for all the ways in which we can have our funny bones tickled. More recently, it has become clear that such a synthesis is unattainable and that humour is multifarious, diverse and uncontainable. As Robin Andrew Haig points out, 'humor is a multifaceted phenomenon, so that no one theory satisfactorily explains or predicts all aspects. The pragmatic stance is to apply several theories to cover all eventualities'.[8] With this in mind, it is useful to examine a few of the techniques and topics – including incongruity, taboo and derision – that Dahl uses to various effects and purposes.[9]

Incongruity

Incongruity is a common tool for humourists, involving setting up a particular set of expectations and then suddenly pulling the rug out from under the reader's or listener's feet. As Christie Davies notes:

> ambiguity and incongruity are central to most jokes, for jokes depend on the teller playing with hidden meanings that are suddenly revealed in an unexpected way. Typically a joke consists of a single text which is compatible with two different scripts that are radically opposed to one another … The skilled joke-teller begins as if he were telling a mundane tale or asking a routine question and the listener, though suspicious, goes along with this until the punch line suddenly switches the joke to a radi-cally different script. First our expectations and interest are aroused by the story, whose purpose we cannot fully discern, and then suddenly all is resolved from a direction we didn't expect.[10]

We can think of incongruity as playing with categories: we sort things into categories, which incongruity then disorders. Jonathan Miller gives the example of a comedy sketch in which someone asks, 'Following the nuclear holocaust, how soon will normal public services be resumed?' and the answer is, 'That's a very fair question. Following Armageddon, we do hope to have public services working fairly smoothly pretty soon after the event. In all fairness, though, I ought to point out that it must needs be something in the nature of a skeleton service.'[11] Miller goes on to dissect the humour in several ways, but most relevant here is his point that in treating Armageddon as if it is an ordinary, common-or-garden natural disaster, we have a serious disordering of categories: 'We are amused by a discrepancy; that is, the discrepancy between the magnitude of Armageddon in the form of a nuclear holocaust, and the extraordinary triviality of public services.'[12]

Disgust and horror are also predicated upon incongruity. As Mary Douglas famously put it, dirt is 'matter out of place',[13] or, in other words, something that is dirty or disgusting is something that is incongruous – it is not what or where we expect it to be. Such incongruity can be simply disgusting, but if a playful mood prevails and no one is likely to be badly hurt, we can have both humour and disgust springing from the single moment of disordered categories. *The Twits* (1980) abounds in examples, such as when Dahl describes in lovingly gross detail all the items in Mr Twit's beard that do *not* belong in beards, including 'maggoty green cheese' and 'the slimy tail of a tinned sardine' or when Mrs Twit serves up spaghetti with tomato sauce, cheese and squishy worms.[14] Our pleasure in reading these passages arises from incongruity: the humorous, disgusting images of icky things nestling precisely where they don't belong.[15]

Incongruity can also wobble precariously between humour and horror. In reading Raymond Briggs's picture book *When the Wind Blows*, for example, the reader is often tipped off balance and left unsure how to react. In this book, an older couple prepare for an impending nuclear holocaust in a hopelessly naive way that emphasises the fact that it is impossible to make meaningful preparations for such an event.[16] We can laugh at them as they bicker with each other and go about trying to create a safe shelter in their house by propping doors against an inner wall, but this laughter turns to horror once the blast hits and they continue, afterwards, to try to keep a stiff upper lip and wonder when government services will resume, even after they turn a hideous shade of greeny-white, begin to lose their hair, and start bleeding from radiation poisoning.

Like Briggs, Dahl also plays with incongruity in ways that could be humorous or horrifying. In the scene in *Matilda* when Miss Trunchbull visits Miss Honey's classroom, for example, the reader, like the students, may be both transfixed and moved to hilarity by the terrible things that Miss Trunchbull does. She barks and bellows astoundingly inappropriate things at the children; she picks up one child by his hair and another by his ears; and she claims that her idea of the perfect school is one which has no children in it.[17] In another scene, she picks up a little girl by her pigtails and launches her like an Olympic hammer. Throughout these scenes, Dahl creates incongruity through disordering the category of 'normal adult behaviour': we simply do not expect adults to say and do the things that Miss Trunchbull says and does. Given the bare descriptions of her actions, it is easy to see that this could be simply horrifying – a tale of hideous abuse. But Dahl makes the situations humorous in two ways: first, in every case, Dahl is careful to let us know that there are no serious consequences to the children. This ensures that each scene stays on the side of slapstick and never dissolves into the horror of actual blood, gore and broken bones. For example, the little girl who was flung by her pigtails quickly recovers and totters back to the playground.[18] Second, Miss Trunchbull is completely calm and matter of fact about the possible consequences of what she is doing, even as she performs actions that are wildly misaligned with our expectations of normal adult behaviour. When she picks up Eric by his ears, she starts by simply pinching them, making him say 'Ow! You're hurting me!' Her reply is 'brisk', a word that we associate with appropriate adult behaviour, though not when coupled with what she does next, which is to lift him from his seat by his ears and hold him aloft.[19] We certainly might expect a brisk answer from a headmistress, but we do not expect her to lift students right out of their seats by their ears. Further, her calmness intensifies the humour because it contrasts so wildly with the potentially explosive nature of her action. Similarly, her matter-of-fact reaction after tossing the little girl by her pigtails contributes to the humour: she dusts off her hands and simply says, 'Not bad … considering I'm not in strict training', before striding away.[20] This is one of the few moments in the text when she speaks like a normal human being, which is humorously incongruous with what she has just done to the little girl.

A particularly clear example of how Dahl humorously disrupts age categories may occur when an adult reads aloud to a child the poem 'The Crocodile' from *Dirty Beasts*. This poem begins as simply a rather gruesomely amusing discussion about how Crocky-Wock the crocodile likes to prepare his meals – of children. Boys, we are told, taste best with mustard, but mustard does not go with the 'plaits and curls' of little girls, who are much tastier with 'butterscotch and caramel'. So far, so good – it is gross, but it is also rather funny; we do not feel too threatened because these are imaginary, unnamed, unspecific children who are being covered in gooey sauces. At this point, the poem shifts into a parental voice, saying typical, soothing things about bedtime – at first. But then things turn scary. The narrator claims to hear something coming up the stairs and urges, 'Go lock the door and fetch my gun! / Go on, child, hurry! Quickly, run!'[21] Tension builds line after line until suddenly Crocky-Wock bursts upon them, with his 'shining teeth' and 'greedy smile'. The disordering of categories will be most strongly felt if the story is read aloud by a parent, because then we experience a double disruption: the bedtime story turns into a bloodbath, and the soothing parental voice becomes a harbinger of doom. As with so much of Dahl's work, we are on a knife's edge here between humour and horror. If a mood of playfulness and safety has been established, then one can imagine the delighted screams and the delicious and humour-filled enjoyment of category disruption that might be triggered by a parent reading this poem aloud. However, if the child is abused and if the home does not feel like a safe place, then the category disruption may be taken as horrifying and frightening instead of humorous.

A comparison of two of Dahl's shorter works demonstrates how he uses incongruity and disordered categories for two quite different effects, creating humour in *The Magic Finger* and horror in 'The Swan'. Though both texts are about the same length, 'The Swan', a short story collected in *The Wonderful Story of Henry Sugar and Six More*, is aimed at an older audience, while *The Magic Finger*, a brief, illustrated book, is for a younger audience.[22] This split is also reflected in the subject matter and in the way that Dahl deals with disordered categories and disrupted bodies in each.

In 'The Swan', Peter Watson, a young boy who loves birds, is tormented by his schoolmates, two thugs who hunt and shoot birds. Their horrific acts towards Peter include tying him between the rails of a railway track and forcing him to lie there while a train rushes over him. He survives, and they move on to a new torture: despite Peter's pleas to spare a nesting swan's life, they kill it, butcher it, and tie the now severed wings to his arms. Having done this, they force him at gunpoint to climb a tree and then take turns shooting at him. In the only fantasy moment of the otherwise hideously realistic text, Peter, tormented beyond endurance when he is actually hit by a bullet, launches himself into the air and uses the wings tied to his arms to fly home, where he collapses into his mother's arms. The incongruity and disordering of the bodies in this story – the butchering of the swan, the hideous mingling of human and swan body when the wings that have been so horribly severed are tied to Peter's tortured body, the moment when the bullet actually penetrates him – are all treated in such a way as to cause the reader to be horrified and sickened. The strong disgust reaction generated by these actions is aimed at condemning hunters, equating them with thugs and bullies of the very worst kind, and implying that they are not fit to be a part of decent society.

Hunters are dealt with in a very different way in *The Magic Finger*. The resulting message is the same – people should not hunt and shoot birds – but the use of *humorously* disordered bodies means that the horror is muted and a mood of laughter prevails. In this book, a young girl is blessed with a 'magic finger' which she uses to turn her neighbours, who are hunters, into semi-birds. Like the boy in 'The Swan', the human family in *The Magic Finger* retain many of their human features – heads, bodies, legs – but have bird wings instead of arms. At the same time, the birds that they have been hunting turn into semi-humans. When the birds take over the humans' house, the human family is cast out and must create a nest and gather appropriate food for themselves. Here, the disordered bodies are humorous rather than grotesque for at least two reasons. First, Dahl does not focus on danger or distress, but instead explores how exactly such a little family might pull together to over-come various obstacles – and they do so in ways that are both inventive and charming. For example, Mr Gregg figures out how to build a nest and the children collect twigs for him using their mouths since they have no hands. When it appears that they might have to eat worms, Mrs Gregg assures them that she can mince them up so small they'll never know what they are eating. As it turns out, they manage with some apples instead, but it is a comforting, reassuring moment in the text. Second, their transformation fulfils a deep-seated human desire: as one of the children says, 'Oh, isn't it lovely! … I've always wanted to know what it feels like to be a bird.'[23] As a result, instead of being horrified by the disordered bodies, the reader can vicariously experience being a little birdie snug in a warm, cosy nest.

Once we have experienced the pleasures of flying and nesting, Dahl then confronts us with the dangers experienced by birds. In the morning, the birds come out of the human house with guns and threaten the nesting family. When the mother pleads for her children's lives, the birds point out that the father and his boys had wantonly killed six bird children the day before. Because of their disordered bodies and their experience of the pleasures of flight and nesting, everyone – father, mother, children and readers – is now struck with a feeling of kinship rather than enmity towards the birds. With that, the horror of what they have done becomes clear to everyone in the family and they swear never to hunt again. The mother, transformed back into her own body, even buries the bodies of the young birds, creating a cemetery and memorial rather than a meal, while the father takes a hammer to every gun in the house and the sons feed wild birds from a bag of barley. As the narrator says, 'they seemed to have gone completely dotty',[24] but the dottiness is presented as positive eccentricity rather than horrifying strangeness. With *The Magic Finger*, thus, we have the potential for horror in the disordering of the bodies, but because of the humorous way that Dahl deals with the family's experiences as hybrids, the feelings spill over into pleasure. In a sense, we are jollied into understanding and condemning the consequences of hunting rather than horrified into it, as we are with 'The Swan'.

Humour and the taboo

Both humour and disgust have close ties with the taboo: violating a cultural taboo can be met either with laughter or with the crinkled nose and primly drawn back skirt that signal disgust, or with a mixture of the two. Further, humour – in tempering disgust – can help us to cope with the social forces that surround and shape us. Children in particular may experience anxieties regarding taboo subjects as they wrestle with making their unruly bodies conform to arbitrary or bewildering social standards of cleanliness and invisibility. In the throes of dealing with these anxieties, they often find jokes about bodies and bodily functions particularly funny.[25] Texts that play humorously with such taboo topics scrape uneasily against childhood's somewhat furtive desires: the desire to secure control over one's own body, the desire for one's body to be free of the control of others, the desire to have control over the all-powerful adults in one's life and, of course, the taboos placed upon expressing all such illicit desire. As Dahl engages in humour of the taboo (particularly coarse scatological humour or humour of the 'material bodily lower stratum' as Bakhtin puts it), we again find ourselves teetering precariously between laughter and disgust.[26]

Dahl's poetry for children provides a rich vein of examples of humour of the taboo. The very title of the first poem in *Dirty Beasts*, 'The Pig', evokes the grotesque: pigs are often associated with filth and one way to express disgust with a person is to call him or her a pig. Aside from the title, the poem does not start in the register of disgust, because Dahl's pig is special: he has 'a massive brain' which he uses to read, do maths, and puzzle about the meaning of life, and he is illustrated by Quentin Blake as clean, pink, and surrounded by books and scientific instruments. However, once he uses his intellect to work out that the meaning of *his* particular life is to be chops, sausage and bacon, he devises a plan to save his skin: the next morning, when the unsuspecting Farmer Bland strolls into the sty, the pig leaps upon him and eats him 'from head to toe'. Upon reading this poem the first time, when I realised what the pig was going to do I gave a gasp of horrified laughter, finding myself awash in that ambivalent feeling of 'I can't believe Dahl's going to do this' that comes up so often when reading his work.

Much of the humour in this poem comes from the way that Dahl revels in gustatory disgust. First, he forces us to confront exactly what we ourselves are eating: under a picture of the horrified (and rather cute) pig, who has just discovered that he's going to be eaten, Dahl catalogues all the parts of a pig that we eat. It is surprisingly gruesome to have one's favourite cuts of meat reeled off by the animal himself, particularly when it is an animal who does not wish to be eaten but yet recognises the commercial and culinary value of his own body parts:

> They want my bacon slice by slice
> To sell at a tremendous price![27]

Second, Dahl dwells lovingly on the pig's feast of Farmer Bland, noting that he 'chew[ed] the pieces nice and slow' and that once he was done, the pig 'felt absolutely no remorse'. Thus, we move from a rather queasy discussion of the things that we *do* eat to an even queasier discussion of things we definitely do *not*. The highly taboo subject of cannibalism (for the pig is anthropomorphised to the extent that his eating the farmer amounts to this) is made both horrifying and yet funny and understandable by Dahl's depiction of the pig, who is, after all, only acting in defence of his own life. In the rest of the collection, in addition to animals eating humans (which also occurs in 'The Crocodile', 'The Lion' and 'The Ant-Eater'), we are also treated to bums being stung or poked full of porcupine quills, cowpats raining from the sky, and a tummy that shrieks demands for chocolates and sweets. It is not surprising that the jacket copy uses both 'unmentionable' and 'irreverent' to describe the goings-on. Much of the humour in these poems relates to bodily functions, illicit body parts and other taboo subjects. Catriona Nicholson notes that such humour is particularly appealing to young readers, quoting two such readers who pinpoint 'rudeness' as a key to Dahl's success. As Nicholson notes, Dahl 'shamelessly exploits the notion that a particular form of pleasure is to be found in risqué humour and juvenile references to bodily functions'.[28]

Derision

Frank MacHovec writes that 'derision theory is based on the premise that we laugh down at others. Its basic drive is to humiliate, to subjugate, to disparage. The feeling tone is hostile and aggressive, its attitude negative and pessimistic'.[29] Because it can be so mean spirited, derisive humour in children's literature often disturbs adult readers – after all, we are deeply invested in the process of civilising children, and an important part of this process is teaching them not to be cruel to others. It is not surprising, then, that when Dahl uses derision – making fun of fat people or suggesting that outer ugliness indicates inner lack of character, for example – it can trigger disgust in readers, who find such messages low and contemptible. Another critique that can be levelled at the use of derisive humour is that it results in shallow, one-dimensional characters who do little to deepen our understanding of human nature. However, it is important to note that such derisive portrayals can also be used in the service of more complex purposes, and this is precisely what Dahl does in his novel *Danny, the Champion of the World*.[30]

For the most part, *Danny* is not a very funny book. Much of it is taken up with sympathetically tracing the complex relationship between Danny and his flawed but deeply loving, bereaved father. However, throughout the novel, Dahl makes careful use of derision in order to place the reader in a position in which the closing scene *can* be funny. Generally speaking, in order to find a situation humorous, the reader needs to be securely positioned as an insider to the joke rather than as the butt, but it is a bit tricky to get the reader into this position in a book as dark and ethically ambiguous as *Danny*. Although his mother has long been dead, Danny has had an idyllic childhood living in a gypsy caravan with his father, a mechanic and filling-station owner. However, early in the novel, Danny is shocked to learn that his beloved, idolised father is a poacher – and not simply out of necessity. In explaining his secret to Danny, his father rhapsodises about the excitement of the chase and the satisfaction of outsmarting the gamekeepers and the landowner whose animals he is killing. Danny is further both dismayed and thrilled to find that all of the authority figures in his small village take part in the illegal activity with enthusiasm, from the policeman to the vicar's wife.

The bulk of the book is thus spent getting the reader to nestle securely and comfortably inside this circle of morally compromised characters. Danny (and by extension the reader) is reassured over and over again that his father's actions are justified as well as pleasurable, that everyone does it, that the gamekeepers are nasty people, and that the person who is ostensibly being harmed – the landowner, Mr Hazell – richly deserves to have his livestock poached. It is in the character of the landowner in particular that Dahl makes use of derision. From his first appearance, the landowner is presented as a flat character who is wholly vile; he is a 'roaring snob' who 'barks' orders at the eight-year-old Danny.[31] He has 'tiny, piggy eyes' and 'a smug superior little smile'.[32] At the same time, Dahl makes it clear that Danny's father does not have any means of fighting Mr Hazell openly: after he refuses to sell the man petrol and tells him to pick on someone his own size, the very next day a health inspector comes to see if the caravan is 'a fit place for humans to live in'.[33] When the caravan passes inspection, Mr Hazell proceeds to use all of his official power and authority to try to drive Danny and his father out: 'Hardly a week went by without some local official dropping by to check up on one thing or another, and there was little doubt, my father said, that the long and powerful arm of Mr Hazell was reaching out behind the scenes and trying to run us off our land.'[34] In addition to making the reader despise Mr Hazell's underhand ways, this also gives Dahl the opportunity to elevate Danny's father, as he passes even the most stringent inspections, demonstrating that he is a scrupulous business owner and a loving, caring parent.

Given the set-up, then, we are prepared to laugh when we come to the final scene. Danny and his father have drugged Mr Hazell's pheasants and collected more than a hundred of them for distribution among the villagers. The vicar's wife is the one who makes the deliveries, with the birds tucked into her baby's carriage, so that the baby's innocence (and that of the vicar's wife herself) masks the illegal activity that they are carrying out. The scene devolves from anticipation and suspense into slapstick as Danny, his father, and the village doctor stand outside the filling-station watching the vicar's wife coming towards them. Instead of strolling sedately (as one might expect of a vicar's wife with no guilty stain upon her soul), she pushes the carriage at high speed, looking more and more frantic as she approaches. Chaos erupts as the birds shake off the last of the drugs, come whooshing drunkenly out from under the screaming baby and, too woozy to fly far, roost all over the filling-station. When Mr Hazell drives up and tries to claim them, the law is on Danny's father's side: once the animals are off his land, they no longer belong to Mr Hazell. In the *coup de grâce*, the pheasants exact a gooey, disgust-laden revenge. The village policeman (who is complicit in the poaching and who has been insulted by Mr Hazell in the course of getting the full story) suggests that they try to drive the birds back across the road and onto Mr Hazell's property. Too drugged to fly properly, the birds straggle drunkenly over Mr Hazell and his beloved, pampered Rolls Royce, as Danny describes: 'They were all over the roof and the hood, sliding and slithering and trying to keep a grip on that beautifully polished surface. I could hear their sharp claws scraping into the paintwork as they struggled to hang on, and already they were depositing their filthy droppings all over the roof.'[35] Finally, in the guise of being helpful, the policeman shoos both Mr Hazell and more than a dozen of the birds into the car, where the birds fly frantically around Mr Hazell's head, presumably continuing to deposit droppings all over him.

The scatological humour here is both disgust-laden and replete with the triumph of the underdog over the powerful. Although Danny's father breaks the law – not just knowingly, but gleefully – Dahl suggests that he lives by a higher moral code, one that decrees that humans treat each other with the respect due to equals rather than abuse the power that can be accrued through such artificial means as money and class status. But we are only able to take up this position and laugh at Mr Hazell's misfortune because Dahl has spent the early part of the book deriding him as a villain who gets what he richly deserves, from people with whom we identify despite their status as habitual law breakers. The final touch that both maintains the humour and allows us to remain firmly on the side of Danny and his father is that amid all of this disgusting imagery there is no mass slaughter of pheasants. Although more than a hundred of them were drugged and earmarked for the roasting oven, in the end, only six ingested so much of the sleeping powder that they simply never woke up. The rest of the birds fly off in the opposite direction from Mr Hazell's land and his shooting party and thus, presumably, make it to freedom. Their revenge on Mr Hazell and their triumphant escape from destruction are very satisfying, while the remaining six die a peaceful and painless death rather than being shot to painful, bloody pieces. Had we concluded with dozens of dead birds, or even just a few wounded, bleeding ones, the reader's laughter could have quickly turned to queasy disgust, distancing the reader from Danny and his father. It is a tricky balancing act, given the illegality of poaching and the potential for a bloodbath, but Dahl firmly guides his readers past the potential land mines to create a happy and humorous ending.

Childhood, humour and power

As Paul Lewis notes, 'because the presentation of a particular image or idea as a fitting subject for humor is based on value judgments, the creation and use of humor is an exercise of power: a force in controlling our responses to unexpected and dangerous happenings, a way of shaping the responses and attitudes of others and a tool in intergroup and intragroup dynamics'.[36] For this reason, he says, we should always ask not just *how* something is funny; we also need to consider to whom it is funny and what this suggests: 'how do these jokes embody or reinforce value systems; how do they serve psychic, social, cultural or political objectives?'[37] Disgust, too, can function in this way, marking the boundaries of the socially and morally acceptable. As Robert Rawdon Wilson argues, 'disgust is a regulating affect, a method that societies promote to control individual behaviour, but it is also a bully's device for gaining control over others'.[38] By controlling who or what is perceived as disgusting or humorous in a text, the author invites us to extrapolate the implied moral message to the real world around us.

Thus, both disgust and humour can be aligned with issues of power – a subject of great interest to children. Martha Wolfenstein,

in a discussion of childhood and humour, notes the special circumstances of children:

> Being a child is a predicament fraught with special difficulties. Children
> are little and they greatly long to have the bigness and powers of the
> adults and their marvellous-seeming prerogatives; they often feel
> oppressed by adult superiority and coerced by adult moral rules. Children
> undergo much frustration and disappointment; they experience many
> anxieties which are hard for them to master. From an early age children
> avail themselves of joking to alleviate their difficulties. They transform the
> painful into the enjoyable, turn impossible wishes and the envied bigness
> and powers of the adults into something ridiculous, expose adult preten-
> sions, make light of failures, and parody their own frustrated strivings.[39]

Gail Munde's work on children's humour preferences is very useful
to consider in relation to these issues. She performed a study that
compared 'children's selections of humorous books with adults' selections of humorous books for children'.[40] What is most striking about
her results is how the adult selectors preferred to use humour in the
service of a more serious purpose. As Munde puts it, 'Adults chose
books that were funny, to be sure, but in many cases books that were
didactic, almost as if humor needed a social or moral lesson in order
to be valuable.'[41] She goes on to note that children preferred humour
that was 'an end unto itself and often was entirely gratuitous'.[42]
Children, particularly of the youngest age group studied, preferred
'humor resulting from situations in which the undervalued, underestimated, misunderstood, overlooked, low-status, or physically awkward
protagonist turned the tables on the powerful, be it adults, their own
peer group, pirates, or imaginary monsters'.[43] For a slightly older age
group (8- to 10-year-olds), Munde says, 'defiance of authority was
the predominant theme in children's choices'.[44] Her many examples
suggest that for both adults and children, humour is predicated upon
issues of status and power, which children recognise that they do not
have but wish that they did. Dahl seems to have understood this and,
in his writing, acknowledges these feelings, giving young readers
multiple outlets for their frustrations and aggressions through the
humorous ways in which his small characters often get the better of
those who have more power.

In *Matilda*, for example, Dahl dismantles typical assumptions about
adult–child relationships in a scene that demonstrates how he intertwines disgust and humour with issues of power. Matilda and her new
friend Lavender are approached by an older child, Hortensia, during
break. Dahl describes Hortensia in lovingly disgusting terms: she

is a 'rugged ten-year-old with a boil on her nose'[45] who digs through
a bag of potato crisps and spews chewed-up flakes at Matilda and
Lavender as she regales them with humorous/disgusting tales of her
battle with the Trunchbull. Dahl puts his finger on the issue of power
when Matilda, after hearing Hortensia's stories, says, 'It's like a war', and
Hortensia replies, 'You're darn right it's like a war ... and the casual-
ties are terrific.'[46] This subversive view of adult–child relationships is
likely to appeal to child readers in the way that Munde discusses, for,
of course, having established that Matilda and the other children are
locked into an uneven power struggle with the hideous adults around
them, Dahl goes on to have them triumph in a most satisfactory and
humorous way.

Further, with the dirty tricks that Matilda plays on her parents,
Dahl makes use of derision, thus increasing the level of subversiveness.
Matilda's practical jokes on her father are clearly intended to make
him look ridiculous and stupid. After she puts superglue into his hat,
we are invited to laugh at the spectacle of him wearing a porkpie hat
with his purple-striped pyjamas.[47] Matilda's mother comes off no
better, being shallow, self-satisfied and smug. Such derision makes the
adults appear foolish and undercuts the status and authority that we
normally associate with adulthood. In more conventional children's
books, adults are often held up as positive role models for child
readers, or at least, adult behaviour may be critiqued in serious ways,
rather than in ways that invite ego-puncturing derisive laughter.

However, it is important to notice here that while Dahl's methods
might be subversive, he uses derisive humour and disgust to endorse
values that the most conservative parents could applaud. As Peter
Hollindale notes, Dahl is 'both conservative and subversive' and
'Matilda, having saved Miss Honey, needs her'.[48] The character of
Matilda functions quite subversively in many ways: she is exceedingly
intelligent – much more intelligent than her parents – and she outwits
the adults around her in humorous ways. But at the same time, she
is not self-sufficient; one of the most striking images in the novel is
Quentin Blake's final line drawing of Matilda and Miss Honey clinging
to each other and gazing out at the reader. Matilda is clever, but she
cannot survive on her own. She needs a sympathetic adult to care for
her and for whom she can care in a mutually satisfying and balanced
relationship. Further, in deriding Matilda's parents and in inviting the
reader both to laugh at and to feel superior to them, Dahl suggests
to readers that we do not want to act like them. Both humour and
disgust are used here to critique certain kinds of behaviour as socially
unacceptable. When Miss Trunchbull or Mr Wormwood is held up

as the butt of derisive laughter, Dahl suggests that their actions are outside the boundaries of socially acceptable behaviour and he taps into the scapegoating functions of both humour and disgust, creating outcasts who can be expelled in a symbolic cleansing of the group that remains inside the social boundaries. Whether we laugh at them or are disgusted by them – or some combination of the two, as is usually the case with Dahl – we know that we cannot act like these derided characters if we want to remain part of the socially powerful in-group.

Many of Dahl's works offer this uneasy mixture, featuring conservative, adult-pleasing morals wrapped in subversive tales of powerless youngsters who eventually triumph. We can see this at work most clearly in *Charlie and the Chocolate Factory*. Aside from Charlie, the children are all one-dimensional examples of naughtiness or even 'sinfulness' – selfishness, greed, gluttony – while our hero is a model child by adult standards: he is kind, loving, respectful of his elders, brave and resourceful in the face of adversity, and thus a worthy heir to the chocolate factory. In the lengthy lead-up to the actual factory tour, Dahl is careful to manoeuvre the reader onto the 'right' side before starting the disgusting fun. We are clearly meant both to identify with and to pity Charlie, who not only is sweet-natured and generous, but also is slowly starving,[49] a plot situation guaranteed to capture reader sympathy.[50] We are, therefore, firmly on the side of the conventionally 'good' boy when we finally arrive at the chocolate factory and meet the other four children. Each of them has a specific fault, such as gluttony or arrogance, and each ends up with a seriously disordered body, so that their faults become literally scarified – impressed upon their disordered bodies as a symbol of their excesses and as a warning to the reader not to behave in socially disruptive ways.

Each moment of transformation is both humorously and disgustingly incongruous. Veruca Salt, for example, is carried off by squirrels, which can be seen as furry, cuddly and cute when dealt with one at a time, but which become monstrous in the quantities required to carry her. As they swarm her, pin her down, decide she is a 'bad nut', and drag her to the rubbish chute, our reaction teeters between humour and horror because their categorisation fluctuates so disturbingly: they should be individually carrying nuts, but they are collectively carrying a person; they're cute, but there are too many of them; they are furry, but they are swarming. This is a particularly visceral scene in the 2005 movie: we get close-ups of their sweet little faces with cute wiggling noses, and then we get a horrifying vision of them swarming over Veruca like a squirming fur coat.[51] The scene makes me laugh, but it also makes me want to violently brush off my arms, shoulders and head. When Veruca emerges much later, she is covered in smelly, disgusting rubbish. Dahl sets this denouement up as her just desserts, casting her down from the heights of superiority and making her literally wallow in garbage. Each of the children has a similar experience, and at the end of the novel, we are invited to laugh at them as they make their way to the front gates of the factory, returning to the outside world with their inadequacies and faults marked upon their disfigured bodies. In a sense, Dahl and his readers can have their Wonka bars and eat them too: we get to revel in the kind of disgusting, subversive humour that is bound to offend those invested in the status quo, while, at the same time, we learn a 'good lesson' about the rewards of 'proper' behaviour.

As Paul Lewis notes, 'The goal of humor criticism is not to standardize humor appreciation but to refine our understanding of the humor we perceive in literature by helping us see how it is structured, how it functions and how it is related to the expression of values.'[52] Humour and disgust serve the social functions of imbuing us with a particular value system – not just in reflecting that system in our literature, but in teaching us how to react appropriately to various humorous or disgusting stimuli. Lewis notes that 'in *The Poetics*, Aristotle asserts that comedy invites us to laugh at low characters, that is, characters with small defects and minor vices. But the way humor functions in comedy is often more dynamic, more of a process than this: we discover which characters are low by learning to laugh at them'.[53] Nicholas Tucker makes a similar point about how humour can function in children's literature specifically. 'Many children's books ... both amuse children and also provide excellent guidance as to what can be safely laughed at.'[54] We learn what is laughable – and thus what is considered acceptable or unacceptable – in part by our reading. We learn what kinds of behaviours are likely to get you scapegoated (covered in trash, blown up like a blueberry, shat upon by doped-up pheasants, or glued to the floor) by the humorous and/or disgusting outcomes that characters face. In his subversive use of humour and disgust, Roald Dahl delineates specific – and often conservative – social boundaries for his young readers.

Notes

1. A number of critics and other writers have addressed Dahl's use of humour. Of particular note in this regard is Julie Cross's article 'Frightening and Funny: Humour in Children's Gothic Fiction', in Anna Jackson, Karen

Coats, and Roderick McGillis (eds), *The Gothic in Children's Literature: Haunting the Borders* (New York: Routledge, 2008): 57–76, in which she compares Dahl's work with that of Henrietta Branford. For other discussions of Dahl that are relevant to considerations of humour and disgust, see Amanda Bergson-Shilcock, 'The Subversive Quality of Respect: In Defense of *The Witches*', in Nicholas Karolides (ed.), *Censored Books II: Critical Viewpoints, 1985–2000* (Lanham, MD: Scarecrow Press, 2002): 446–51; Bill Brittain, 'Roald Dahl's *James and the Giant Peach*', in Karolides: 264–8; Robert Carrick, 'Roald Dahl', in Darren Harris-Fain (ed.), *Dictionary of Literary Biography*, vol. 255 (Detroit: Gale, 2002): 37–47; David Furniss, 'Keeping Their Parents Happy: Roald Dahl's *Revolting Rhymes*', in Karolides: 351–56; Alice Gould, 'Magical, Funny and Deliciously Disgusting!' *The New Welsh Review* 16 (1992): 55–6; Peter Hollindale, '"And Children Swarmed to Him Like Settlers. He Became a Land": The Outrageous Success of Roald Dahl', in Julia Briggs, Dennis Butts, and M. O. Grenby (eds), *Popular Children's Literature in Britain* (Burlington, VT: Ashgate, 2008): 271–86; Catriona Nicholson, 'Dahl, The Marvellous Boy', in Dudley Jones and Tony Watkins (eds), *A Necessary Fantasy? The Heroic Figure in Children's Popular Culture* (New York: Garland, 2000): 309–26; Margaret Talbot, 'The Candy Man: Why Children Love Roald Dahl's Stories – and Many Adults Don't', *New Yorker*, 11 July 2005; and Mark I. West, 'The Grotesque and the Taboo in Roald Dahl's Humorous Writings for Children', *Children's Literature Association Quarterly* 15(3) (Fall 1990): 115–16.

2. See, for example, Landsberg, who calls Dahl's work 'stories of spite, vengeance, and unbridled aggression' (46), parallels *Charlie and the Chocolate Factory* with the Holocaust, and, addressing *George's Marvellous Medicine*, juxtaposes two quite distinct passages, separated by 50 pages, in order to suggest that George feels orgasmic over his Grandmother's 'rape' and death. Michele Landsberg, 'Liberating Laughter', *American Educator* 16(3) (Fall 1992): 34ff. Individually, Landsberg's readings are intriguing, but the depth of her visible disgust with Dahl makes the lengthy section of her essay dealing with his work feel more like a tirade than dispassionate literary criticism. See also Cameron, whose vitriolic assessment of *Charlie and the Chocolate Factory* in *Horn Book* triggered both a furious response from Dahl and an impassioned outpouring of letters from *Horn Book* readers, both agreeing and disagreeing with Cameron. Eleanor Cameron, 'McLuhan, Youth, and Literature', *Horn Book Magazine* 48(5) (October 1972): 433–40; 'McLuhan, Youth, and Literature, Part II', *Horn Book Magazine* 48(6) (December 1972): 572–9; 'McLuhan, Youth, and Literature, Part III', *Horn Book Magazine* 49(1) (February 1973), 79–85; Roald Dahl, '"Charlie and the Chocolate Factory": A Reply', *Horn Book Magazine* 49(1) (February 1973): 77–8. For a discussion of the *Horn Book* exchanges see Kathleen Krull, 'Revisiting Eleanor, Marshall, and Roald; or, Having a Sense of Humor in the Millennium', *Horn Book Magazine* 75(5) (September 1999): 564–71.

3. George Carlin, 'Seven Words You Can Never Say on Television', in *Class Clown*, prod. Jack Lewis and Monte Kay (Santa Monica, 1972).

4. For discussions of childhood and humour, see Howard Gardner, 'Children's Literary Development: The Realms of Metaphors and Stories', in Paul E. McGhee and Antony J. Chapman (eds), *Children's Humour* (Chichester: John Wiley and Sons, 1980): 91–118; Frederick C. Howe, 'The Child in the Elementary School', *Child Study Journal* 23(4) (1993): 227–363; Mary Renck Jalongo, 'Children's Literature: There's Some Sense to Its Humor', *Childhood Education* 62(2) (November/ December 1985): 109–14; Katharine Kappas, 'A Developmental Analysis of Children's Responses to Humor', *The Library Quarterly* 37(1) (January 1967): 67–77; McGhee and Chapman; Gail Munde, 'What Are You Laughing At? Differences in Children's and Adults' Humorous Book Selections for Children', *Children's Literature in Education* 28(4) (1997): 219–33; Donna Shannon, 'What Children Find Humorous in the Books They Read and How They Express Their Responses', *Humor* 12(2) (1999): 119–49; Thomas Shultz, 'A Cognitive-Developmental Analysis of Humour', in Antony J. Chapman and Hugh C. Foot (eds), *Humour and Laughter: Theory, Research and Applications* (London: John Wiley and Sons, 1976): 11–36; Thomas R. Shultz and Judith Robillard, 'The Development of Linguistic Humour in Children: Incongruity Through Rule Violation', in McGhee and Chapman: 59–90; Nicholas Tucker, 'What's the Joke? A Look at Children's Humour', in John Durant and Jonathan Miller (eds), *Laughing Matters: A Serious Look at Humour* (Harlow: Longman, 1988): 66–74; Karla Wendelin, 'Taking Stock of Children's Preferences in Humorous Literature, *Reading Psychology* 2(1) (Fall 1980): 34–42; and Martha Wolfenstein, *Children's Humor: A Psychological Analysis* [1954] (Bloomington, IN: Indiana University Press, 1978).
5. Roald Dahl, *Charlie and the Chocolate Factory* [1964] (New York: Knopf, 1981).
6. Roald Dahl, *Matilda* [1988] (New York: Matilda, 1990): 81.
7. For discussions of the various theories, see Durant and Miller; Max Eastman, *Enjoyment of Laughter* (New York: Simon and Schuster, 1937); William F. Fry, Jr, *Sweet Madness: A Study of Humor* (Palo Alto, CA: Pacific Books, 1963); Marcel Gutwirth, *Laughing Matter: An Essay on the Comic* (Ithaca, NY: Cornell University Press, 1993); Robin Andrew Haig, *The Anatomy of Humor: Biopsychosocial and Therapeutic Perspectives* (Springfield, IL: Charles C. Thomas, 1988); Paul Lewis, *Comic Effects: Interdisciplinary Approaches to Humor in Literature* (Albany: State University of New York Press, 1989); Frank MacHovec, *Humor: Theory, History, Applications* (Springfield, IL: Charles C. Thomas, 1988); and Neil Schaeffer, *The Art of Laughter* (New York: Columbia University Press, 1981).
8. Haig: 9.
9. We do not have space to look at all of them, of course. A particularly obvious omission from this essay is a discussion of Dahl's use of linguistic humour. However, this particular aspect of his work has been well covered by other critics. For more information, see Carrick; Sándor G. J. Hervey,

'Ideology and Strategy in Translating Children's Literature', *Forum for Modern Language Studies* 33(1) (1997): 60–71; Hollindale; and Talbot. We will also not be covering issues of 'quantity', although Dahl quite clearly makes use of excess in both amusing and disgusting ways. *George's Marvellous Medicine* (1981), for example, is all about exaggeration for humour and pleasurable disgust, from the grossness of George's grandmother to the nearly unending litany of materials for the medicine, to the over-the-top effects that the medicine has on the various 'patients'. Just when you think there's nothing else in a typical household that could possibly go into the medicine, Dahl pounces on another place to access awful stuff and the medicine bubbles even higher.

10. Christie Davies, *Ethnic Humor Around the World: A Comparative Analysis,* (Bloomington, IN: Indiana University Press, 1990): 7.

11. Durant and Miller: 13–14.

12. Durant and Miller: 14.

13. Mary Douglas, *Purity and Danger: An Analysis of Concepts of Pollution and Taboo* [1966] (New York: Routledge Classics, 2004): 44.

14. Roald Dahl, *The Twits* [1980] (New York: Penguin, 2007): 7, 15–16.

15. For an astute and humorous discussion of such images and their impact on one child reader in particular, see West.

16. Raymond Briggs, *When the Wind Blows* (Long Acre: Hamish Hamilton, 1982).

17. *Matilda*: 159.

18. *Ibid.*: 116.

19. *Ibid.*: 153.

20. *Ibid.*: 116.

21. Roald Dahl, *Dirty Beasts* (New York: Penguin, 1986): n.p., emphasis in original.

22. Roald Dahl, *The Wonderful Story of Henry Sugar and Six More* (New York: Knopf, 1977); *The Magic Finger* [1964] (New York: Scholastic, 1998).

23. *Magic Finger*: 27.

24. *Ibid.*: 60.

25. For discussions of such issues in relation both to life and literature, see Howe; Kathryn James, 'Crossing the Boundaries: Scatology, Taboo and the Carnivalesque in the Picture Book', *Papers: Explorations into Children's Literature* 12(3) (December 2002): 19–27; Josepha Sherman and T. K. F Weisskopf, *Greasy Grimy Gopher Guts: The Subversive Folklore of Childhood* (Little Rock, AR: August House Publishers, 1995); Joseph T. Thomas, Jr, *Poetry's Playground: The Culture of Contemporary Children's Poetry* (Detroit: Wayne State University Press, 2007); and West.

26. For further discussion of disgust and the taboo, see Mikhail Bakhtin, *Rabelais and His World*, trans. Helene Iswolsky (Bloomington, IN: Indiana University Press, 1984); Douglas; James; William Ian Miller, *The Anatomy of Disgust* (Cambridge, MA: Harvard University Press, 1997); and Robert Rawdon Wilson, *The Hydra's Tale: Imagining Disgust* (Edmonton, Alberta: Alberta University Press, 2002).

27. *Dirty Beasts*: n.p.
28. Nicholson: 323. As a whole, Nicholson's essay makes perceptive points about Dahl's use of humour, solidly rooted in analysis of his autobiographical text *Boy*, and in her work with young readers who responded astutely to Dahl's work in book-talk sessions. For further discussion of the pleasures of the carnivalesque, see Bakhtin.
29. MacHovec: 31. Also see Gutwirth.
30. Roald Dahl, *Danny the Champion of the World* [1975] (New York: Penguin, 2007).
31. *Danny*: 42.
32. *Ibid.*: 43.
33. *Ibid.*: 45.
34. *Ibid.*: 46.
35. *Ibid.*: 186.
36. Lewis: 13.
37. *Ibid.*
38. Wilson: 13.
39. Wolfenstein: 12.
40. Munde: 221.
41. *Ibid.*: 222.
42. *Ibid.*: 223.
43. *Ibid.*: 224.
44. *Ibid.*: 225.
45. *Matilda*: 102.
46. *Ibid.*: 109.
47. *Ibid.*: 35.
48. Hollindale: 274, 280.
49. Roald Dahl, *Charlie and the Chocolate Factory*: 42.
50. See also Landsberg, who also discusses Charlie's positioning as 'the very model of the deserving poor' (47).
51. *Charlie and the Chocolate Factory*, directed by Tim Burton (Warner Brothers, 2005). DVD.
52. Lewis: xi.
53. *Ibid.*: 33.
54. Tucker: 67.

3

'Don't gobbelfunk around with words':[1] Roald Dahl and Language

David Rudd

Introduction

While it is a truism that anyone who tries to write stories must engage in the arduous process of organising words and sentences, it is also the case that for some authors language becomes more central, as it famously does in Lewis Carroll's 'Alice' books. For Roald Dahl, too, I would argue, the shape, sound and possibilities of language are abiding concerns, often becoming part of the subject matter or plot. The title story of Dahl's teenage collection, *The Great Automatic Grammatizator, and Other Stories*, is a key example.[2] Here, the protagonist, Adolph Knipe, feeds a primitive computer a range of themes, plots, writing styles, vocabulary and proper names in order to have it generate stories. After initial success Knipe seeks to monopolise the market by having other writers sign a contract agreeing not to write any more but, in return for a lifetime's pay, to let the agency produce stories under their names. But this third-person story, written in the narrative past, has a Dahlesque 'twist' towards the end:

> This last year ... it was estimated that at least one half of all the novels and stories published in the English language were produced by Adolph Knipe upon the Great Automatic Grammatizator.
> Does this surprise you?
> I doubt it.[3]

The story finishes:

> This very moment, as I sit here listening to the howling of my nine starving children in the other room, I can feel my own hand creeping

51

closer and closer to that golden contract that lies over on the other side
of the desk.
    Give me strength, Oh Lord, to let our children starve.[4]

The proximal deictic, '[t]his', makes us pause, as we suddenly find
ourselves in the here and now, being hailed directly ('you'); moreover,
a first-person narrator rears his (or, possibly, her) head as we shift into
the present tense.

    In terms of theme, the Grammatizator might be said to provide us
with an effective metaphor for how literature becomes commodified
in mass society, a problem against which the individual artist must
fight; or more briefly, we have a battle between Mammon and Art –
except that our artist is rather clumsy with that sudden shift in person,
let alone his/her improbable omniscience about the Grammatizator.
We might then reconsider that melodramatic ending and the improbable number of children this writer has; moreover, we might note
the similarity of the inventor's name to that of Dahl's publisher at
the time (Alfred Knopf); we might, finally, be drawn to a particular
passage where Knipe explains one of the 'many … little refinements'
he made to his machine:

> '… there's a trick that nearly every writer uses, of inserting at least one
> long, obscure word into each story. This makes the reader think that
> the man is very wise and clever. So I have the machine do the same
> thing. There'll be a whole stack of long words stored away just for this
> purpose.'
>   'Where?'
>   'In the "word-memory" section,' he said, epexegetically.[5]

That final word (referring to extra information that clarifies something
previously said) is slipped in unobtrusively, but is, no doubt, meant to
add to our suspicion that a machine could be behind this – except that,
as Knipe also notes, he first spotted the 'trick' in real writers (and Dahl
might be cited as a key exemplar).[6]

    Who exactly is responsible for this story, then, is, finally, undecid-
able; which points us towards a more abiding problem that all writers
have with words; for language is itself the Grammatizator, with its
standard plots and genres, let alone its orderly lexicon and syntax,
and writers have to struggle endlessly, seeking ways of cheating it,
of making it fresh. Dahl, certainly, was always on the hunt for new,
surprise endings to his short stories; and, more specifically in his
writing for children, continually sought out novel approaches; for
instance, using insects as main characters in *James and the Giant Peach*,[7]

updating fairy stories and nursery rhymes to cater for a more savvy, twentieth-century young audience, and fashioning a language more appropriate for those reared on cartoons, TV, advertising slogans and the like. In this chapter I will explore the various techniques used by Dahl, from the micro to the macro levels of language, suggesting that it is at the phonological level that the language can most readily be disrupted, which will then impact on other areas. However, it is first necessary to understand why Dahl, in particular, set himself so resolutely against the Grammatizator.

Dahl vs the Grammatizator

Part of the reason for Dahl's stand no doubt arises from the fact that the Great Grammatizator, like Great Britain itself, was initially alien to Dahl. He felt an outsider, as the son of Norwegian parents and growing up in a land that, in some respects, appeared hostile (as he records in *Boy*).[8] Moreover, fluent in Norwegian, English was the foreign tongue with which he struggled, as his school reports declare: '[a] persistent muddler. Vocabulary negligible, sentences malconstructed … indolent and illiterate'.[9] He might have cultivated his Received Pronunciation, but he always seems wary of, if not antagonistic towards, the British establishment – indeed, choosing to live abroad for many years. He was a largely self-made man who did not go to university, and who despised many of the products of such a system (in education, in the church and in the armed forces). In short, he more readily sided with the poacher than with the landowner, but nonetheless realised the value of the owner's cultural capital. From within, Dahl could then invent stories where the powerless poked fun at those in charge, pointing out their hypocrisies, and the ugly physicality that he often saw beneath their seemingly culti-vated surface. Like a civilised Caliban, he too could claim, 'You taught me language; and my profit on't / Is, I know how to curse'.[10]

Dahl thus grew up with a tacit understanding of the insights of Benjamin Whorf and Ferdinand de Saussure, that different tongues carve the world up in different ways and that ways of representing the world – objects, ideas, beliefs, values, and *mores* – are, ultimately, arbitrary. However, it is still the case that the language of the powerful defines a particular society's reality, making the ruling class's version seem natural and transparent – as 'how things are'. It is only when things do not fall within their allotted semantic categories that they become troublesome, 'out of order', and need addressing. Seen in these terms, Dahl's obsession with the scatological and violent becomes a powerful way of fighting back, drawing on a tradition – often linked to the working class, to the masses – whose energy derives precisely from upsetting the status quo, and which, furthermore, thereby seems to satisfy deep-seated desires in many readers, too.

Mary Douglas has most eloquently shown how things that confound categories – matter out of place – is labelled 'dirty', and Dahl specifically mines three areas that sit uneasily on the nature–culture fault line: those to do with children, with animals, and with what I shall call 'corporeality'.[11] Children do this by falling between culture (rational, fully developed beings) and nature (animal-like, 'little beasts', 'kids'). Animals, on the other hand, though legitimately typified as part of nature, become problematic when we start to personify them, to see them as having families and possessions, thus encroaching on culture. Finally, corporeality, encompassing the 'natural' elements of our cultural body (eating, drinking, urinating, defecating, having sex, being sexed, birth, death, body shape, bodily change, and so on), disturbs most societies, and is therefore wrapped carefully in euphemism.

Dahl, as noted above, derives his energy as a writer from worrying at these fissures in the social fabric. But he is not, thereby, the aberration that some critics have suggested (for example, David Rees and Eleanor Cameron), seeking to assess him according to traditional literary criteria.[12] I would suggest that he is more appositely located in a tradition that has its roots in orality, reaching back to nursery rhymes, jokes and folk tales – themselves once relayed in ephemeral, chapbook form. In this alternative tradition, we might also find that criticisms concerning the violence, the sadistic behaviour, the pandering to the scatological and grotesque are misplaced, in that they are part and parcel of a distinctive, carnivalesque way of viewing the world: one that can accommodate the earthy folk tale, the music-hall joke, and the creative violence of silent comedy, cartoons and comics (updating the chapbook tradition). Specifically, from a literary point of view, it seems more appropriate to situate Dahl's use of language within the nonsense tradition, which is renowned for its overt and casual treatment of violence and morbidity. Good Victorians like Edward Lear, for example, have works awash with violent death and destruction:

> There was an old person of Stroud,
> Who was horribly jammed in a crowd;
> Some she slew with a kick, some she scrunched with a stick,
> That impulsive old person of Stroud.[13]

And similar, pointed anarchy can be found in Carroll, Hilaire Belloc, Dr Seuss, Spike Milligan, Shel Silverstein and Edward Gorey, to name but a few others in this vein. But, as many commentators have also noted, this nonsense works precisely by clothing itself in the conventions of normality, from which it then departs.[14] In Lear's limerick, for example, we have a senior citizen from a provincial town (old people are the main protagonists in Lear's work), and one who, at the point at which violence breaks out, is discovered to be female. There's a feeling that she's not just fighting the crowd but the whole rulebound form of the limerick, struggling to break free. And, though the form finally holds her (conceding in its last line that she's 'impulsive', in Lear's casual euphemism), she has safely extricated herself from the mob. An orderly frame thus contains – and thereby points up – its violent content.

Of course, semantic containers – words and phrases – also encode their own undoing, which is where the pun comes into its own, as Dahl endlessly demonstrates. It stands to reason, then, that Wonka's 'whipped creams' are not innocent confections; rather, they have felt the lash. Nonsense shows us how such entities and worlds can come to life within language. As we shall see, it therefore tends to resist metaphor and symbolism, where things turn into other things and end up holding 'deeper', underlying meanings. This would ground reality in some sort of transcendent order, whereas nonsense always dissolves and deconstructs fixity: there is always further signification, hence nonsense's preference for the more provisional figures of simile, paronomasia (or pun) and metonymy. The words of nonsense literature, then, never point directly at an underlying signified, never become transparent, such that pure meaning is revealed; rather, nonsense celebrates the word made flesh, where its shape, font, sound, look, position and etymology are all obdurately present – and open to distortion, to being 'horribly jammed', to exploit the pun within that phrase of Lear's. The Vermicious Knids in *Charlie and the Great Glass Elevator* capture this somatic aspect of language when they spell out 'SCRAM' with their bodies,[15] one subsequently thrusting his alphabetical rear-end into the faces of the passengers of the Great Glass Elevator.

Nonsense, then, and Dahl's work especially, always has a sense of the metafictional, of things being on the verge of stepping outside their allotted semantic space – whether it be objects like whipped creams, characters who morph into giant blueberries (Violet Beauregarde in *Charlie*) or, indeed, characters becoming authors (James, for example in *James*). Dahl himself certainly liked to fudge the divide between events in his life and his fiction, famously aligning himself with the BFG, for instance – a character who can announce, 'What I mean

and what I say is two different things', which is just what Dahl was
accused of in a school report: 'I have never met a boy who so persis-
tently writes the exact opposite of what he means.'[16] That 'intolerable
wrestle / With words and meanings',[17] then, or the attempt to hold
out against the Great Grammatizator, was something that Dahl clearly
recognised. But he was, as I've suggested, perhaps also more personally
motivated, having experienced the stuffiness of British society, still an
imperial power, at first hand. Let us now turn, then, to his various
innovations in language, moving from the micro to the macro levels.

Lexical innovation

It is probably at the lexical level that Dahl has had the most obvious
impact on readers, with some of his neologisms – most infamously,
'whizzpoppers' – becoming sniggering, everyday parlance. *The BFG*
is certainly the work where Dahl gives full rein to this feature of his
writing, though elements of it can be traced back to his very first
work, *The Gremlins* (1942). In *The BFG*, 'langwitch'[18] is stretched
and reshaped in a number of ways. A few of his new words are
simply malapropisms, like 'human beans', a term previously used by
the Borrowers in Mary Norton's classic series.[19] But other terms are
new coinages, fashioned in various ways. Some are compound words
('whizzpopper'), but more often Dahl collapses two words into one,
as did Carroll with his portmanteau creations like 'chortle' (to chuckle
and snort). Dahl, for example, has '[d]elumptious',[20] from delicious
and scrumptious, 'horrigust'[21] (horrible/disgusting) and 'repulsant'[22]
(repulsive/repugnant). However, the last example also brings us to a
more common technique of Dahl's, whereby he adds an affix (usually
a suffix) to an existing word (e.g., 'It's filthing! … It's disgusterous! …
It's sickable! It's rotsome! It's maggotwise!').[23]

More credible than these, though, are cases where an existing
word replaces the standard one, but earns its keep by having relevant
phonological and/or semantic connotations; thus the BFG talks about
'natterboxes',[24] where 'natter' not only rhymes with 'chatter', but is
also its synonym. This technique is used in idiomatic phrases, too, such
as 'once in a blue baboon'[25] where not only are rhyme and alliteration
used, but there's the semantic link with blue-faced baboons; likewise,
'[k]eep your skirt on!'[26] uses both rhyme and the semantic field of
clothing; in contrast, 'barking up the wrong dog'[27] uses semantic links
alone, barking being metonymic of the canine.

The same applies with another technique used by Dahl which
draws on phonological elements; namely, the spoonerism. Thus the

BFG talks of 'rommytot' and 'frack to bunt'[28]; Miss Honey likes 'playing with words in that way' too, we are told, and speculates that the Wormwoods' house, '"COSY NOOK"', might more appropriately be named "Nosey cook"'.[29] However, without any semantic dimension these are less effective coinages than others, like 'every crook and nanny' or 'Dahl's Chickens'.[30] Miss Honey's example, for instance, might have had more mileage had it been 'Nosey crook'. Finally in this category are variations on the spoonerism, where Dahl reverses the order of morphological units of words, rather than letters alone, as in 'snapperwhippers', 'curdbloodling' and 'squeakpips',[31] this last, again, proving the most effective with its lexical and semantic dimensions.

Before moving on to consider the phonological features of Dahl's language in their own right, two misconceptions about Dahl's lexis need correction. First is the idea that he used a restricted vocabulary. Admittedly, he liked to use slang and colloquial language, but a cursory glance at *James and the Giant Peach*, for instance, also turns up the following: 'insidiously', 'shrivelling', 'pandemonium', 'martyr', 'tethered', 'harnessed', 'katydids', 'rambunctious', 'wraithlike', 'imbeciles', 'loathsome', 'infuriated', 'deluge', 'sinister', 'melancholy', 'stupor', 'tapered', 'chaperone', 'eccentricity', 'limousine', 'procession' and 'elegant'.[32] A second accusation is that his language – his slang especially – is dated (the frequent exclamations of 'by gum', 'by gosh', 'gee-whizz' and 'golly-gosh', by characters of all ages). However, I would argue that Dahl's strong voice effectively makes these expressions part of his distinctive idiolect. Only occasionally does he seem to hit a false note (e.g., using the term 'perambulator',[33] or having Bruno calling the witches 'crazy punks').[34]

Phonological innovation

It is probably the sound of Dahl's language that is most memorable, making him such a classroom favourite. One of his most popular techniques for this is alliteration. Here, for example, is Mr Twit, delivering a characteristic Dahlesque line: 'I'll swish you to a swazzle! I'll gnash you to a gnozzle! I'll gnosh you to a gnazzle!'[35] Mrs Twit is equally voluble: 'Some beastly bird has dropped his dirty droppings on my head!'[36] Most frequently Dahl alliterates two words ('witless weed! … glob of glue! … fleabitten fungus!' – *Matilda*),[37] but he often achieves a threesome ('foul and filthy fiend! I hope you get squashed and squished and squizzled' – *The Enormous Crocodile*)[38] and even four in a row ('grousing, grouching, grumbling, griping' – *George's*

Marvellous Medicine).[39] Dahl names some characters in similar fashion, like the farmer threesome in *Fantastic Mr Fox*,[40] Boggis, Bunce and Bean, or the grandparents in *Charlie and the Chocolate Factory*: Joe, Josephine, George, and Georgina. Moreover, if Dahl liked a phrase, he was by no means averse to recycling it, as with the description 'grizzly old grunion', applied to both Mrs Twit and George's grandmother.[41]

Once again, it should be emphasised that these techniques often overlap, so assonance deserves mention here, increasing the effectiveness of phrases like 'bloated old blue-faced baboon',[42] whose power depends not just on alliteration but also on the fact that the long /o/ sound of the first two words, 'bloated' and 'old', is paralleled by the /oo/ sound of 'blue' and 'baboon'. Beyond assonance, of course, full rhyme is frequently used by Dahl. Almost all his work, again going right back to *The Gremlins*, includes sections of verse, but he also enjoys creating internal rhymes in his prose, as, for example, in the naming of characters (e.g., the Oompa-Loompas and the Roly-Poly Bird, recalling the precedent of Edward Lear with his Quangle-Wangle and Yonghy-Bonghy-Bò), but also in phrases like 'scrumptious-galumptious, so flavory-savory, so sweet to eat'.[43] The Oompa-Loompas, unsurprisingly given their name, also speak in rhyme, forming a sort of Greek chorus commenting morally on the action, and also allowing Dahl to write in a freer, less inhibited manner:

> '*A bacon rind, some rancid lard,*
> *A loaf of bread gone stale and hard,*
> *A steak that nobody could chew,*
> *An oyster from an oyster stew,*
> *Some liverwurst so old and grey*
> *One smelled it from a mile away,*
> *A rotten nut, a reeky pear,*
> *A thing the cat left on the stair …*'[44]

Such description is reminiscent of much oral playground rhyme ('Great grey globs of greasy, grimy gopher guts', etc.), and it is of note that Dahl extended his subversive verse parodies into three published volumes, the last, *Rhyme Stew*, explicitly warning 'Unsuitable for small people' – rather an ambiguous descriptor![45] In these volumes he uses many of the techniques discussed above, but with added effects, such as his orthographical revisions to ensure full rhymes at times, as in 'Cinderella', from *Revolting Rhymes*: 'There is a Disco at the Palace! / The rest have gone and I am jalous!'[46] Also distorting orthographic convention, and recalling children's lore, is the mock language, 'FIMBO FEEZ!', which Willy Wonka creates in *Charlie and the Great*

Glass Elevator. On closer inspection, this language turns out to be a mixture of phonetic spelling, ellipsis and typographical innovation, as this rather predictable line shows: 'PANTZ FORLDUN IFNO SUSPENDA!'[47]

Typographical innovation

This area is extensive enough to warrant its own section, with Dahl frequently using capitalisation, different fonts and reordering of layout. Thus, *The Witches* opens with 'A Note about Witches', and when he first writes, 'This [story] is about REAL WITCHES', he uses small capitals. Then, to make it more memorable ('Never forget what is coming next', he exhorts us), he starts to express it in larger capitals and italics: '*REAL WITCHES dress in ordinary clothes…*'.[48] *Charlie and the Chocolate Factory* uses even larger emboldened capitals to represent a newspaper headline, and when the article is subsequently read, presents the newspaper's name in large Gothic font before reproducing the standfirst in italics, preceding the report itself.[49] Likewise, when Dahl introduces Mr and Mrs Bucket to us, the print is spaced out across the page, so that it mirrors the characters' placing in the illustration.[50] In *The Giraffe and the Pelly and Me* the length of the giraffe's neck is demonstrated by three increasingly large fonts in capitals, descending the page; however, on the next page, where Dahl wants to demonstrate that the giraffe's neck extends vertically ('HIGHER'), we are clearly meant to read the growing fonts in ascending order.[51]

More radical typographical innovation occurs in *Esio Trot*, from the title on. As Mr Hoppy, the male character explains: 'Tortoises are very backward creatures. Therefore they can only understand words that are written backwards.'[52] We have whole rhymes written backwards in what the Opies term 'back-slang',[53] with lines like 'WORG PU, FFUP PU, TOOHS PU!'[54] As his neighbour and would-be consort, Mrs Silver, comments, 'there's an awful lot of poos in it. Are they something special?', which of course is exactly what Mary Douglas indicated, dirt being matter out of place.[55] This becomes even more powerful when such language is spoken by a man not only of the establishment, but of God. In *The Vicar of Nibbleswicke*,[56] we learn that the eponymous Vicar suffers the same affliction as tortoises, 'a very rare disease called Back-to-Front Dyslexia', which results in some unfortunate advice in church, telling his congregation how to drink the communion wine: 'What you must do is pis. Pis gently. All of you, all the way along the rail must pis, pis, pis'; and then advises them not 'to krap all along the front of the church before the service'[57] – meaning, of course, that they should park their cars elsewhere. Clearly, this works far better delivered orally than read off the page.

Syntactical innovation

This section is necessarily brief for, as others have noted, grammatical rules are rarely tampered with when writers play language games (and morphological innovation, another aspect of grammar, has been dealt with elsewhere).[58] Thus Carroll's 'Jabberwocky', despite its many neologisms, is still written in standard sentences with discernible nouns, adjectives and verbs. Dahl's work is much the same – though sentence fragments are more apparent in his *oeuvre*. It is only with the giants in *The BFG* that we find systematic deviation from standard English. I say 'giants' because, although the BFG apologises that he cannot help 'saying things a little squiggly',[59] all the giants seem to have this sociolect. Thus they all (fairly) systematically use singular forms of the verbs 'to be' and 'to have', regardless of person, and whether singular or plural: 'I is', 'you is', 'we is', 'we was',[60] 'Human beans ... has'[61]; other verbs, though, are used in their regular form.

Semantic innovation

More common than grammatical changes are semantic shifts (though many of the above techniques also result in changes of meaning). Figurative language is often responsible for these shifts but, like many other nonsense writers, Dahl seems keen not to lose sight of the original meaning (which metaphors can tend to obscure); hence, as noted earlier, his preference for similes and puns, where both frames of reference, the original alongside the transgression, are maintained. Often, then, when Dahl uses a metaphor, the simile will already have been unpacked. Thus the BFG is referred to as having 'truck-wheel ears', but earlier Dahl has noted that each ear is 'as big as the wheel of a truck'.[62] Most of Dahl's similes are highly effective, often being deployed to delineate characters, perhaps most infamously George's grandmother, with her 'small puckered up mouth like a dog's bottom'.[63] Dahl is not averse to 'recycling' an apposite simile, either. Thus fat Augustus Gloop appears as though 'blown up with a powerful pump', similar to Miss Trunchbull's imperious look ('inflated by a bicycle-pump').[64] Metaphors are certainly not absent, however, and come into their own in the plentiful insults characters hurl, Miss Trunchbull being a key exponent:[65] 'This *clot*, ... this *blackhead*, this *foul carbuncle*, this *poisonous pustule* …'; 'You ignorant little slug! … You witless weed! You empty-headed hamster! You stupid glob of glue!'.[66]

Puns are equally plentiful, and there are many examples that I have given earlier, 'human beans' being a favourite. In *The BFG* Dahl particularly enjoys punning on the names of countries; thus 'Greeks from Greece is all tasting greasy', 'Human beans from Chile is very chilly', in contrast to the 'Hottentots', of course.[67] This process is technically known as *adnominatio*, where a proper noun becomes interpreted either literally or homophonically. Dahl actually has Willy Wonka explore this process in relation to Veruca Salt: 'You *do* have an interesting name, don't you? I always thought that a veruca was a sort of wart that you got on the sole of your foot!'[68] There are many other motivated names, too; for example the Wormwoods, Miss Trunchbull and Miss Honey from *Matilda*, or, less obviously, perhaps, Charlie Bucket; as Wonka comments: 'A grown-up won't listen to me; he won't learn. He will try to do things his own way and not mine. So I have to have a child'.[69] In other words, Charlie's surname suggests he's an empty vessel, a *tabula rasa*.

This notion of words creating their own reality is a key one in nonsense literature, and Dahl exploits it relentlessly. Obviously granting words such latitude can be seen as a subversive act, but it also has deeply traditional and literal aspects, seeking to impose a version of the world sanctioned by the written word. Thus, in a poem called 'The Ant-Eater' in *Dirty Beasts*, the protagonist's relative is eaten by his pet because some Americans

> However hard they try, they can't
> Pronounce a simple word like AUNT.[70]

Because of a 'mispronunciation', this woman is reclassified as an 'ant', and is therefore fair game for the boy's pet.

Likewise, because we speak about dilemmas having horns, then it is reasonable to suggest that one could '*be tossed / On the horns of a furious Dilemma*' (in *James and the Giant Peach*).[71]

These moves frequently point out how language helps us order the world in particular, ideologically charged ways, as I noted earlier. Thus, from a pelican's point of view, it is logical that a fishmonger, like a 'fish-*pie* … fish-*cake* and a fish-*finger*', should be 'good to eat'.[72] Dahl thus frequently draws our attention to what has been termed 'situated knowledge' – the notion that our views are always coloured by our particular perspective.[73] Most commonly Dahl makes us aware of this through inversion, showing us, for example, what hunting means from an animal's perspective – as for the ducks in *The Magic Finger*[74] or the foxes in *Fantastic Mr Fox*. Likewise, 'The Pig' in *Dirty Beasts* is about such an animal, who resents being defined as food in terms of bacon, ham, pork and so on, and so turns the tables and consumes the farmer. In *Danny*, too, the case in favour of poaching is eloquently made, helped by the obnoxious description of the landowner, Mr Hazell. And, in other tales again, one can see that our preconceptions about childhood (being a passive, ineffectual, naive state) are being challenged – in *Matilda*, perhaps, especially. This young character also certainly challenges notions of what is appropriate reading matter for children, but then Dahl had done this throughout his work, pushing at the boundaries of what was acceptable subject matter and at its forms of expression. His punning title, *Revolting Rhymes*, seems to play on this very notion, criticising traditional versions of tales as 'phoney':

> And made to sound all soft and sappy
> Just to keep the children happy.[75]

Narrative style

Sentences do not exist in isolation, of course, but are part of larger units of discourse, from which we get a better notion of a writer's style. 'The Great Automatic Grammatizator' has already been discussed, with its rather clumsy shift into the first person at the end. But such shifts occur elsewhere as well. Noriko Shimoda Netley has noted the move from 'we' to 'I' to 'one' in the opening pages of *Matilda*, arguing that Dahl moves from being a sympathetic child-centred narrator to a rather cynical adult, before retreating to a more inclusive position. In the closing pages of *James and the Giant Peach* and *The BFG* Dahl is more overt in shifting the narratorial perspective:

> [James] thought it would be nice if one day he sat down and wrote [his adventures] as a book.
> So he did.
> And that is what you have just finished reading.[76]

and

> But where, you might ask, is this book that the BFG wrote?
> It's right here. You've just finished reading it.[77]

These unexpected twists in the closing lines simply reverse the problems raised by the Grammatizator story: that if it really is an individual's perspective, he knows too much. Even in Dahl's books told in the first person (*The Magic Finger*, *Danny*, *The Witches* and *The Giraffe*), the same is true. Dahl seems partially aware of this problem, and in *The Witches* there is an opening chapter entitled 'A Note about Witches'. It stands apart from the main narrative and seems to be written by an adult ('As far as children are concerned...' and 'I do not wish to speak badly about women').[78] However, having two first-person speakers is not without its own confusions.

Personally, though, I think this supposed awkwardness uncovers a deeper quality of Dahl's writing, which is that he, like Enid Blyton, is an author who draws on techniques more closely associated with the oral tradition. Known as a witty raconteur and storyteller (his own children being his primary audience), Dahl seems to carry this style into his writing, where we always have intrusive, opinionated narrators; we have already seen this in *The Witches*, above, and in *Matilda* Dahl also imposes himself, speculating that he'd like to write teachers' reports in order to gain revenge on those parents who endlessly praise their offspring. He proceeds to give some examples before reining himself in: 'But enough of that. We have to get on'.[79] His use of 'we' here, and his frequent hailing us as 'you', also enacts a more oral notion of audience, which extends to us being introduced to Charlie as though he were physically present: 'How d'you do? And how d'you do? And how d'you do again? He is pleased to meet you.'[80]

In other words, Dahl's voice always comes through regardless of who the narrator ostensibly is. This, in turn, explains why his characters are such ciphers, all speaking in much the same style – and why, occasionally, their speech sounds inappropriate, as for example, when Danny's father uses the word 'splendiferous', or Bruce Bogtrotter in *Matilda* exclaims, like someone out of Billy Bunter, 'I mean, dash it all'.[81] It is Dahl we hear, relaying their feelings. This slippage, moreover, can run in two directions, such that sometimes, though it is the narrator speaking, the character's thoughts or feelings come through (in what is known as free indirect discourse). For example, regarding Wonka's Chocolate Factory, the narrator gives us Charlie's view: 'Oh, how he loved that smell!'.[82] However, that exclamation, 'Oh, how', together with its dedicated punctuation mark, suggests that Charlie's own feelings are infusing the telling.

Furthermore, in arguing that Dahl is always present through his characters, the division between his fiction and his factual writings becomes increasingly hard to maintain (as a number of commentators have detailed).[83] Dahl himself seems less concerned with this, running together both forms in collections like *The Wonderful Story of Henry Sugar*; and, both there and elsewhere (*Boy* and *Going Solo*),[84] giving us the supposed background to many of his stories. However, even here, as is made explicit in *Boy*, he is careful to distance himself from the label 'autobiography', preferring the more accommodating 'tales of childhood'. As a raconteur retelling his stories, then, it also becomes clearer as to why material is recycled, and why some characters crop up in different stories (the oral tradition is renowned for drawing on a common stock of figures). Thus the BFG is foreshadowed in *Danny*, Muggle-Wump and the Roly-Poly Bird appear in *The Enormous Crocodile* and *The Twits*, the Vermicious Knids appear in *Charlie and the Great Glass Elevator*, but are also mentioned in both *James* and *The Minpins*. In fact, the Minpins themselves, from Dahl's last, posthumous picture book, seem very close relatives of the creatures in his first book almost 50 years earlier, the Gremlins, who also, traditionally, inhabit woods and wear suction-boots. Not only did Dahl use modern-day folk figures here, but again played loose with fact, claiming the gremlins as his own: 'this I believe was the first time the word had been used'.[85] Dahl, then, did not simply use his own works as intertexts, but drew extensively on others' works, too, especially nursery rhymes, folk and fairy tales (again, most overtly in his verse retellings). Some of these are obvious borrowings, like the Duchess's vocal plea in *The Giraffe*:

> '*My diamonds are over the ocean,*
> *My diamonds are over the sea,*
> *My diamonds were pinched from my bedroom,*
> *Oh, bring back my diamonds to me.*'[86]

Others are more subtle, as in the Keatsian comment that Miss Trunchbull's 'face … was neither a thing of beauty nor a joy for ever'.[87]

I do not intend to detail all the features of oral storytelling that Dahl exhibits, but one last aspect deserves mention; namely, the way he makes his stories sound as though they are unfolding in the here and now, before the reader's eyes. I shall mention two techniques that Dahl uses to achieve this. First, by writing in the present tense, as in 'Here comes Charlie' at the beginning of *Charlie*, where Dahl also uses the proximal deictics 'this' and 'these' to effect a sense of our being *in medias res*. Related to this is a second technique: stimulating our senses. In *Charlie*, and especially in the opening pages, the visual immediacy of the writing is deftly supported by the illustrations, without which the deixis would be meaningless. Likewise in *The Twits*, the directive,

'Take a look at her', precedes a picture of Mrs Twit, below which we are asked, 'Have you ever seen a woman with an uglier face than that? I doubt it'[88]; and in *The Witches* we have him cheekily instructing his audience thus: 'She [i.e. a witch] … might even be your lovely school-teacher who is reading these words to you at this very moment. Look carefully at that teacher'.[89]

Leaving aside the sterling work of his illustrators, though (most notably Quentin Blake), Dahl's own writing is powerful in conjuring up visual images; and he also seeks to invoke other senses. It is writing that begs to be read aloud, and the phonological devices mentioned earlier help capture the energy of his stories' usually brash exterior, besides the graphemic representation of onomatopoeia, as in this example from *The BFG*: '*Eeeeowtch!* … Ughbwelch! Ieeeech!'[90] Other visual conventions are there to assist the reader, too, like the italics in the last example or, elsewhere, capitals and exclamation marks (Eleanor Cameron, early on, rather unfairly claimed that '[t]he exclamation mark is the extent of [Dahl's] individuality'[91]). Dahl also attempts to invoke our senses of taste and smell with his exacting descriptions, as in the verse detailing the fate of Veruca Salt descending the rubbish chute, quoted earlier. The reaction he creates is almost visceral – but then his humour usually manages this sort of response anyway.

As I also made clear in the case of Blyton,[92] such immediate, sensory gratification creates the sense of being present, of the story unfolding like a daydream, a fantasy; moreover, it is one in which the physically powerless overcome their oppressors through superior brain power. In short, such stories indulge 'His Majesty the Ego, the hero alike of every day-dream and of every story'[93] – though one would want to add that, in the process, this ego, male or female, enjoys much id-like indulgence, too.

Conclusion

I have suggested that Dahl had a particular animosity towards what he saw as the Great Grammatizator, which can be seen to represent the language of the establishment, of a Great Britain that, reluctantly, he found himself a part of. He learned its ways, certainly, but kept himself on its margins, both geographically and mentally. His stories clearly reflect this notion of being a bit of an outsider, both in the modes in which he chose to write (tales of fantasy and the macabre, tales for children) and in the style of his writing. The energy of this work comes, I have postulated, from the way Dahl exploits the fissures and fault lines of our culture, places where matter is seen to be out of place, not sitting comfortably in its time-honoured categories. Specifically, Dahl explores the tenuous and ambivalent status of children and animals and, relatedly, the corporeal reality that lies beneath all our cultural pretensions. By inverting many of the conventions of our society (empowering children over adults, animals over humans), Dahl opens up a carnivalesque space where many of society's categorisations can be rethought.[94] A cat may look at a king, certainly, and in Dahl's world a giant may also fart before royalty, in this case Her Majesty the superego. His subversions, though, appear not merely in his plots but also, as I have detailed, down at the micro levels of language, confounding the 'natural' ways that we encode things in sound and sense. Small shifts in the patterning of phonemes and morphemes can result in our rethinking what we are saying, simultaneously releasing sounds and senses usually repressed. In the words of Mr Hoppy, replying to Mrs Silver, 'Poo is a very strong word in any language'[95] – but, as he might also have added, thereby a very funny one.

Notes

1. Roald Dahl, *The BFG* (London: Penguin, 1984): 28.
2. Roald Dahl, 'The Great Automatic Grammatizator', in *The Great Automatic Grammatizator, and Other Stories* (London: Penguin, 1997): 9–34.
3. 'The Great Automatic Grammatizator': 33.
4. *Ibid.*: 34.
5. *Ibid.*: 21.
6. For example, the 'dendrochronologist' mentioned in *Charlie and the Great Glass Elevator* (129) or the 'katydid' in *James and the Giant Peach* (71).
7. Roald Dahl, *James and the Giant Peach* (Harmondsworth: Penguin, 1973).
8. Roald Dahl, *Boy: Tales of Childhood* (London: Penguin, 1986).
9. Roald Dahl, 'Lucky Break', in *The Wonderful Story of Henry Sugar, and Six More* (Harmondsworth: Penguin, 1978): 147–75, at 160.
10. Shakespeare, *The Tempest*, I.ii.517–18.
11. See Mary Douglas, *Purity and Danger: An Analysis of the Concepts of Pollution and Taboo* (London: Routledge, 1991).
12. David Rees, 'Dahl's Chickens: Roald Dahl', *Children's Literature in Education* 19(3) (1998): 143–55; Eleanor Cameron, 'McLuhan, Youth and Literature, Part 1', *The Horn Book Magazine* (1972): 433–40.
13. Edward Lear, *The Complete Nonsense of Edward Lear*, ed. Holbrook Jackson (London: Faber and Faber, 1947): 169.
14. See, for example, Elizabeth Sewell, *The Field of Nonsense* (London: Chatto and Windus, 1952) and Susan Stewart, *Nonsense: Aspects of Intertextuality*

in Folklore and Literature (Baltimore, MD: Johns Hopkins University Press, 1979).

15. Roald Dahl, *Charlie and the Great Glass Elevator* (London: Penguin, 1975): 58–9.
16. *The BFG*: 49; 'Lucky Break': 160.
17. T. S. Eliot, *Four Quartets* (London: Faber and Faber, 1959): 26.
18. *The BFG*: 44.
19. See Mary Norton, *The Borrowers Omnibus* (London: Dent, 1990). The first book in the series, *The Borrowers*, was published in 1952.
20. *The BFG*: 64.
21. *Ibid.*: 78.
22. *Ibid.*: 50.
23. *Ibid.*: 51.
24. *Ibid.*: 46.
25. *Ibid.*: 88.
26. *Ibid.*: 88.
27. *Ibid.*: 120.
28. *Ibid.*: 59, 73.
29. Roald Dahl, *Matilda* (London: Penguin, 1989): 92.
30. *The BFG*: 73, 113.
31. *Ibid.*: 88, 84, 99.
32. *James and the Giant Peach*: 40, 50, 55, 59, 62, 63, 71, 78, 81, 82, 88, 92, 93, 94, 99, 104, 105, 107, 107, 110.
33. *The BFG*: 49; *James and the Giant Peach*: 55.
34. Roald Dahl, *The Witches* (London: Penguin, 1985): 92.
35. Roald Dahl, *The Twits* (London: Penguin, 1982): 43.
36. *The Twits*: 84.
37. *Matilda*: 218.
38. Roald Dahl, *The Enormous Crocodile* (London: Jonathan Cape, 1978).
39. Roald Dahl, *George's Marvellous Medicine* (Harmondsworth: Penguin, 1982): 8.
40. Roald Dahl, *Fantastic Mr. Fox* (Harmondsworth: Penguin, 1974).
41. *The Twits*: 41; *George's Marvellous Medicine*: 8.
42. Roald Dahl, *Danny, the Champion of the World* (Harmondsworth: Penguin, 1977): 155.
43. Roald Dahl, *The Giraffe and the Pelly and Me* (St Helens: The Book People, 2008): 18.
44. Roald Dahl, *Charlie and the Chocolate Factory* (London: Penguin, 1985): 126.
45. Roald Dahl, *Rhyme Stew* (London: Penguin, 1992).
46. Roald Dahl, *Revolting Rhymes* (London: Penguin, 1982): 6.
47. *Charlie and the Great Glass Elevator*: 46.
48. *The Witches*: 7.
49. *Charlie and the Chocolate Factory*: 30–2.
50. *Ibid.*: 13.
51. *The Giraffe and the Pelly and Me*: 34–5.

52. Roald Dahl, *Esio Trot* (St Helens: The Book People, 2009): 18.
53. Iona and Peter Opie, *The Lore and Language of Schoolchildren* (Oxford: Clarendon Press, 1959): 320.
54. *Esio Trot*: 17.
55. Douglas.
56. Roald Dahl, *The Vicar of Nibbleswicke* (London: Penguin, 1992).
57. *The Vicar of Nibbleswicke*: 37, 27, 34.
58. See note 6, above.
59. *The BFG*: 50.
60. *Ibid.*: 48.
61. *Ibid.*: 28.
62. *Ibid.*: 42, 25.
63. *George's Marvellous Medicine*: 8.
64. *Charlie and the Chocolate Factory*: 33; *Matilda*: 144.
65. See Knowles and Malmkjær; for example, they discuss the animal and military metaphors associated with Miss Trunchbull. Murray Knowles and Kirsten Malmkjær, *Language and Control in Children's Literature* (London & New York: Routledge, 1996): 137–9.
66. *Matilda*: 120, 148.
67. *The BFG*: 26, 61, 37.
68. *Charlie and the Chocolate Factory*: 69.
69. *Ibid.*: 157.
70. Roald Dahl, *Dirty Beasts* (Harmondsworth: Penguin, 1986).
71. *James and the Giant Peach*: 40.
72. *The Giraffe and the Pelly and Me*: 10.
73. See Donna J. Haraway, *Simians, Cyborgs and Women: The Reinvention of Nature* (New York: Routledge, 1991).
74. Roald Dahl, *The Magic Finger* (Harmondsworth: Penguin, 1974).
75. *Revolting Rhymes*: 5.
76. *James and the Giant Peach*: 111.
77. *The BFG*: 208.
78. *The Witches*: 9.
79. *Matilda*: 8–9.
80. *Charlie and the Chocolate Factory*: 14.
81. *Danny*: 20; *Matilda*: 120.
82. *Charlie and the Chocolate Factory*: 18.
83. For example, Mark I. West, *Roald Dahl* (New York: Twayne, 1992), chapter 8; Jeremy Treglown, *Roald Dahl: A Biography* (London: Faber and Faber, 1994): 19–24.
84. Roald Dahl, *Going Solo* (London: Penguin, 1988).
85. 'Lucky Break': 170. The *OED* provides written examples from 1941, this first one (by C. Graves) claiming that the term originated in the Great War (i.e., 1914–18), vol. 6: 824.
86. *The Giraffe and the Pelly and Me*: 44.
87. *Matilda*: 83.

88. *The Twits*: 14.
89. *The Witches*: 10.
90. *The BFG*: 60.
91. Cameron: 439.
92. David Rudd, *Enid Blyton and the Mystery of Children's Literature* (Basingstoke: Palgrave Macmillan, 2000).
93. Sigmund Freud, 'Writers and Day-dreaming' [1908], *The Standard Edition of the Complete Psychoanalytical works of Sigmund Freud*, IX (London: Hogarth Press, 1959): 143–53, at 150.
94. For a more detailed example, also drawing on children's readings, see David Rudd, *A Communication Studies Approach to Children's Literature* (Sheffield: Pavic Press, 1992).
95. *Esio Trot*: 19.

4

'The problem of school': Roald Dahl and Education

Pat Pinsent

Introduction

In one form or another, education figures extensively in the work of Roald Dahl. His memoir, *Boy* (1984), reveals schooldays blighted by violent or even sadistic teachers.[1] The same subject is also prominent in his shorter, 'factual', piece, 'Lucky Break' (1977). The accuracy of these recollections has subsequently been challenged, but it could be argued that this picture reflects part of Dahl's self-construct as someone whose ability, unrecognised by those in authority, triumphed despite, rather than because of, the endeavours of his teachers. A similar emphasis is to be found in much of his fictional writing. The contrast in *Matilda* (1988) between the angelic Miss Honey, who recognises her pupil's potential, and the brutal Miss Trunchbull, who is adamant about the limitations of young children, is consistent with Dahl's views about the weaknesses of the educational system. It appears that Dahl's self-edited recollections of the schools he had experienced created in him a tension between appreciation of the sterling qualities of those teachers who encouraged in their pupils a love of learning, and in particular of literature, and those schools and teachers who wanted children to fit their preconceived notions about children as the products of the educational system.

Dahl seems to have held strong beliefs about education. His conviction about the importance of handing on a literary heritage to the young is evident. This is explicit in *Boy* and 'Lucky Break', and among his novels is especially noteworthy in *Matilda*, where he refers to a number of major writers and shows a particular enthusiasm for Dickens. Implicitly Dahl's appreciation of the importance of story is reflected in his gift for stimulating his readers' interest throughout his own tale telling. Also evident is his belief in children's innate potential: for instance, nothing that Matilda's parents could do would suppress her considerable abilities. Dahl's views about other aspects of the curriculum can also be discerned in his writing, which favours individual endeavour and outdoor pursuits. *Danny, the Champion of the World* (1975), for example, mirrors the kind of voluntary activities featured in the author's own early life.[2]

Given Dahl's ambivalence about schooling, it is perhaps ironic that his fiction has been widely used in classrooms to foster interest in reading, particularly among boys. To a certain extent this phenomenon has been 'client driven', because of the considerable popularity of his work as part of children's voluntary reading, as attested by various surveys. In a way that he might not have relished, his ostensibly 'subversive' texts have been appropriated by teachers and several titles by or about him have appeared in series designed to be read in school, sometimes by less able readers.[3]

Dahl's own schooldays

While it is perhaps unusual to begin a consideration of a writer's views about education with a discussion of passages about being caned, this may be justified in the case of Dahl on the grounds of the vivid writing and the fact that this aspect seems to have been central to his recollections of his schooldays. Probably these descriptions of the savage beatings that he and his friends endured at the hands of brutal teachers are the aspect of Dahl's autobiographical writing that is most remembered by his young readers, particularly because such practices are, fortunately, outlawed in today's schools. In 'Lucky Break: How I Became a Writer', an autobiographical piece included in *The Wonderful Story of Henry Sugar* (1977), a lengthy passage vividly depicts the punishment incurred as a result of his asking another boy for a pen nib. The eight-year-old boy is depicted as knowing that the caning will produce on his body long corrugated blue-black welts with 'brilliant scarlet edges'. Dahl describes the first stroke:

> *Swish! … Crack!*
> Then came the pain. It was unbelievable, unbearable, excruciating. It was as though someone had laid a white-hot poker across your backside and pressed hard.
> *Swish! … Crack!*
> The second one landed right alongside the first and the white-hot poker was pressing deeper and deeper into the skin.

Swish! ... Crack!
The third stroke was where the pain always reached its peak ...[4]

Seven years later, in *Boy*, which Dahl claims is 'not an autobiography' but simply a record of 'a number of things' which 'made such a tremendous impression on me that I have never been able to get them out of my mind',[5] he intensifies the impression of barbarity by including no fewer than three chapters ('Mrs Pratchett's Revenge', 'Captain Hardcastle' and 'The Headmaster') with equally lengthy graphic accounts of punishments administered respectively at Llandaff Cathedral School, St Peter's in Weston-super-Mare (repeating some of the wording above) and Repton Public School. In the last instance the perpetrator is described as being Dr Fisher, who later became Archbishop of Canterbury, and Dahl cites Fisher's brutality as a reason for having 'doubts about religion and even about God. If this person, I kept telling myself, was one of God's chosen salesmen on earth, then there must be something very wrong about the whole business'.[6] Jeremy Treglown's biography, however, reveals convincingly that, while Dr Fisher was indeed strict, he was not in fact the perpetrator of the beating described.[7]

The passage quoted above, together with the reiteration and amplification of this kind of material in the later text, demonstrates the aspect of education that made most impact (both literally and figuratively) on Dahl. It also displays the power of his writing, with its ability to engage the reader empathetically through the senses. The quoted passage, for instance, enlists the visual effect of the colourful evidence of the beating, as well as the sound and the physical sensations involved. Dahl's emphasis on this aspect of schooling makes apparent the message he wishes to convey – that children are helpless victims at the mercy of the school system, unappreciated by most of their teachers. The question of whether his memories were accurate in relation to Dr Fisher seems also to have been secondary to the point he wanted to make about religion.

Dahl's accounts of his own schooling are not, however, all negative. A slightly later passage in 'Lucky Break' describes how, every Saturday morning, in the absence of the masters (who all went to a local pub), the boys aged ten and over would be read to by Mrs O'Connor, 'a great and gifted teacher, a scholar and a lover of English Literature'. Over three years, she would talk to the boys about the 'great landmarks of English Literature, together with their dates', making 'one hundred items in all' come alive. He concludes, 'Dear, lovely Mrs O'Connor! Perhaps it was worth going to that awful school simply to experience the joy of her Saturday mornings.'[8] These fond memories seem to provide the foundation for his personal devotion to literature and the importance he attaches to it in the school curriculum. Again it is easy to appreciate how Dahl's message is intensified by his use of language. Coming just after passages which emphasise the pain and distress attendant on his schooling, the description of this comfortable middle-aged woman 'with her whacky clothes and her grey hair flying in all directions'[9] gains force from the contrast with what has gone before, together with the fact that the brutal masters were all 'boozing at the pub',[10] a phrase which creates a sense of dereliction of duty (even though it was Saturday morning!).

Another aspect of his education which seems to have influenced Dahl's writing is his conviction that his abilities were undervalued by his teachers. His autobiographical story 'Lucky Break' reveals how deeply affected he still was, more than 40 years later, by the adverse criticism of his English composition that he had received at school. He quotes school reports which describe him as 'incapable of marshalling his thoughts on paper', and being 'a persistent muddler. Vocabulary negligible, sentences mal-constructed', 'indolent and illiterate' and '[c]onsistently idle. Ideas limited'. He adds, 'Little wonder that it never entered my head to become a writer in those days'.[11] In parallel with this it is worth looking at a passage near the end of *The BFG* (1982) which may perhaps reflect Dahl's own sense of failure followed by his pride in his subsequent achievements as a writer: the eponymous character, whose faulty speech has throughout the book provided a rich source of comedy, expresses the desire to learn to speak properly. What is more, he is taught by Sophie, the protagonist, 'to spell and to write sentences'. He develops a fondness for Dickens, and in due course becomes 'a real writer', in fact the actual author of *The BFG*, though he is too modest to put his name on it.[12] Dahl himself confounded the low expectations of his teachers by getting some very respectable grades in his School Certificate, and winning one of only seven places out of 107 applications to work for the Shell Company after leaving school. Fifty years later, Dahl clearly still resented his housemaster's failure to congratulate him or 'shake me warmly by the hand. He turned away muttering, "All I can say is I'm damned glad I don't own any shares in Shell."'[13] This reluctance to acknowledge his ability seems to have left Dahl with the conviction that all too much of school education was devoted to keeping down rather than fostering the talents of its 'victims'. The ambiguity of his love–hate relationship with education is constantly to be detected in his writing.

The ideal curriculum

Despite the negative picture of his own education that Dahl creates, his fiction often also conveys an impression of the kind of values and behaviour that he wishes to be inculcated in the young, together with a very strong indication of the qualities he deplores. For instance, the intrepid journey of Little Billy into the (suggestively named) Forest of Sin (*The Minpins*) in defiance of his mother's mollycoddling and her expressed fears about the terrible creatures that inhabit it, results in the child meeting the miniature people and having exciting experiences which include defeating the Gruncher and riding on a swan.[14] Similarly, *Fantastic Mr Fox* revels in the ingenuity and clever exploits of the eponymous hero, while making apparent the greed of the poultry farmers. Through the vividness of his characterisation Dahl is clearly attempting to educate his readers in 'right' values.

A story in which Dahl's views about how to educate a child are very explicit is *Danny, the Champion of the World* (1975). This full-length book is an amplification of a short story, 'The Champion of the World', first published in the 1960 edition of the (adult) collection *Kiss Kiss*, later reappearing in 2000 in *Skin and Other Stories*, published in the Puffin Teenage Fiction series.[15] This short story centres on a plot devised by two men to use drugged raisins as a lure in order to capture the pheasants from the estate of Mr Victor Hazel and thus ruin his shooting party. The same plot, against the same landowner (whose name is now spelt Hazell), is also an important theme in the longer novel, but whereas the short story does not include a young protagonist, the novel is narrated by Danny, whose education by his widowed father is at least as important as the tale about the pheasants. The book is very clearly aimed at a young readership; nevertheless the final words also express a forceful message to parents:

A MESSAGE
to Children Who Have Read This Book …

a stodgy parent is *no fun at all*

What a child wants
and deserves
is a parent who is
SPARKY.[16]

Dahl's intention of ensuring that readers' sympathies lie with Danny's father (despite his questionable morals) could hardly be more explicit.

From the beginning of the novel, Danny's father is shown as a caring parent. The little boy is brought up to help his father at a filling-station, with the result that early in his life his father says, 'you must be easily the best five-year-old mechanic in the world'.[17] The father expresses his hope that Danny will become a famous design engineer, for which he will need a really good education, but at the same time he is reluctant for the boy to go to school, which he sees as a 'problem' to be deferred until, at the age of seven, Danny is able to 'take a small engine to pieces and put it together again'; only then does his father decide he is ready to start school.[18] Danny's home education does not however cease at this point – his father shows him how to make and fly a kite and then a fire-balloon, builds a tree house with the boy, creates stilts and a bow and arrows, all of which he teaches Danny to use; for the boy's eighth birthday he makes him 'an amazing machine … from four bicycle wheels and several large soapboxes'.[19] It is clear that Dahl has chosen to associate Danny's father with activities intended to make most boy readers feel somewhat envious of Danny (possibly to the detriment of their own parents!). The subtext appears to be that the education of boys in particular should ideally be practical, with an emphasis on finding things out for themselves, and a delight in doing, rather than sitting down in school to learn lessons.

Another aspect of the education which Danny's father bestows on the young boy is an imaginative love of nature and of animals. He tells Danny about the Big Friendly Giant (the BFG, an early appearance of the eponymous character of the 1982 novel) who goes around at night catching children's dreams and making them even better.[20] His father also teaches him the names of trees, flowers and all the wild creatures, and enables him to recognise birds from their calls, and to look at their nests without touching.[21]

The visual and auditory images employed in passages such as these leave no doubt as to the respect for small creatures and the love of the beauty of the natural world that, via Danny's father, Dahl is seeking to generate in the young reader. As Matthew Grenby observes, 'Dahl's fantasy of a son's greater love for his father than his friends flies in the face of most school stories', but it is clearly fundamental to the author's views about both the nature and the content of the best kind of education.[22]

Danny's home, despite being associated with a filling-station, is 'an old gipsy caravan … on a small country road surrounded by fields and woody hills', a location which contrasts with the unlovely 'squat ugly red-brick' school building, where 'boring' words about its foundation are encountered daily,[23] instead of the interesting messages about insects or flowers which Danny imagines his father writing on the stone. Images such as these intensify the impression that Danny's real education is at the hands of his father and outside school.

Danny's father's curriculum is also ostensibly subversive, as Danny imagines him writing, 'I'LL BET YOU DON'T KNOW THAT IN SOME BIG ENGLISH COUNTRY HOUSES, THE BUTLER STILL HAS TO IRON THE MORNING NEWSPAPER BEFORE PUTTING IT ON HIS MASTER'S BREAKFAST-TABLE'.[24] While this sentiment is consistent with Dahl's hostility throughout his work towards pomposity, greed, and large landowners generally, it could be argued that from the social perspective of 1970s Britain, it is hardly revolutionary. In fact, Dahl's evident delight throughout his fiction in meting out unpleasant punishments to those of whose behaviour he disapproves suggests a somewhat populist attitude towards the desirability of retribution. In this book he confines himself to showing how Mr Hazell's splendid car is despoiled, inside and out, by pheasant droppings, but the penalties incurred, for instance, by Aunts Sponge and Spiker in *James and the Giant Peach* and the eponymous characters in *The Twits* are significantly worse.[25]

Dahl would presumably argue that such retribution gives a clear indication to the young reader about the right way to behave, but Peter Hunt questions, 'Can such a zestful exploitation of childish instincts for hate and revenge, prejudice and violence, be as innocent as it appears?'[26] Justification for Dahl's portrayal of vicious characters can, however, be suggested to lie in terms of the 'cartoon effects' which Hunt admits, as amplified in Seth Lerer's description of Dahl's technique as 'caricature and sharp parody'. Lerer sees the bad characters from *Charlie and the Chocolate Factory* (1964) as 'creatures out of some medieval book of sin',[27] a description which is also applicable to much of the rest of Dahl's writing. It could, for instance, be argued that the parallels between Dahl's villains and the Vices in morality plays result from similarly didactic intentions in both cases – to deter an unsophisticated audience from indulging in unsocial behaviour. The character of Avarice from the fifteenth-century play *The Castell of Perseverance*, for instance, declaims at some length to his human audience:

> Pay not thi serwautys here serwyse
> Thy neyborys loke thou dystroye ...
> Here no begger thou he crye;
> ... bye and sell be fals weytys...[28]
> [Don't pay your servants for their service
> Make sure you destroy your neighbours ...

Don't listen to the cry of beggars;
... buy and sell using false weights ...]

The representative of humanity, 'Humanum Genus', is sorely tempted and only when he is on the verge of being carried off to hell is he rescued from the devil by the power of God's (personified) Mercy. The blatantness of the evil recommended here differs little from the behaviour of the three farmers in *Fantastic Mr Fox* (the speeches of Gluttony in the play could equally have been cited), as summarised in Dahl's rhyme:

> Boggis and Bunce and Bean
> One fat, one short, one lean.
> These horrible crooks
> So different in looks
> Were nonetheless equally mean.[29]

While Dahl's didactic intent, especially in the portrayal and the punishment of villains, may seem crude to adults today, it has well-established precedents in the classics of allegory, other parallels being found in, for instance, Bunyan's *Pilgrim's Progress*.

Fictional teachers, good and bad

The influence of Dahl's own education is certainly to be detected in his depiction of teachers in his fiction. His characterisation of the many teachers who appear in his novels tends towards a degree of polarisation which reflects his ambiguous sentiments towards these powerful figures who have the potential to impart a love of knowledge and of literature yet all too often, in his view, are associated with sadism and small-mindedness. One of the earliest examples of a teacher who puts down a pupil and is therefore punished is in *The Magic Finger* (1966) where 'poor old Mrs Winter' misguidedly asks the little girl who is first-person narrator to:

> 'Stand up ... and spell cat.'
> 'That's an easy one,' I said. '*K-a-t*.'
> 'You are a stupid little girl!' Mrs Winter said.
> 'I am not a stupid little girl!' I cried. 'I am a very nice little girl!'
> 'Go and stand in the corner,' Mrs Winter said.
> Then I got cross and I saw red, and I put the Magic Finger on Mrs Winter good and strong, and almost at once ...
> Guess what?

Whiskers began growing out of her face! They were long black whiskers, just like the ones you see on a cat, only much bigger. And how fast they grew! Before we had time to think, they were out to her ears.[30]

Soon Mrs Winter also grows a tail, and the narrator goes on to disclose that if anyone is wondering 'whether … she is quite all right again now, the answer is No. And she never will be'.[31] It is surely not fanciful to see this punishment as a form of retribution against the teachers who regarded the young Dahl as stupid.

Generally speaking, Dahl's revenge against the unpleasant teachers he recalls in his own memoirs takes the form of the negative way in which he portrays them in his writing, both fiction and non-fiction. The most vividly depicted corporal punishment in his fiction is doled out to the title character of *Danny, the Champion of the World* by Captain Lancaster, who has 'fiery carrot-coloured hair and a little clipped carroty moustache and a fiery temper … [he watches his pupils] with pale watery-blue eyes … and [makes] queer snuffling grunts through his nose, like some dog sniffing round a rabbit hole'.[32] Even before Captain Lancaster's brutality is revealed, this description is calculated to antagonise young readers, creating as it does a combination of control and predation. The description of Danny being punished is preceded by a second reference to the teacher's eyes and snuffles (lest the reader remain oblivious to his unattractive attributes); the beating is inflicted because Danny gives a friend the answer to a mental arithmetic problem. The incident of the beating is completely extraneous to the plot, and seems to be there solely to emphasise both the evil of school (despite the other teachers being kinder) and, afterwards, the compassion of Danny's father in his response to the injury inflicted on his son. The description of the actual beating, with its reference to a hot poker, recalls that from 'Lucky Break' quoted above:

> The long white cane went up high in the air and came down on my hand with a crack like a rifle going off. I heard the crack first and about two seconds later I felt the pain. Never had I felt a pain such as that in my whole life. It was as though someone were pressing a red hot poker against my palm and holding it there. I remember grabbing my injured left hand with my right hand and ramming it between my legs and squeezing my legs together against it. I squeezed and squeezed as hard as I could as if I were trying to stop the hand from falling to pieces. I managed not to cry out loud but I couldn't keep the tears from pouring down my cheeks.[33]

The emphasis on the physical pain inflicted is likely to create an empathetic response in young readers, though, by its date of publication, corporal punishment of this nature would be unlikely to be experienced by the majority of schoolchildren. Whether because of this social change or not, Dahl's negative portrayal of other teachers tends to be confined to other modes of description in his later works.

Probably the most memorable pairing of good and bad teachers, involving comments on teaching methods and the appreciation (or lack of it) they show about pupils' qualities, is to be found in *Matilda*. This precociously intelligent child has, unlike Danny, a very unpleasant father, and resents being told by him that she is stupid when she knows this is untrue.[34] At school she encounters Miss Trunchbull, 'a gigantic holy terror, a fierce tyrannical monster'.[35] As the evil headmistress admits, 'I wish to heavens I was still allowed to use the birch and belt as I did in the good old days!'[36] In default of the usual means of corporal punishment, Miss Trunchbull replays her Olympic career of throwing the hammer by launching across the playground a child whose hair is too long. Miss Trunchbull has very fixed ideas about children's potential – echoes of Dahl's negative school reports here – and refuses to believe that all the members of the first class have been taught so well that they can already spell 'difficulty'.[37] Her own preferred method of teaching a boy to learn to multiply involves dangling him in the air by his hair while he recites, 'Two sevens are fourteen'.[38] She admits to her own dislike of children and denies ever having been small herself,[39] thus showing herself incapable of empathy with her pupils. Inevitably this monster gets her come-uppance at the end of the book, when her villainy in depriving her niece, also a teacher in the school, of her rightful inheritance is exposed. Miss Trunchbull collapses in a coma and finally vanishes from the school and village, to everyone's relief.

This niece, Miss Honey, is the contrasting good teacher whom Matilda encounters. Miss Honey's methods involve interesting approaches to teaching spelling, and a wide curriculum, but possibly her most significant characteristic is her ability to recognise the potential of all the children in her class, especially that of the precocious Matilda. Early in her acquaintance with the child, she realises that Matilda is a mathematical prodigy,[40] and she is also impressed by the child's knowledge of literature. Her efforts to convince the headmistress of Matilda's abilities are, of course, fruitless, because Miss Trunchbull has a rule 'that all children remain in their own age groups regardless of ability'[41] – a possible gibe at the inflexible rules that prevailed in educational policy throughout much of the immediate post-war period.[42]

Another person whom Dahl offers as a contrast to Miss Trunchbull's presuppositions about the low abilities of children is the local librarian, Mrs Phelps, who provides Matilda with reading matter that starts at the level appropriate to her pre-school age, but very soon gives her *Great Expectations* and other works of Dickens, evidently Dahl's particular favourite author. Like Miss Honey, Mrs Phelps responds to Matilda as an individual rather than someone of a specific age who can only be given reading recommended for that age. Over the next six months, under Mrs Phelps' guidance, Matilda reads 14 more of the classics of English literature, and is then encouraged to take books home, thus widening her repertoire. There seems little doubt that Dahl is recalling in this friendly librarian the character of Mrs O'Connor, as noted above in the discussion of 'Lucky Break'. Thus he is presenting in fictional form his convictions about the power of reading, convictions that undoubtedly shaped his presentation in story form of what he felt schools should and should not be doing to their pupils.[43]

Dahl's popularity in the classroom and outside

In view of the hostility towards schooling expressed in so much of Dahl's writing, it is perhaps ironic that his books, even those expressing the most negative views of teachers, have in recent years found a firm foothold in schools. In putting them on the shelves, teachers and librarians have, of course, been aware of their popularity with children and in particular their appeal to reluctant male readers. A survey of 34 schools of all types and age groups, involving 8,834 children (4,360 girls, 4,474 boys) carried out by the National Centre for Research in Children's Literature at Roehampton in 1996 (before the advent of Harry Potter) revealed that Dahl was by far the most popular author among pupils aged between 7 and 16.[44] He received 2,212 mentions, roughly equally divided between boys and girls, and twice as many as the runner-up, Enid Blyton, with 1,014.[45] In fact, all of the six books named as favourites by children aged between 7 and 11 are by Dahl.[46] The reasons for Dahl's popularity are likely to lie in the way in which his books offer the qualities which, in answering the more general questions, the young respondents mentioned preferring, notably that books should be 'funny'.[47] This recalls Dahl's sixth requirement in his advice to writers in 'Lucky Break': 'It helps a lot if you have a keen sense of humour. This is not essential when writing for grown-ups, but for children, it's vital.'[48] It is also worth noting that the survey disclosed that the most frequent source of books borrowed was school, though there is no way of knowing whether or not such books included ones by Dahl.

For some reason, Dahl's work seems not to have incurred the prohibitions from teachers and librarians that Blyton's had suffered earlier, perhaps because by the period when he was most popular, teachers were more concerned about getting their pupils to read than about the literary and political aspects of his books. Dahl's work also seems to have a greater appeal to adults than has Blyton's, so that teachers still enjoyed it themselves, rather than 'growing out' of it as they did with Blyton. This may result from Dahl's ostensibly 'subversive' attitude towards aspects of society that his readers may also have deplored, for instance in his resistance against commercial interests as shown in *Fantastic Mr Fox*. Blyton's greater tendency to address young readers directly in order to make her moral explicit is likely also to have been a deterrent to most mature readers. Whatever the reason, Dahl's books appear frequently in publishers' lists of books produced with school consumption in mind. A 1975 list of the New Windmill series[49] published by Heinemann, often targeted at reluctant readers, includes at least seven of his titles: *Boy*, *Danny, the Champion of the World*, *The Wonderful Story of Henry Sugar*, *George's Marvellous Medicine*, *The BFG*, *The Witches* and *Going Solo*. The majority of these are still in print in the current list for this series, together with collections of short stories that include Dahl's.[50] Another instance of a book being directed towards an implied school audience is Chris Powling's life, *Roald Dahl*, in the 'Profiles' series of the educational publishers, Evans Brothers.[51] Presumably the publishers had the intention of extending the knowledge of the boy readers who, enjoying Dahl's fiction, are likely to have wanted to know more about him, as well as providing an available reference book for school-based research projects.

Conclusion

Whether or not Dahl would have approved the extensive use of his books in schools, they clearly remain popular with children today, though faced perhaps with a greater level of competition from more recent best-sellers than was the case in the late 1990s. The messages that his books convey are therefore an integral part of the education of a large number of young children. These messages may at times conflict with the values of today's curriculum: for instance, Dahl's books, even if purged of potentially racist elements such as the original ethnic origins of the Oompa-Loompas in *Charlie and the Chocolate Factory*, are still lavish in class and gender stereotypes. Their potentially cruel caricatures may also fail to foster tolerance based on mutual understanding, may imply that the best answer to bullying is retribution in kind, or show children disrespecting their elders; additionally, they are very irreverent in their portrayal of teachers in particular. Another factor that might have been expected to deter educationalists from promoting his novels among the young is the fact that Dahl's language might often have been described in the past as vulgar: the BFG's reference to the propensity of giants to indulge in 'whizzpopping' (farting), has endeared the book to generations of children.[52] While this is clearly less likely to be seen as a negative factor in today's society, the question could arise as to whether the fact that these books encourage children to enjoy reading justifies their officially sanctioned presence in schools.

There seem to me to be several reasons why Dahl's books should be recognised as contributing positive elements to the educational curriculum. Most obviously, as already indicated, they are popular with children who might otherwise have a resistance to reading. Provided that these books are not the only ones they encounter, Dahl's novels can positively enhance children's imaginations by opening up a vast range of possibilities, including what they might do if they possessed the powers of some of the characters. In *Children Talk about Books*, a series of interviews with six children aged between 8 and 15, Donald Fry reports on an eight-year-old girl who has enjoyed reading Dahl's *The Magic Finger*. Helen relates her own feelings of anger to the uncontrollable behaviour of the narrator of this book, and, Fry suggests, 'Her re-reading of the story now marks her developing interest in the world around her and in the forming of judgements of what is right and wrong.'[53] Equally, some of the carnivalesque elements, of the world being turned upside down, can help channel the feelings of anger and passivity felt by children against authority figures such as parents and teachers.

Another factor in favour of books which can be seen by adults as relatively crude in their characterisation is that there is an age when children positively need stereotypes. Appleyard supports the idea that children of the age when they are most likely to be attracted to Dahl's books, between about 7 and 12, like to know where they are as far as fictional characters are concerned.[54] There is also the likelihood that such adult characters as Miss Trunchbull and Mr Hazell can help children to develop the understanding that the theoretical values with which the educational system is seeking to endow them are not always fully lived out by the adults whom they actually meet.[55] This is not to suggest that educators should fail to apply correctives where Dahl's books may be establishing unsatisfactory racial, gender or class stereotypes, but rather that such instances afford material for discussion which is probably best handled within a school situation.

While there will always remain elements of Dahl's work which attract controversy and will, as Peter Hunt indicates, continue to polarise critical opinion, there seems little doubt that they will also carry on attracting young readers even in the very different social situations of the future.[56] The vigour with which he portrays situations and characters, especially those related, in one way or another, to the world of education, has a natural appeal to those who are in the process of undergoing the educational experience – particularly if the element of respect for those in authority is conspicuously absent.

Notes

1. Roald Dahl, *Boy* [1984] (Oxford: Heinemann, 1986).
2. Roald Dahl, *Danny, the Champion of the World* [1975], illus. Jill Bennett (London: Heinemann, 1985).
3. Evidence about the use and popularity of his books in schools is to be found later in this chapter.
4. Roald Dahl, *The Wonderful Story of Henry Sugar and Six More* (London: Jonathan Cape, 1977): 203–4.
5. *Boy*: 9.
6. *Ibid.*: 132.
7. Jeremy Treglown, *Roald Dahl* [1994] (London: Faber and Faber, 1995): 21–2.
8. *The Wonderful Story of Henry Sugar*: 210–12.
9. *Ibid.*: 210.
10. *Ibid.*: 210.
11. *Ibid*: 216.
12. Roald Dahl, *The BFG* [1982], illus. Quentin Blake (London: Heinemann, 1984): 223–4.
13. *Boy*: 152.
14. Roald Dahl, *The Minpins*, illus. Patrick Benson (London: Jonathan Cape, 1991).
15. Roald Dahl, *Skin and Other Stories*, ed. Wendy Cooling (London: Puffin, 2000).
16. *Danny, the Champion of the World*: 208.
17. *Ibid.*: 22.
18. *Ibid.*: 23.
19. *Ibid.*: 30.
20. *Ibid.*: 17–18.
21. *Ibid.*: 108.
22. Matthew Grenby, *Children's Literature* (Edinburgh: Edinburgh University Press, 2008): 92.

23. *Danny, the Champion of the World*: 10, 110.
24. *Ibid.*: 111.
25. Roald Dahl, *James and the Giant Peach* [1961], illus. Nancy Ekholm Burket (Harmondsworth: Puffin, 1973): 42; *The Witches Plus Three Other Titles* (includes *The Witches* [1983], *Esio Trot* [1990], *The Twits* [1980], *The Giraffe and the Pelly and Me* [1985]), illus. Quentin Blake (London: Ted Smart, 1999): 351.
26. Peter Hunt, *Children's Literature* (Oxford: Blackwell, 2001): 57.
27. Seth Lerer, *Children's Literature: A Reader's History from Aesop to Harry Potter* (Chicago: University of Chicago Press, 2008): 302. Roald Dahl, *Charlie and the Chocolate Factory* [1964], illus. Faith Jaques (Harmondsworth: Puffin, 1973).
28. Peter Happé, *Four Morality Plays* (Harmondsworth: Penguin, 1979): 113.
29. Roald Dahl, *Fantastic Mr Fox*, illus. Tony Ross (London: HarperCollins, 1991): 14.
30. Roald Dahl, *The Magic Finger* [1966], illus. Tony Ross (London: Puffin, 1989): 11–12.
31. *The Magic Finger*: 12.
32. *Danny, the Champion of the World*: 113–14.
33. *Ibid.*: 120.
34. Roald Dahl, *Matilda* [1988] (London: Puffin, 2007): 23.
35. *Matilda*: 61.
36. *Ibid.*: 83.
37. *Ibid.*: 140.
38. *Ibid.*: 144.
39. *Ibid.*: 145.
40. *Ibid.*: 69.
41. *Ibid.*: 82.
42. Although the 1944 Education Act advocated education according to 'age, aptitude and ability', the clear-cut division between primary and secondary schools that it imposed, and the introduction of the 'Eleven-plus' examination, led to a degree of rigidity that could disadvantage pupils who did not fit easily into the system.
43. It is of some interest in this context that the published version of *Matilda* was adapted, on the advice of its original editor, Stephen Roxburgh, from an initial version which laid much less emphasis on the brilliant abilities of the heroine, or the way in which these are recognised by an ideal teacher. Treglown gives a detailed account of the changes, and of how Dahl incorporated these without showing any gratitude to the man who had suggested them (Treglown: 231–45). In the original, Matilda inflicts various tortures on her parents without the justification given in the final version by their stifling of her talents (which are in the early version only disclosed at a later point in the story), while the counterpart of Miss Honey is responsible for her own poverty because of her indulgence in gambling. Miss Trunchbull is, however, characterised in a

similar way to that in the final version. This suggests that Dahl found much more enjoyment in depicting villains than in countering them with 'good' characters, and also reveals how persistent was his compulsion to depict the negative aspects of school education.

44. Kimberley Reynolds et al. (eds), *Young People's Reading at the End of the Century* (London: Children's Literature Research Centre, 1996). Younger pupils were not asked about authors, though they were requested to name favourite books; *Charlie and the Chocolate Factory* figured among the five most popular with this age group, being particularly favoured by boys (Reynolds et al.: 73).

45. It is perhaps relevant also to note that the most popular illustrator with all age groups was Quentin Blake, frequently associated with Dahl (Reynolds et al.: 75).

46. *The BFG, The Twits, Matilda, Charlie and the Chocolate Factory, Fantastic Mr Fox, The Witches.*

47. Reynolds et al.: 70.

48. *The Wonderful Story of Henry Sugar*: 201.

49. Listed in *Danny*, endpapers.

50. Information about the current list derived from www.pearsonschools andfecolleges.co.uk (accessed 25 April 2012).

51. Chris Powling, *Roald Dahl*, illus. Stephen Gulbis [1983] (London: Evans Brothers, 1993).

52. Reticence about bodily functions is less noticeable in today's children's fiction. One of many twenty-first-century examples which might be cited is in Eoin Colfer's *Artemis Fowl* (London: Viking, 2001), where the dwarf, Mulch, tunnels through rock by 'ingest[ing] several kilos of earth a second, [processing it rapidly and] eject[ing] it at the other end'. In order to facilitate this process, Mulch 'open[s] the bum-flap on his tunnelling trousers' (162, 173). The reaction of delighted disgust felt by many readers to this behaviour, as well as the dwarf's vomiting up 'a thoroughly slimed goblin [which] collapsed retching on the floor' (167), is undoubtedly part of this book's appeal to some young readers.

53. Donald Fry, *Children Talk about Books: Seeing Themselves as Readers* (Milton Keynes: Open University Press, 1985): 16.

54. J. A. Appleyard, *Becoming a Reader: The Experience of Fiction from Childhood to Adulthood* (Cambridge: Cambridge University Press, 1990): 62.

55. These points are amplified in my book, *Children's Literature and the Politics of Equality* (London: David Fulton Books, 1997), especially at 25 and 63.

56. Peter Hunt, *An Introduction to Children's Literature* (Oxford: Oxford University Press, 1994): 23.

5

The Unlikely Family Romance in Roald Dahl's Children's Fiction

Ann Alston

The dilemma of Dahl

Tim Burton's film adaptation of *Charlie and the Chocolate Factory* concludes by suggesting that Willy Wonka was the true winner in the rags-to-riches tale because he was given the gift of a family. The film's narrator tells the audience that Willy Wonka had gained a family and that this life-fulfilling pleasure exceeded even the riches and sweetness of owning a chocolate factory.[1] Yet in Dahl's texts the sweetness of family is confused, abstract and often discarded as cultural myth. In *George's Marvellous Medicine* the aim of the book is to 'improve' (poison) Granny; in *Matilda* the heroine is pitched head-to-head with her parents in an ongoing battle that ends with them living in different countries; and in *James and the Giant Peach* James's repugnant aunts are squashed to death as the peach rolls over them in James's bid for freedom. If all Dahl's texts dealt with family in this manner, then this chapter would be relatively straightforward, but the delight of Dahl is that his work refuses such easy categorisation. The family in *Charlie and the Chocolate Factory* conforms to the Victorian 'poor but happy' cliché; Mr Fox in *Fantastic Mr Fox* is a replica of the archetypal Victorian patriarch; and Danny's father in *Danny, the Champion of the World* is nurturing, loving and creative. Single adults and couples who are childless are often represented negatively: the single women in *The Witches* threaten literally to consume children, Miss Trunchbull in *Matilda* is sadistically violent, and the Twits are portrayed as self-obsessed and destructive. While Dahl's fictional families do not always conform to the conventions of family, those who reject what Dahl seems to regard as essential, that is, a cordial adult–child relationship, tend to come to bad ends. Dahl's fiction for children speaks to the twentieth-century world of the independent child and simultaneously looks back to the fairy story and the cautionary tale of the nineteenth century. Despite the Gothic aspects of Dahl's work, with its humour, horror and reliance on carnivalesque traditions, he is, I suggest, a writer in the Romantic mode. For when it comes to family in his fiction, it is the child who metaphorically becomes the 'father of the man' and brings the phenomena of family and childhood to those who have forgotten the spontaneity and wonder of youth.

Adult vs child

The distrust of adults prevalent in much of Dahl's writing for children has its origins in his own experience. In the autobiographical *Boy*, Dahl records with reference to his prep-school matron that from his own nine-year-old perspective and from that of his schoolmates, 'it made no difference whether she was twenty-eight or sixty-eight because to us a grown-up was a grown-up and all grown-ups were dangerous creatures'.[2] Away from the protective home of his mother and sisters the young Dahl was at the mercy of the frequently – to a child – unjust and often cruel adults within the British public school system, and his fictional child protagonists are regularly subjected to similar periods of loneliness and suffering at the hands of adults. In *James and the Giant Peach* James has 'a happy life … with his mother and father in a beautiful house by the sea' until they are eaten by a giant rhinoceros and he is sent to live with his child-beating aunts, Sponge and Spiker[3]; Sophie in *The BFG* endures life in an orphanage where punishment consists of being locked in the cellar with the rats and starved[4]; the eponymous heroine of *Matilda* and her peers live in fear of their headmistress, Miss Trunchbull; and in *The Witches* all children are the object of adult hatred. Family in itself does not always afford ample protection to the child. In *George's Marvellous Medicine*, George is left to the mercy of his grandmother's 'complaining, grousing, grouching, grumbling, [and] griping',[5] while Matilda's parents look upon her as 'nothing more than a scab'.[6] The adults who reject and abuse children have no redeeming features either physically or morally speaking. Julie Cross argues that this hyperbolic negative depiction of the adult characters, typical in cartoon-like characters such as Miss Trunchbull or James's aunts, gives children 'the satisfaction of laughing at a stupid adult'.[7] Indeed, there is no shortage of material documenting Dahl's support for the victimised child and condemnation of the cruel adult. Christine Hall and Martin Coles go so far as to suggest that there is 'almost a two-fingered gesture to the adult world in some of his books'.[8] It is perhaps this anti-authoritarian stance that has led to parents, schoolteachers, librarians and critics suggesting that these texts are 'not good for children'.[9] Their discomfort is possibly in response to Dahl's rejection of the idealised world that parents and other adults prefer to offer the child reader – when authors present the world as they might like it to be rather than how it really is.[10] Dahl's fiction offers, veiled in humour and parody, the cruelty of the adult, and represents the family, home and school as potential places of torture and misery; his books rely on the grotesque and have been condemned, especially by critics such as Dieter Petzold and David Rees, for being too clear cut in classifying adults as either good or bad.[11]

Imposter mother figures

There is no denying the excess of adult cruelty, neglect and corruption in Dahl's fiction for children – and non-parental figures who act *in loco parentis* are most guilty. These abhorrent guardians tend to be women who refuse to embrace their traditional caring roles. In *James and the Giant Peach*, James's aunts are described as 'two ghastly hags' who refer to James not by his 'real name' but as 'a disgusting little beast' or a 'filthy miserable creature'.[12] Tellingly, after a day selling tickets to people wishing to see the marvellous giant peach, Aunt Sponge and Aunt Spiker cannot feed the starving James as they are too busy counting their money and instead send him out into the garden for the night in order to pick up rubbish. This is a neat reversal of the Cinderella story in terms of gender for James; the wicked stepsisters remain equally vindictive and unloving but James, rather than finding a prince, in turn discovers a bizarre family set-up of over-sized and charismatic yet caring insects. The peach the insects live in is a model of growth and fertility while, in contrast, the aunts' house and its setting are representative of the aunts' lack of nurture and love: Gothic and foreboding, the aunts' house is a 'queer ramshackle house on the top of a high hill', surrounded by a lifeless garden.[13] Like the aunts, the house and its environs are bleak and sterile. Aunt Sponge has 'small piggy eyes, a sunken mouth, and one of those white flabby faces that looked as if it had been boiled', while Aunt Spiker has 'a screeching voice and long wet narrow lips, and whenever she got angry or excited, little flecks of spit would come shooting out of her mouth as she talked'.[14] Aunt Sponge's small eyes emphasise her inward-looking self – the life has been boiled away, and the mouth is sunken, incapable of communicating with the outside world – while Aunt Spiker is similarly unwelcoming with her thin, narrow lips.

Dahl's obsession with unnatural femininity figured in facial features is also evident in *The Witches*, where the Grand High Witch's face is described as 'foul and putrid and decayed. It seemed quite literally to be rotting away at the edges, and in the middle of the face, around the mouth and the cheeks, I could see the skin all cankered and worm-eaten, as though maggots were working in there'.[15] The face, with the mouth as centrepiece, is a symbol of death, not only with regard to the Witches' desire to consume the children, but also in their decision to remain childless. Women who refuse to embrace their roles as the fertile producers and carers of children are depicted as sterile, repulsive characters. As Anne-Marie Bird deftly argues, behind the witch's mask of normality lies a 'grotesque being who not only rejects the Judeo-Christian construction of woman as procreator but transgresses it totally in that she wishes to murder children'.[16] A good woman, Dahl's texts imply, can be recognised through her capacity for love, and her ability to sacrifice herself in order for her children to flourish, while a bad woman can equally be recognised through her deficiency in love and her failure to make such a sacrifice. This ideologically conservative stance has won Dahl few friends in feminist circles: in a post-feminist world he seems prescriptive and narrow in his positioning of women and the family. Interestingly enough, the single men who appear in Dahl's fiction are not always subject to the same ideological suspicion; the BFG is friendly, as implied by his name, and Willy Wonka is eccentric but not unjust or mean.

To grow up or shrink away

Growth is an essential theme in Dahl's accounts of family and childhood. The deviant adult represented in his fiction will, at worst, threaten literally to consume the child, and at best rebuke them for growing up. The good adult, Dahl implies, should encourage and help children to grow emotionally through good storytelling (the grandmother in *The Witches*, Danny's father in *Danny, the Champion of the World*, the BFG) and through providing intellectual as well as bodily sustenance. It is the ongoing act of growing that frustrates the adult: in *George's Marvellous Medicine*, the protagonist's grandmother's repulsive characteristics are made clear to the reader when she chastises George for that 'nasty childish habit' of growing, and Miss Trunchbull in *Matilda* dislikes children, claiming to have 'been large' all her life.[17] Although, in contrast to the Witches or James's aunts, the grandmother in *George's Marvellous Medicine* must have produced children – George's mother is her long-suffering daughter – her mouth is now 'puckered up like a dog's bottom' and she is as old and sterile as the aunts. George's grandmother is demonised precisely because of her refusal to embrace her grandson and to encourage metaphorically his proper growth.[18] Indeed, the 'happy' conclusion of *George's Marvellous Medicine* sees George, encouraged by his father, feed grandmother enough of the marvellous medicine to make her shrink away to nothing. As she vanishes, George's father, Mr Kranky, remarks, 'That's what happens to you if you're grumpy and bad-tempered', while his wife agrees, commenting, 'Ah well, I suppose it's for the best, really. She was a bit of a nuisance around the house.'[19] Normal family life can now be restored as the grandmother's stunted emotional growth is embodied in her shrinking into nothingness.

A similar fate awaits the adults in *The Twits*. Again, their deviance from the 'norm' is apparent in terms of both their repulsive physical appearance and their behaviour. The narrator insists on telling the reader that Mrs Twit 'had quite a nice face when she was young. The ugliness had grown upon her year by year as she got older … If a person has ugly thoughts, it begins to show on the face.'[20] Mrs Twit – like Dahl's other evil women such as the Witches, George's grandmother, James's aunts and Miss Trunchbull in *Matilda* – becomes increasingly repulsive as she grows away from childhood but evades her proper nurturing role. She and her husband are effectively at war, and their childlessness is hardly surprising given the following battle. In one of their many 'battles', Mr Twit, by adding a small piece of wood to Mrs Twit's walking stick each day, has convinced his wife that she is shrinking. Mr Twit then mischievously offers to 'stretch' his wife by tying her feet down and giving her balloons to hold. Unable to resist temptation, Mr Twit then cuts the ropes from her feet and Mrs Twit floats away, leaving Mr Twit to celebrate while drinking a beer. Mrs Twit, while flying through the sky, realises that by releasing the balloons slowly she can return to the ground and control her journey. Mrs Twit's landing is aptly violent as the narrator tells the reader that a 'bundle of balloons and petticoats and fiery fury landed right on top of him, lashing out with the stick and cracking him all over his body'.[21] Mrs Twit is now 'on top' both literally and metaphorically. Her use of the stick to beat her husband suggests her appropriation of masculinity in the phallic imagery, emphasising her refusal to adhere to her traditional gender role. It is significant that this childless, unloving pair are eventually outwitted by the monkey, his family and the animals working together. The Twits, who have abused their encaged monkeys by insisting they live their lives performing upside-down tricks, receive their comeuppance when the monkeys escape and turn the Twits' house upside down by gluing furniture and carpet to the ceiling, leaving a patch of glue for the Twits themselves to fall into when they turn their bodies upside down. As the Twits are left to shrink with their heads stuck to the floor (in a similar way to how they caught the birds by painting the tree branches with glue) the reader is told that, after a few weeks, 'There was nothing more left in this world of Mr and Mrs Twit'.[22] The Twits, as with many of Dahl's dubious adults – James's aunts are squashed into nothingness, the Witches are themselves transformed into mice and killed by the hotel staff – have no place in the world and so are entirely removed from it. They are not missed because they have no family to grieve for them; the world is a better place in their absence. A refusal to nurture in the sense of children and family – that is, reproductively – is paralleled by an inability to grow spiritually. Adults like Mr and Mrs Twit or James's aunts have never had to, or wanted to, put children first and consequently they have become more and more self-centred. Dahl's stories suggest that adults can only learn and grow through and with their children; that nurturing and prioritising the young forces adults to lose their selfishness and become better-rounded individuals. The adults who ignore their children (the Wormwoods) or neglect to have children (the Twits, the Witches) are destined to vanish literally and metaphorically; their memories and stories will not survive the generations.

The small will overcome the mighty

The conclusions of Dahl's texts are often carnivalesque, establishing 'liberation … from the established order' and enabling the child to become empowered while adult authority shrinks away into nothingness.[23] The children (usually) grow up as the texts progress, but the adults, in refusing to embrace childhood in all its Romantic wonders, simply shrink away or become obliterated – consumed, so to speak, by the next generation. As Catriona Nicholson argues, 'Dahl's ability to combine within each story his distinctive brand of humour, fantastic adventure and strong measure of adult ridicule or exposure is a winning formula … Such tales of triumph signify children's capacity for self preservation in the face of adult threat and show that boys and girls can overcome adult oppression.'[24] Almost all Dahl's child heroes are depicted and described as small in contrast to the adults around them, perhaps most obviously in the *BFG*, where Quentin

Blake's cover illustration shows Sophie sitting on the palm of the
giant's hand. But equally in *The Witches*, the unnamed boy protagonist
is turned into a mouse; *Danny, the Champion of the World* opens with
a photographic representation of baby Danny. In what is perhaps
Dahl's best-known book, *Charlie and the Chocolate Factory*, Charlie's
place in the family hierarchy is made clear as he is only introduced
to the reader *after* his grandparents and parents, and the reader is told
Charlie is a 'small boy'. Throughout the text, Charlie is repeatedly
described as 'little' and significantly he is illustrated as a tiny figure
against the immensity of the chocolate factory's gate.[25] Locked out
from the privileged heavenly site of capitalism, consumerism and
desire, Charlie faces a difficult journey in his bid to escape from his
silenced and impoverished position. Along with his Grandpa Joe,
however, Charlie is given the space and the intellectual stimulation,
figured in the stories told to him by his family, to grow. Finally, the
heroine of *Matilda* is a 'tiny girl'[26] whose intellectual development is
enhanced through literature: Blake's illustrations frequently show her
with a book in her hand and juxtapose her with high library shelves
or with broadsheet newspapers towering over her. Despite her size
she remains undaunted by the adult world that surrounds her. This is
most clearly signified in the physical, intellectual and spiritual antith-
esis between Matilda and her head teacher, Miss Trunchbull, though
it is also apparent in the differences between Matilda and her parents,
particularly her mother's 'unfortunate bulging' figure'.[27] What Dahl's
heroes have in common is not just their vulnerability in the face of
adult power but their ability to overcome adversity and their adversar-
ies and to triumph in Dahl's empowering wish-fulfilment fantasies.

The conundrum of *Matilda*

This empowerment of the child is at its most apparent and most
complicated in relation to the family in *Matilda*. Superficially,
Matilda's nuclear family seems the epitome of suburban normality:
Matilda is not abused or starved or beaten as James is, she does not
want for home comforts like Charlie, and her parents own a comfortable three-bedroomed house.[28] As Miss Honey observes, Matilda's
residence 'could not have been cheap to buy and the name on the
gate said COSY NOOK. Nosey cook, might have been better …'.[29]
Miss Honey's words alert the reader to the all-important wordplay
that so often signals rebellion and change in Dahl's texts. The facade
of the ideal family consisting of two parents, a boy and a girl, and
a detached house, is undermined by Miss Honey reading the sign

both literally and figuratively: the image suggested by the name 'Cosy Nook' is dispelled as soon as Miss Honey hears the television playing loudly inside and Mr Wormwood, who proves to be a nosey crook, opens the door and challenges his visitor.[30] By contrast, Dahl devotes a whole chapter to Miss Honey's cottage and, in opposition to the sounds emanating from the Wormwood household, the walk to Miss Honey's front door is preceded by her recital of Dylan Thomas's poetry. Fittingly, since Miss Honey is often described as small and child-like (she has a 'porcelain figure'), her cottage is compared to a doll's house and the reader is told it might have come out of 'a fairy-tale'.[31] Miss Honey possesses the essential elements of the perfect parent, not only in her love for children but in her love of wordplay and literature. Miss Honey's preference for the old rather than the new is represented by her recital of poetry and distaste for the modern in terms of the television, and this also translates into her preference for the old and rustic in terms of architecture and furnishings. When, with Matilda's help, she regains her family home, in marked contrast to that of the Wormwoods it is described as 'a lovely red-bricked house with its weathered old red tiles and its old chimneys …'.[32] Miss Honey keeps with an older, simpler lifestyle in terms of entertainment, food, decor and, of course, traditional concepts of motherhood.

The Wormwoods and Miss Honey are continually represented as binary opposites, not merely in names but in actions. The Wormwoods embody the (negative) image of the modern family: they watch television rather than read; Mrs Wormwood takes the easy option and feeds her family take-away food while Miss Honey makes a distinct sacrifice by giving up her own meagre portion of bread to feed Matilda; Mr Wormwood is a crooked second-hand-car dealer while Miss Honey teaches; and Mrs Wormwood is overweight, plastered in make-up and has bleached hair, while Miss Honey is 'slim and fragile' with light brown hair.[33] Miss Honey represents the epitome of control and fits in with nature, not changing the body she has been given, while Mrs Wormwood represents the fake with her make-up and dyed hair and in addition is condemned by her inability to control her weight. The closure of the text sees Miss Honey holding the 'tiny' Matilda in her arms while the Wormwoods flee in their car with the 'tyres screaming'.[34] The text interrogates the ideal nuclear family: Mr Wormwood, its head and the main breadwinner, is reminiscent of Barrie's Mr Darling in *Peter and Wendy*: both fathers are infantilised as they search for attention and respect – in Mr Wormwood's case he hides at the back of the line when he believes there to be a ghost in the house, and in turn Mr Darling reneges on his pledge to drink

some unpleasant medicine. Both examples expose the father as unde-
pendable and weak. Dahl's and Barrie's texts reveal the deficiencies
of the nuclear family and render it an idealised cultural construction.
But in this negative representation, signalled by the families' inability
to adhere to the customs of 'good' ideological families (for example,
sharing specific meals in certain settings), the texts implicitly advocate
what they seem to denigrate. *Matilda* insists that a good parent will
choose a respectable career, cook good nutritious food, impart a love
of literature and language, and, perhaps most significantly, the adult
will be willing to learn from the child. Miss Honey fulfils all these
requirements as she gazes at Matilda 'in wonder'[35] but the narrative
closure, with effectively the one-parent family replacing the nuclear
family, seems radical. The biological family, then, is not necessarily the best or only alternative. Indeed, in *James and the Giant Peach*
the eccentric insects provide a more worthwhile family than James'
biological aunts; in *The BFG* Sophie finds the perfect father figure
in a giant rather than a human; and it is implied that the boy in *The
Witches* is equally happy, or perhaps even better off, with his grandmother than with his parents.

This, then, is the complexity of Dahl; the signifiers of what make
a good family remain conventional but at the same time the reality
of the single mother as the ideal mother in *Matilda* seems radical and
forward looking. Miss Honey has a 'pale oval Madonna face'[36] and
is almost child-like with her doll-like physique and virginal features.
The ideal mother, based on the Virgin Mary, marks an impossible
ideal but one that is prevalent in children's literature's presentations
of good mothers. Traditionally, children's literature exposes women
as 'bad' through their lack of maternal warmth and instinct and this
is evident in countless fairy tales, in C. S. Lewis's Narnia and in the
many abhorrent women in Dahl's texts. The culmination in an all-
woman family at the conclusion of *Matilda* may appear empowering
and radical in its praise of a single mother but it arrives at this point
through a very typical rejection of all those who fail to adhere to
the normative, middle-class signs of good domesticity and family
life. Matilda, through her intelligence and special powers, has single-
handedly managed to restore justice and a home and inheritance to
Miss Honey; she has also broken what Perry Nodelman terms the
home–away–home pattern, prevalent in children's fiction, and has
replaced her unsatisfactory family with an idyllic one.[37] In many
ways she is as empowered as any child character could be, yet once
normality is restored she loses her powers, and it is no coincidence
that she is returned to a family where bread and jam is eaten in the

archetypal kitchen that has the perfect domestic signifier of order and tradition in the Welsh dresser included in Blake's illustration. Matilda is returned to a family that is well nourished not just by good simple food but by good literature. Fittingly, it is no coincidence that when Matilda asks Miss Honey to adopt her, Miss Honey is standing in a bed of roses pruning them with clippers. Diligent as ever, this 'English rose' of a teacher is set to bring up the next generation.[38]

The idealised father figure and the power of two

If the privileging of the Miss Honey type suggests that there is no place for the non-maternal woman in Dahl's fictional worlds, then there is also little room for the father who is unable to conform to the stereotype of provider for, and physically imposing protector of, the family. Mr Wormwood is described as 'skinny', 'hardly the kind of man a wife dreams about', and is clearly a coward.[39] He is the complete opposite of fathers such as 'fantastic' Mr Fox, who is literally the traditional hunter-gatherer able to save his family through cunning, or the strong and protective BFG. In less fantastic worlds, Danny's 'sparky' father in the social realist text *Danny, the Champion of the World* is resolutely masculine and fulfils his son's expectations of fatherliness. While the father is mocked and essentially eliminated in *Matilda*, he plays a pivotal role in *Danny, the Champion of the World* and *Fantastic Mr Fox*; effectively, these texts are the stories of the fathers rather than of the child, especially in the case of *Fantastic Mr Fox*. In *Danny, the Champion of the World*, Danny tells the reader that 'my father, without the slightest doubt, was the most marvellous and exciting father any boy ever had'. He has 'brilliant blue eyes' and is, in contrast to the Twits, an 'eye-smiler'.[40] In addition, the home is rich with signifiers of a good family:

> The caravan was our house and our home ... My father said it was at least a hundred and fifty years old ... For furniture, we had two chairs and a small table, and those apart from a tiny chest were all the home comforts we possessed. They were all we needed ... I really loved that old gipsy caravan. ... Most wonderful of all was the feeling that when I went to sleep, my father would still be there, very close to me sitting in his chair by the fire, or lying in the bunk above my own.[41]

Miss Honey's cottage is reminiscent of fairy tale settings and Danny's caravan also has a romance and history of its own that tells a folkloric story of Englishness and tradition. Where Miss Honey has only some boxes to sit on at mealtimes, Danny and his father have two chairs and a small table. Neither home has any modern accessories such as Dahl's bête noire, the television, allowing the central characters to focus solely on each other. As Danny states, 'all through my boyhood, from the age of four months onward, there were just the two of us, my father and me'.[42] The best familial relationships are, Dahl seems to suggest, between one adult and one child, as seen in *Danny, the Champion of the World*, *The Witches*, *The BFG* and *Matilda*. Indeed, in the latter the entire plot is pointedly aimed at ensuring the disappearance of all other characters who might intrude on this relationship.

Danny enjoys an idyllic, almost womb-like, existence in his early years since he lives alone with his father and does not attend school. Instead, as he listens to his father's stories he states that he 'didn't have a worry in the world'.[43] Yet, if the idyllic and archaic lifestyle of Danny and his father in their gipsy caravan sits uncomfortably with their means of earning a living by repairing cars and selling petrol, then Danny's father's foray into poaching pheasants from the local landowner also interrogates the representation of the father in this figure who is at once 'a thief' and a 'gentle loving man'.[44] There is an important, Dahlesque, stance in Danny's awakening to the flaws of adults in general, but most markedly his father. Here the intrusive nature of Dahl's narrator is particularly evident:

> You will learn as you get older, just as I learned that autumn, that no father is perfect. Grown-ups are complicated creatures, full of quirks and secrets. Some have quirkier quirks and deeper secrets than others, but all of them, including your own parents, have two or three private habits hidden up their sleeves that would probably make you gasp if you knew about them.[45]

It is curious that even in a book dedicated to the equal relationship of father and child the grown-ups are set apart as altogether different creatures from children. But in this address Dahl, albeit it with an authoritative voice, draws the child readers towards him in order to share the secrets of the adult world. This is precisely what Danny's father also proceeds to do as he shares with Danny an alluring midnight feast of bread, butter, cheese, jam and cocoa while justifying and imparting to him a love of poaching. Danny's father tells his son, and implicitly the reader, the secrets of poaching; he justifies in Marxist terms stealing from the rich, and he is, the text unambiguously declares, a fantastic father. In their shared quest to poach the pheasants from Mr Victor Hazell's land, father and son work alongside each other as equals. Danny, though, is the mastermind behind the plot, further emphasising the importance of a young creative mind. Father and son defeat authority in both staying away from school and stealing from the wealthy.

In an address surely aimed at adult readers, and the adults the child readers will one day become, the book concludes with:

A MESSAGE
to Children Who Have Read This Book

When you grow up
and have children of your own
do please remember something important

a stodgy parent is no *fun at all*

What a child wants
and deserves
is a parent who is
SPARKY[46]

Where Perrault's morals placed at the end of his fairy tale retellings would warn against temptation and disobedience, in the twentieth century the warnings are aimed at the adults and their parenting skills. The child and the importance of his or her welfare is central to the text, and only a 'sparky' parent will do. Nicholson argues that Dahl is a 'pied piper' writer who, shedding truths and secrets as he goes, is devoutly followed by the child reader.[47] She goes on to suggest that Danny's father bears a strong resemblance to Dahl himself, locked away in the caravan at the bottom of the garden telling stories:

> Dahl's male protectors, in their different ways, bear strong resemblances to the writer. In his early books, which began life as bedtime stories for his own children, there is a strong sense of benign paternalistic Dahl cast in the role of hero to the young hero. With his long, stooped stature and fatherly benevolence, his love of language (albeit confused), the BFG can be regarded as a self portrait of the writer.[48]

The family and its storytellers

The BFG, Danny's father and Dahl have much in common. All are large, gentle giants who share a love and understanding of children; all rally against various authorities in society; and, perhaps most importantly, all engage and play with language to produce stories. Stories are passed from generation to generation; they are part of the child's heritage and, as such, in Dahl's texts good storytellers automatically qualify as good parents. In support of Nicholson's argument that Dahl bases Danny's father in part on himself, it is Danny's father who first tells readers of the BFG in his bedtime story, and the story he tells of the bullfrog attracting his mate is also told in Dahl's account of his time in Africa and the army in *Going Solo*.[49] Danny's father is at his most idealised when telling stories, for although he 'was not an educated man and I doubt if he had read twenty books in his life … he was a marvellous storyteller'.[50] Similarly to Danny, Charlie Bucket, although starved of food and home comforts, is nourished by the 'stories that the old people told; and thus for perhaps half an hour every night this room would become a happy place, and the whole family would forget it was hungry and poor'.[51] In *The Witches* the child narrator explains that in 'order to forget our sadness, my grandmother started telling me stories'.[52] In Sophie's company, the BFG learns to master words that have been such a 'twitch-tickling problem to me all my life' and writes the book the reader has just completed.[53] Stories fuel relationships in these texts and without them, exposed to the tortures of the television as in *Matilda* or in Mike Teavee's case in *Charlie and the Chocolate Factory*, families fail. Matilda wishes that her parents would read to make them better people but she is unable to persuade them to embark on a literary adventure. This is in stark contrast to Sophie's role in educating the BFG, who is open to language and ideas and reads 'all of Charles Dickens (whom he no longer called Dahl's Chickens) and all of Shakespeare'.[54] Sophie also teaches the BFG to become a 'real writer'. He is willing to learn from her, and yet his unique play on language is lost as he conforms to adult language structures to produce his book.[55] Nonetheless, the message remains: children and adults must remain open to learning from each other.

The romantic conclusion

In each good familial relationship in Dahl's children's books it is the child who reignites life and inspiration in the adult. For the parent–child relationship to work in Dahl it seems that the adult partner must, at least initially, also be the underdog. Miss Honey is abused and left penniless by her aunt, the BFG lives in terror of the bullying man–eating giants, Danny's father is poor and looked down upon by characters such as Mr Hazell, and all of Charlie Bucket's family face poverty and starvation. The adult must understand and empathise with the vulnerable child and his or her plight and, in each of the cases above, the adult and child share this fate and overcome it together. In what is a prevalent nineteenth-century notion, the child actually saves the man. For Danny's father it is implied that the child served to lessen the grief of widowhood; as Danny states, 'I think all the love he had felt for my mother when she was alive he now lavished upon me'.[56] Charlie's grandparents are brought back to life when he comes home from school, with Grandpa Joe leaping out of bed to join Charlie at the gates of the chocolate factory, and the BFG is liberated by Sophie as together they defeat the other giants.

Quite apart from setting the adult and child against each other, then, what Dahl suggests very strongly is that the family will only survive if its members work together and respect each other's needs and quirks. Kimberley Reynolds argues, citing Dahl as an example, that the 'Great Tradition of children's literature has always been characterised by its elevation of childhood and its questioning of adult wisdom and ortho-doxy'.[57] Certainly, this is apparent in the way unpleasant or deviant adult characters are mocked in Dahl, but it is also worth noting that the adult characters who do privilege the children in their lives are the ones who conclude the tales happily and at peace. Dahl, then, does not do anything so radical as he is often accused of: indeed, his approach to children and adults is largely Romantic and conservative. The text suggests that the underdogs – here, the children – will rise against authority which is often corrupt, unjust and violent, but although the weak may over-come the strong, chaos in a Bahktinian sense will not reign because the ideologically stable signifiers of family will be restored in the guise of good dinners, traditional surroundings and inherited stories and histo-ries. The characters who refuse to have, or to nurture, their adoptive children/grandchildren are demonised and offered no redemption; they, like Mrs Twit, become uglier and uglier until in various ways they are eliminated from the text. This perhaps suggests something rather sinis-ter, ideologically speaking, about single men and women who choose to remain child-free and consequently serves to promote the values of family and marriage albeit through negative examples. What is perhaps most alarming in terms of the traditional and idealised institution of the nuclear family is the emphasis placed on relationships between just two members. Dahl's texts prioritise one particular kind of relationship, that of parent–child in various guises; they rarely deal with sibling relation-ships, and indeed, the best families are made up of single parents: the boy in *The Witches* is happy to live out his existence as a mouse precisely because he will then die at the same time as his guardian. Charlie is perhaps an exception to this, but even here, the main relationship in the book is between Charlie and the youthful Grandpa Joe. Each of the child characters who find – and in the case of Matilda or James, engineer – new families, also rejuvenate their adult partners. The onus then remains on the adult to recognise the child, to learn from the child and be inspired by him or her, suggesting that it is the child who is empowered to create the perfect child-centred family. This is undoubtedly a modern phenomenon born of Romantic traditions, as Dahl insists that without children and stories we are nothing.

Notes

1. *Charlie and the Chocolate Factory*, directed by Tim Burton (Warner Brothers Pictures, 2005).
2. Roald Dahl, *Boy: Tales of Childhood* [1984] (Harmondsworth: Penguin, 1986): 181.
3. Roald Dahl, *James and the Giant Peach* [1961 USA, 1967 UK] (London: Penguin, 2010): 7.
4. Roald Dahl, *The BFG* [1983] (London: Penguin, 2010): 30–1.
5. Roald Dahl, *George's Marvellous Medicine* [1981] (London: Penguin, 2007): 2.
6. Roald Dahl, *Matilda* (London: Penguin, 1988): 10.
7. Julie Cross, 'Frightening and Funny: Humour in Children's Gothic Fiction', in Anna Jackson, Karen Coats and Roderick McGillis (eds), *The Gothic in Children's Literature: Haunting the Borders* (New York: Routledge, 2008): 57–76, at 60.
8. Christine Hall and Martin Coles, *Children's Reading Choices* (London and New York: Routledge, 1999): 53.
9. Deborah Cartmell, 'Screen Classics', in Janet Maydin and Nicola J. Watson (eds), *Children's Literature. Approaches and Territories* (Basingstoke: Palgrave Macmillan, 2010): 281–95, at 290.
10. Perry Nodelman, 'The Other: Orientalism, Colonialism, and Children's Literature', *Children's Literature Association Quarterly* 17(1) (1992): 19–35, at 30.
11. For further criticisms of Dahl's work see: Dieter Petzold, 'Wish Fulfilment and Subversion in Roald Dahl's Dickensian Fantasy *Matilda*', *Children's Literature in Education* 23(4) (1992): 185–93; David Rees, 'Dahl's Chickens: Roald Dahl', *Children's Literature in Education* 19(3) (1998): 143–55.
12. *James and the Giant Peach*: 12, 8.
13. *Ibid.*: 8.
14. *Ibid.*: 11–12.
15. Roald Dahl, *The Witches* [1983] (Harmondsworth: Penguin, 1985): 66.
16. Anne-Marie Bird, 'Women Behaving Badly: Dahl's Witches Meet the Women of the Eighties', *Children's Literature in Education* 29(3) (1998): 119–29, at 125.
17. *George's Marvellous Medicine*: 4; *Matilda*: 151.
18. *George's Marvellous Medicine*: 2.

19. *Ibid.*: 103–4.
20. Roald Dahl, *The Twits* [1980] (London: Penguin, 2007): 6–7.
21. *The Twits*: 34.
22. *Ibid.*: 87.
23. Mikhail Bahktin, *Rabelais and his World* (Bloomington, IN: Indiana University Press, 1984): 10.
24. Catriona Nicholson, 'Dahl, the Marvellous Boy', in Dudley Jones and Tony Watkins (eds), *A Necessary Fantasy? The Heroic Figure in Children's Popular Fiction* (New York and London: Routledge, 2000): 309–26, at 324.
25. Roald Dahl, *Charlie and the Chocolate Factory* [1964 USA/1967 UK] (London: Penguin, 2007): 57.
26. *Matilda*: 6.
27. *Ibid.*: 6.
28. *Ibid.*: 16.
29. *Ibid.*: 86.
30. *Ibid.*
31. *Ibid.*: 60, 178, 180.
32. *Ibid.*: 229.
33. *Ibid.*: 60.
34. *Ibid.*: 232.
35. *Ibid.*: 75.
36. *Ibid.*: 60.
37. Perry Nodelman, *The Pleasures of Children's Literature* (New York: Longman, 1996): 147.
38. *Matilda*: 227.
39. *Ibid.*: 28.
40. Roald Dahl, *Danny, the Champion of the World* [1975] (London: Penguin, 1994): 12–13.
41. *Danny, the Champion of the World*: 5–7.
42. *Ibid.*: 1.
43. *Ibid.*: 25.
44. *Ibid.*: 30.
45. *Ibid.*: 25.
46. *Ibid.*: 216.
47. Nicholson: 313.
48. *Ibid.*: 317.
49. Roald Dahl, *Going Solo* (London: Penguin, 2010): 62.
50. *Danny the Champion of the World*: 9.
51. *Charlie and the Chocolate Factory*: 22.
52. *The Witches*: 4.
53. *The BFG*: 44.
54. *Ibid.*: 198.
55. *Ibid.*: 198.
56. *Danny, the Champion of the World*: 3.
57. Kimberley Reynolds, *Children's Literature in the 1890s and the 1990s* (Plymouth: Northcote House, 1994): 72.

6

'When one is with her it is impossible to be bored': An Examination of Roald Dahl's Contribution to a Feminist Project in Children's Literature

Beverley Pennell

Introduction

Like all literature, Roald Dahl's children's books reflect the cultural context of their production. For this study of Dahl's representations of women and girls, the significant aspects of his cultural context include the reconceptualisation of childhood that occurs in the second half of the twentieth century, and the challenge second-wave feminism poses to the traditional Western gender order that occurs from the late 1950s onwards. Dahl's *oeuvre* offers a literary record of the cultural shifts in both these areas of social life. His representation of the shifting power differentials in adult–child relationships is an established hallmark of his children's novels.[1] Aligned with shifting representations of adult–child relationships are Dahl's shifting representations of female characters and the reshaping of female storylines. This study examines Dahl's reconfigurations of conceptualisations of 'girl', 'woman' and 'family' across two decades, from *The Magic Finger* (1966) to *The BFG* (1982) and then to *Matilda* (1988).[2] The criteria guiding the selection of these focus novels were that the texts foreground 'girlhood' and/or female gender issues by having a female character in the primary storyline, and that the storyline represents significant interaction between a girl character and adult characters. The focus novels meet these criteria and attempt the complex task of reconfiguring patriarchal narrative conventions and story constituents to represent the individualisation of female subjects, which was the primary goal of liberal feminism.[3]

Examination of *The Magic Finger* and *The BFG* demonstrates Dahl's early experimentation in disrupting patriarchal ideology and indicates the complexity of the process of degendering literary narratives, that is, the undermining of the gender binaries inherent in patriarchal social orders.[4] The examination also illustrates how, in these novels, matters of 'girlhood' may be as much about 'childhood' as about being female. In contrast, *Matilda* foregrounds the relational dimensions of girl–adult interactions, not just child–adult interactions, and represents democratic interpersonal relationships between girls and women. Dahl's girl characters are often transgressive in their resistance to presumptuous displays of adult power. By itself this does not indicate that a children's text has a feminist ideology; however, this *is* the case with *Matilda*. This novel presents a wide range of girl and women characters and it is, in part, this range of female characters, and their intertwined storylines, that enable readers to reflect on the life choices of Western women. The examination of the three novels demonstrates that effective power shifts in child–adult and male–female relations require more than the representation of subjective changes on the part of dominated groups, such as children/girls and women. Dahl's novels employ narrative strategies that allow girl characters to be self-reflexive about, or alert to, their gender positioning in the public sphere and in the private sphere. Such reflexivity leads readers to conclude that what is required is the alteration of the hierarchical structure of gendered social relations. Dahl achieves this complex feminist literary project in *Matilda*. In this novel the feminist project is more important than the childhood project, as it ruptures the convention of patriarchal storylines that expects female characters to follow a unitary life course where girls are always 'proto–mothers' whose destiny lies in the private sphere.[5]

Any study proposing a feminist orientation in Dahl's *oeuvre* conflicts with the accusations of misogyny directed at him.[6] Indeed, such accusations are a part of the 'controversial nature' of Dahl's work.[7] Dahl's recuperation with regard to misogyny charges begins with Bird's (1998) comparative study of Dahl's *The Witches* and Roeg's (1989) film adaptation of the novel of the same name.[8] Bird argues that in Dahl's novel, unlike Roeg's film, 'evil is not gender specific' but rather is present in 'all-powerful adults'.[9] That is, in Dahl's novel the witches represent adult power, not female power. After all, the witches are 'not actually women at all', but are 'demons in human shape'.[10] Defence of Dahl is complicated because two of his narrative preferences, for the comic mode and for the fairy tale genre, have misogynistic conventions.[11] Consideration of these aspects of Dahl's novels is necessary here as each of the focus novels evidences Dahl's success as a humorous writer and his preference for problematisations of fairy tales and the narrative possibilities that the conventions of low fantasy afford.[12] Scholars of comedy argue that employing the conventions of misogynistic humour offers sure success in engaging readers, especially males, and making them laugh out loud, while female readers read against themselves, accepting that this is how men have traditionally constructed comic representations of women.[13] Dahl's representations of married couples and mothers reveal the use of traditionally gendered comic stereotypes and demonstrate how 'natural' these traditional representation appear and how readily gendered stereotypes can be employed to achieve a successful comic effect.[14] This is the case in the representation of Mr and Mrs Gregg in *The Magic Finger*. Consider, for instance, the hysteria and helplessness Mrs Gregg displays[15] and the stereotypical dialogue as Mr Gregg takes charge of saving the family once they are birds.[16] Space precludes any detailed discussion of the comic here apart from the analysis of Miss Trunchbull's character in *Matilda*. Miss Trunchbull is read as one of Dahl's comic grotesque characters, another aspect of Dahl's *oeuvre* that earned opprobrium, as did his use of invective and comic violence.[17] His critics included those with a conservative view of childhood innocence and an inability to read comedy.[18]

Consideration of the fairy tale genre is also integral to the examination of the focus novels. The significance of literary genres in gender stereotyping is well established in children's literature scholarship.[19] Genres consist of widely endorsed discourses and narrative conventions. They have ideological significance, inviting readers to 'to feel in a certain way towards the characters, to anticipate their actions and fates, and, in fact, invok[ing] ready-made systems of morality and meaning'.[20] Misogyny, especially with regard to older women, is a convention of the fairy tale genre.[21] Marina Warner argues that 'All over the world, stories which centre on a heroine, on a young woman suffering a prolonged ordeal before her vindication and triumph, frequently focus upon women as the agents of her suffering.'[22] Nevertheless, Warner argues that fairy tales always evidence a 'desire' to 'vindicate the feminine', as the 'misogyny of the fairy tales engages women as participants and not just as targets; the antagonisms and suffering the stories recount connect to the world of female authority as well as experience'.[23] Furthermore, Warner argues that, in the twentieth century, fairy tale writers found 'a territory of freedom to express their rebellion … '.[24] Dahl is one such writer who activates the subversive possibilities of fairy tales. As is typical in fairy tales, Dahl's girls and women characters are unfortunate or disadvantaged. However, rather than needing heroic rescue by princes, the female characters are agential, and devise schemes that remove them from the adults who persecute them psychologically, physically, or both.[25] Dahl's narratives show that the hierarchical operations of power employ symbolic violence,[26] and his storylines revel in the subversion of such power, especially when wielded by adults over children.

The Magic Finger as a proto-feminist project

The first focus text, *The Magic Finger*, is a comic low fantasy novel set in the countryside, where the fairy tale character of the witch is invoked. A young witch who hates hunting is the novel's first-person narrator, thus enabling close reader and narrator/character alignment. In the orientation the unnamed eight-year-old narrator addresses readers, joking about giving the incorrect ages of two characters, the Gregg brothers, Philip and William. In expectation of active readers, the narrator corrects her mathematical mistake, because she knows that readers will check her additions.[27] Being a young witch, the girl has trouble controlling her magic powers.[28] Commonly in feminist fantasy literature a young witch's uncontrolled power is called 'wild magic' and is akin to female sexual power. John Stephens and Robyn McCallum argue that in feminist literature the 'outbreaking of wild magic, and the need to learn how to control it, is roughly equivalent to the episodes in the early life of the male hero in which he tests the boundaries of his strength'.[29] This reversion of the fairy tale's witch links the feminist project and the story of the competent child because it locates the witch's magical powers in the narrator's 'magic finger'. The magic finger gives the narrator supernormal powers to punish people when she is roused to righteous anger. The magic finger may be read in many ways. It locates the girl's power within her person rather than in an external object like a wand. It also connects the human emotion of anger with the witch's magic wand as well as with the symbolic phallus: the girl turns red and gets 'very, very hot all over', the tip of her right forefinger tingles 'most terribly' and 'a sudden sort of flash comes out of me, a quick flash, like something electric'.[30] Yet another possible meaning is that the magic finger is a vulgar affront to powerful adults, symbolising an offensive gesture, as in 'giving someone the finger' and pointing the finger of blame. There are, then, reasons to argue that this is a powerful child, as much as a powerful girl.

The reconceptualisation of childhood, as enshrined in the United Nations' (UN) *International Convention on the Rights of the Child* (1989), formalises ideas that emerged in the decades after the Second World War, when Dahl comes to the forefront in children's literature. The UN convention requires that both states and parents acknowledge the 'evolving capacities' of the child. This reconceptualisation of childhood as a time of increasing competence and self-determination circulates in dialogue with the traditional conceptualisations of childhood as a time of innocence and dependence. Dahl's novels are child-centric and they certainly represent child subjects as having increasing cognitive and physical capabilities; in closures, his child characters are always agential, that is, they have the power to effect changes in their world. In some cases, Dahl's child characters have extraordinary competencies in the 'real' world, as well as supernormal fantasy powers. The question arises as to whether the girl narrator in *The Magic Finger*, with her special power, is to be understood as an agential child or specifically as an agential girl. To frame the problem differently, does the reader see *The Magic Finger* contributing to a proto-feminist project or to a pro-childhood competence project? If the decision to designate the narrator as a 'girl' is assumed to be significant, that will influence the answers to these questions.

In traditional paradigms of childhood, Bronwyn Davies argues that 'Children are defined as *other* to adults in much the same way that women are other to men. Children have to learn to be both outside adult discourse and to participate with adults both in terms of adult's concepts of children and of adult–child relations.'[31] Here Davies argues that children need to be self-reflexive about how adult discourse positions them. Dahl's novels typically represent self-reflexive child characters, as is the case with the narrator of *The Magic Finger*, drawing the child reader's attention to the narrative structures and positioning them to interrogate the representations of child subjectivities and the metanarratives of childhood. Of course, the representation of gendering is an integral part of these meta-narratives.[32] *The Magic Finger* contains elements of the emergent reconceptualisation of childhood in that it overturns the traditional understanding of childhood as a carefree time with children dependent on, yet separated and protected from, the adult world. The young narrator is passionately concerned about social issues and assaults the barriers that would deny her a voice on matters in the public sphere, hunting in this case. From a new millennial perspective, *The Magic Finger* represents a desire to dismantle the barriers between the worlds of the child and adult. The novel's orientation, or opening sequence, exemplifies the normal operations of power employed against a child who opposes adult behaviour: she is rebuffed. The girl opposes blood sports and when she confronts Philip and William's father, Mr Gregg, about his duck and deer hunting she is ignored or ridiculed.[33] Is the undignified dismissal of the narrator's opinions a response to a child, or more specifically a response to a girl?

The girl is self-reflexive about her teacher, Mrs Winter's, and Mr Gregg's subordination of her because she is a child. The novel's first embedded narrative is a flashback that demonstrates the girl's magical powers. When Mrs Winter publicly declares the girl 'stupid' for misspelling 'cat',[34] the girl protests at the teacher's abuse. As the teacher shows no remorse, the girl activates her uncontrollable super-powers and the teacher finds herself with a cat's whiskers and tail and the class's ridicule. The girl and the reader have a sense of superiority over the teacher.[35] With Mr Gregg, when the girl tries to protest about his hunting trips, he first ignores her and then, when she shouts her opposition to the killing of a deer, commands her 'to go home and mind her P's and Q's'.[36] Here Dahl represents adult power as quintessentially a matter of symbolic violence perpetrated against the child.[37] In her unapologetic shouting at adults and the use of her special powers against them, the girl is a transgressive child, not just a transgressive female. The novel's second embedded narrative tells of the Gregg family's punishment by metamorphosis into ducks, a delightfully ludicrous event and clearly pro-nature ideologically. Unlike Mrs Winter, the Greggs are not forever condemned, because they repudiate hunting. Their time spent as ducks, experiencing flying, nest building and fear of human-sized ducks with guns, leads the family to new respect for all animals. Admiration for their feathered friends leads to the comic turn that has the family change its name from Gregg to 'Egg'.[38]

Establishing the case for feminist ideology in *The Magic Finger* requires an examination of genre, character and storyline. Readers' alignment with the first-person narrator is a familiar strategy in children's novels and readers assume that the narrator is reliable, or trustworthy. The girl is powerful, then, as her point of view controls the story. The girl is ultimately agential with regard to transforming the attitudes of male characters towards the patriarchal practice of hunting. However, this transformation requires the use of magical powers since her attempts to use reason to achieve this outcome fail: 'Every time I went over to their farm I would try my best to talk them out of it, but they only laughed at me'.[39] Is she laughed at because she is a girl and because she is exhibiting traditional female traits of bossiness and nagging? Is she laughed at because protesting against blood sports is a 'girly', soft-on-violence attitude? However we answer those questions, the means by which the girl achieves her victory remains one of traditional femininity, namely witchcraft. Mr Gregg mentions the idea of a 'witch' as one possible explanation for the metamorphosis of the family into ducks.[40] Significantly, in the resolution, it is clear that the girl will continue to use her powers to wage her anti-hunting programme with the Coopers, the next set of 'hunting mad neighbours'.[41] The girl declares her magicality as she tells the (Gr)Eggs that the Coopers will be 'nesting in the trees tonight, every one of them'.[42] The novel's closure represents the girl's ongoing reforming zeal, rather than offering a conservative return to the normal, as is typical in comic resolutions.[43] *The Magic Finger* is certainly a proto-feminist novel that presents the story of an agential girl. The novel also certainly contributes to the shift in understandings of childhood as a time of ever-increasing competence: the girl child refuses to remain a captive of the private sphere and asserts her right to a voice in the public sphere; she successfully schemes so that male characters foreswear a patriarchal practice. The cultural narratives of childhood and of gender are closely intertwined here.

The BFG and second-wave feminism

Dahl's contributions to feminism as well as to the reconceptualisation of childhood in children's literature, as distinct cultural projects, are clear in the second focus text, *The BFG*. This novel reflects the cultural context of second-wave feminism because it makes femininity visible as the courageous Sophie, a normal girl without magical powers, negotiates her relationship with a character from fairy tales, the giant, who calls himself the BFG. Sophie is a heroine in an adventure storyline, very much a traditional patriarchal genre. In this adventure the female character holds the moral purpose and shows a taste for action. Mark West recognises Sophie's significance as 'a spunky girl who is not easily intimidated' and that a 'noteworthy feature of the plot is that it is driven by decisions made mostly by Sophie', indeed, Sophie 'makes plans, takes risks, and exercises leadership'.[44] The intelligent, and increasingly confident, Sophie takes her place in the public sphere of the storyworld, dealing with matters of life and death for the world's children. The resolution of the primary storyline requires the containment of nine child-eating giants. Sophie devises the plan to achieve this and the giants' successful capture is possible because of the trust and confidence that the BFG has in Sophie's ability. Here barriers between the world of the child and the adult are dissolved and the novel represents a democratic interpersonal relationship between the girl child and the aged giant. While *The BFG* successfully reconfigures female subjectivity and elements of the adventure genre, this examination shows how the novel's resolution and denouement rein in the feminist ideology, with the reinstatement of the gendered conventions of the romance genre.

The BFG, then, represents aspects of the values and ideas that second-wave feminism espoused. Second-wave feminism, from the mid-1960s onwards, articulated women's claims to the same rights to individualisation as men: that is, to independence as economic units and the right to operate autonomously in the realm of public life. Feminists outlined demands for a reorganisation of the dominant Western social structure and its embedded gender regimes. Feminism named the traditional male-dominated social structure as 'patriarchy': a social structure that assumed that women were 'naturally' subservient to, and dependent upon, men. Liberal feminists argued that the idea of the 'separation of spheres' for men and women underpins this social structure, with the private sphere being the place for women and childrearing.[45] Patriarchy assumes that the ideal social arrangement has women away from the public sphere, a view second-wave feminism contested. Chambers argues that the ongoing problem of women's invisibility in public life results from their subordination in the patriarchal social structure of the family.[46] Contesting patriarchal social structures in literature requires reconfigured representations of female characters operating in the public sphere – beyond the home – and thereby symbolically articulating social change and contesting patriarchal expectations. A complex matrix of changes was needed in literary texts in order to reflect changes in female subjectivity as well as in the traditional gender order.[47] The first strategy employed was the reconfiguration of female character attributes by allowing attributes from the traditional schema of masculinity to be added to the traditional schema of femininity, as happens with Sophie's character in *The BFG*. The strategy of diversifying female experiences followed, enabling the representation of democratic interpersonal relationships between girls and a range of male and female child and adult subjects, incorporating social differences such as age, ethnicity and social class. *The BFG* diversifies femininity in a significant, if restricted, way because the orphaned Sophie joins forces with the powerful, high-status character, the Queen of England, in order to overcome the threat facing the nation's children. The next strategy to be reconfigured in order to achieve a feminist shift was genre, with elements of patriarchal genres being reshaped in terms of the roles female subjects played in the primary storylines. Changes in genre elements gave female characters access to, and agency in, story events that occurred in the public sphere. In *The BFG* Sophie is the central character in the primary storyline of an adventure narrative. Ultimately, of course, feminist reconfiguration of literary texts required the production of new female metanarratives, and this is what Dahl achieves in *Matilda*.[48]

Dahl reconfigures Sophie's female character attributes to include attributes from the traditional schema of masculinity, such as courage and rationality. This strategy is evident in the novel's orientation when the arrival of the BFG in Sophie's English village signals a magical intervention in the real world. To begin Sophie's adventures, Dahl mixes low fantasy and the fairy tale genre. It is the 'witching hour' when the world outside Sophie's window 'didn't look real', for the 'houses looked bent and crooked, like the houses in a fairy tale'.[49] On this night, Sophie sees the black-cloaked giant, with his suitcase and dream-blowing trumpet, gliding along the street and peering into each house. Sophie survives the terror of being kidnapped from her bed by the BFG, but the obtrusive narrator comments on how frightening Sophie's experience would be, thus indicating her bravery.[50] Sophie is told that she can never be released because she has seen a giant.[51] She is courageous as she fears for her life, expecting that the BFG will eat her.[52] She is self-reflexive about her powerless position and controls her fears as she strategises about how to humour the BFG.[53] The same self-reflexivity is shown later when she considers ways to convince the Queen of the urgent need to act against the evil giants. Sophie learns that the BFG is a 'nice and jumbly Giant', 'a dream-blowing giant' who is hundreds of years old, so Sophie should respect him as an 'old sage and onions'.[54] Later, Sophie and the BFG return to London and Buckingham Palace to gain the Queen's support for their plan to capture and imprison the child-eating giants. Here the child female subject is agential in the public sphere and democratic interpersonal relations are represented between the child and adult female subjects.

The BFG also employs the feminist strategy of diversifying female experiences in the public sphere and this is achieved by using the high fantasy genre. This is most significant because it is in the unfamiliar secondary worlds of Giant Country and Dream Country that Sophie develops emotionally and intellectually as she engages with other ways of being and thinking. Giant Country is off the map, humorously located in the blank pages at the back of the atlas[55] and is geographically unlike England[56] and occupied by ten giants,[57] nine of whom eat 'human beans'.[58] Sophie learns all about giants and giant history: they are eternal,[59] 'time-twiddlers' and supernatural in that they are not born of a mother but rather 'they simply *appears*'.[60] Sophie learns the BFG's own (hi)story and his philosophy of life which means that, unlike the other nine giants, he refuses to eat children. In indirect focalisation, Sophie realises that 'this extraordinary giant is disturbing her ideas' and 'leading her to mysteries that were beyond her understanding'.[61] Sophie and the BFG have metaphysical discussions about the fact that, unlike giants and most other species, human beings kill 'their own kind'.[62] The BFG argues that 'Grown-up human beans is not famous for their kindnesses' but Sophie protests that this generalisation is unfair.[63] The BFG argues the need for care of nature, animals and plants, even arguing that plants are sentient beings and insisting that he hears the screams of picked flowers.[64] Later, Sophie convinces the BFG to act against the other giants because of his belief in the harmony that should exist between all living things. The BFG has previously confronted the other giants about their dietary preferences and he tells Sophie that he would like 'to find a way of disappearing them'.[65] However the BFG does not see himself as agential; being only 24 feet in height, the BFG is a 'runt' of a giant and bullied by the other 50-foot giants.[66] Sophie insists that they act; she is prepared to face all necessary dangers herself and devises a plan. In the climax of the adventure, the capture of the giants, Sophie saves the day, ingeniously sticking a 'three-inch-long brooch pin' into the foot of an awakening giant to help subdue him.[67] The item of feminine attire is a valuable gift Sophie received from the Queen and this feminine ornament is ironically resignified as a weapon.

While *The BFG* reconfigures female character attributes and aspects of genre so that its feminism is explicit, the novel does not achieve a new metanarrative for its main female character. Indeed, the incorporation of elements of the 'Beauty and the Beast' romance tale undermines the feminist ideology of the novel. The giant/beast becomes the beloved figure of the female subject, a father figure in this case, rather than the lover/husband. There are exchanges of familial kisses that indicate Sophie and the BFG's deepening attachment. When Sophie queries the BFG about his justification for kidnapping her, he says that 'I did not steal you very much … After all you is only a tiny girl'.[68] The inadequacy of this patriarchal rationalisation is deflected by the BFG's joke about size and his humorous idiosyncratic use of English. Sophie's relationship with the BFG transforms him. For instance, when he presents himself to the Queen, he is 'dignified',

and has 'the grace of a nobleman'.[69] The beast schema is a convention of the romance genre and the elements that Dahl employs in the
resolution restore the patriarchal social order, much as Roeg does in
his reversion of *The Witches*. In both cases, readers see, in Bourdieu's
terms, masculine domination reinstated.[70]

The novel's feminism is also undermined by Sophie's relegation
to the role of the BFG's mentor and teacher.[71] Sophie teaches the
BFG the skills he needs to become a writer and storyteller. Possibly
as a postmodern textual feature, or perhaps as artistic hubris, the
twist in the tale is that *The BFG* has Dahl's name on it as the author
because the BFG is too shy to use his own name.[72] Thus there is a
trick revealed in the novel's resolution when the obtrusive narrator
and the author are identified as one and the same: Dahl is the BFG,
the keeper of children's dreams and nightmares. A consequence of
this storyline for the female character is that she returns to being of
secondary importance, the traditional female role in patriarchal literature. The conservative bent of the comic mode and romance genre is
clear, as closure returns the world order to the way it is traditionally
understood. This contrasts with the subversive fantasy closure of *The
Magic Finger*.

Matilda's subversion of idealisations of 'girl', 'woman' and 'family'

By the late 1980s children's literature was making femininity visible,
employing a diverse range of female subjects and successfully reconfiguring female character attributes and patriarchal genres. These
strategies enabled literary texts to offer reconceptualisations of 'girl',
'woman' and 'the family'. Patriarchal idealisations of these concepts
were problematised and alternatives were represented that allowed
the articulation of liberal feminism's individualisation of the female
subject in literary texts. *Matilda* incorporates these aspects of feminist
literary reconfigurations and particularly problematises the traditional
nuclear family. *Matilda* offers a new female metanarrative that ruptures
the post-Second World War expectation that all female subjects will
follow a unitary life course that includes motherhood and containment in the private sphere. In *Matilda*, a new female metanarrative
is constructed in the stories of Matilda and her teacher, Miss Honey.
These characters are juxtaposed with the storylines of Matilda's mother
and Miss Trunchbull, the school principal. However, while Matilda and
Miss Honey are represented in realist mode, Matilda's mother and
Miss Trunchbull are represented in comic mode and so must be read

differently. Matilda's and Miss Honey's metanarrative is that of the educated professional woman with the potential for economic and social independence. *Matilda* clearly makes a significant contribution to the feminist project. The limitation of this second-wave feminist meta-narrative, from our historical perspective, is that the female characters' economic independence remains an extension of the mothering roles of 'education, care and service' and the issue of relational dimensions of masculinity and femininity is not recognised.[73]

Pressure on the concept of the family comes from many social forces post-Second World War. Ariès's research into the history of childhood was prompted by the regulatory nature of the Western family and its child-rearing practices because, as he argues, under-standings of childhood are intrinsically linked to patterns of family life.[74] Certainly, the concept undergoes a substantive reconcepualisa-tion of its constitution and of its significance in Western social life as a result of feminist scholarship. Arguing the complex interconnected-ness of social structures, John Stephens writes that:

> Attempts to change a society's concepts of gender occur in the context of a sense of larger social change, a sense that the modern world calls into question the explanatory force of the systems of the past – whether social, ethical or religious – and that categories once thought of as fixed and stable, such as gender or the family, may in fact be relative.[75]

Stephens argues here that social categories like the family and gender are mutable concepts. Such ideas were provocative and prompted a conservative backlash towards the end of the twentieth century. A counter-discourse of 'family values' emerged in an attempt to halt the disruption to traditional family life implicit in women's demands for equal opportunity in the workplace and equality of labour contributions in the home. As Chambers argues, 'Politicians and institutions who promote the idea of a crisis in family values claim it to be related to a crisis in gender identities that can only be resolved by a return to traditional gender roles.'[76] For women, the implicit requirement of the 'family values' ideology is that they return to a secondary role in the social structure and relinquish their claims to the full individualisation that male subjects enjoy. Chambers argues that the conservative backlash has political support: 'Public poli-cies continue to shore up the ideal of the male breadwinner and to pathologise mothers without a male partner or who wish or need to enter paid employment, and also other types of living arrangements and sexual relations that do not conform to the nuclear ideal.'[77] The backlash is also evident in the arts, as Roeg's film version of Dahl's *The*

Witches demonstrates. Bird argues that the film's ideology reinstates patriarchal attitudes towards women, making women responsible for 'the collective ills of contemporary society'.[78] Dahl's *Matilda* undoubtedly exhibits the feminism that provokes a conservative 'family values' backlash. The novel repudiates idealisations of the nuclear family and suggests that 'familial bonds' may be non-existent among biological kin and that family should not necessarily mean a household legitimated and financed by men. West argues that in '*Matilda* the family is not much more than a collection of individuals who live in the same house', but argues that this is not typical because family was the one social structure that Dahl valued.[79]

Disruptive children's novels, like Dahl's, dismantle oppositional and hierarchical representations of adult–child relations and male–female relations in order to represent ways of being and interacting that enable genuine transformations to democratic interpersonal relations between children and adults, males and females. One way Dahl achieves this is through genre mixing and mode switches. If genres offer 'ready-made systems of morality and meaning',[80] then genre mixing may bring conflicting ideological systems into dialogue. Genre mixing is integral to Dahl's increasing success with contributions to a feminist project in children's literature, particularly in *Matilda* where the novel employs, and reconfigures, three traditional female genres: the family story, the school story and the fairy tale. In *Matilda* there are shifts between the realist and the comic modes. Several studies of gender and children's literature show that the comic mode has the resources to represent transformed gendered social structures.[81]

In the first chapters of *Matilda,* child readers are positioned to weigh the idealised myths of family against the dysfunctional relationships in Matilda's family, the Wormwood household. Dahl offers a brutal reconfiguration of the traditional family story. The negative representation of Matilda's family is signified in the family name, Wormwood. Five-year-old Matilda is described as a 'genius' and 'precocious' as soon as Miss Honey meets her, with Miss Honey defining precocious as 'having amazing intelligence early on'.[82] Miss Honey's comment that, 'When one is with her it is impossible to be bored'[83] shows her understanding of the possibility of a democratic intersubjective relationship with this little girl. Yet Matilda's family story is one of parental psychological abuse connected to her gender. Mr Wormwood favours Matilda's brother and humiliates her. As is common in second-wave feminist ideology, there is a misandric element[84] in the representation of Mr Wormwood, as a criminal and a boastful bully. Matilda hates her father because of 'being told constantly that she was ignorant and stupid when she knew she wasn't'.[85] She is self-reflexive about her disempowerment as a child, and significantly, as a girl and daughter,[86] and this injustice leads to transgression. As Matilda's only weapon is her intelligence, she uses this to take her revenge, as is typical of Dahl's characters,[87] devising pranks that are 'suitable punishment'.[88]

Matilda is most subversive with regard to family in its resolution, where the Wormwoods' lack of parental feeling for their daughter is unequivocal. Matilda's parents are unconcerned about leaving her behind with Miss Honey, as they flee to Spain to escape the law. However, it is not entirely a matter of abandoning her. Rather, the Wormwoods defer to Matilda's assertion of her competence to make decisions about her own life.[89] Her mother says, 'Why don't we let her go if that's what she wants', and her father agrees, 'It's fine with me'.[90] Importantly, this resolution does not incorporate Miss Honey into the traditional mothering role. While Miss Honey is delighted to be responsible for Matilda, the relationship that Miss Honey and Matilda have is not one of child dependency. Matilda is a competent child in Miss Honey's eyes because Matilda has been agential in promoting Miss Honey's welfare. There is the representation of an interpersonal relationship that argues for mutuality and reciprocity of care between adults and children. Here Dahl envisions the postmodern family, where 'family' signifies 'subjective meanings of intimate connection rather than formal blood or marriage ties'.[91] The novel's final comment about the Wormwoods and about family is offered metonymically. As the Wormwood's car, minus Matilda, disappears 'for ever into the distance',[92] it is Matilda's brother who looks back and waves. This implies that Matilda's brother, rather than her parents, has to negotiate the social arrangements presaged by Matilda and Miss Honey as a new family unit.

Matilda contains two Cinderella stories. There is Matilda's own story, a young Cinderella, and there also is that of her teacher, Miss Honey, the adult Cinderella. In the novel's final chapters, elements of the fairy tale genre are elaborated in the realist mode and then subverted. Miss Honey's storyline makes the fairytale connection to Cinderella overt with the forest setting and the princess/teacher in need of rescue. Significantly, in terms of feminist reversion of the patriarchal storyline, there is a double rescue, with each female subject rescuing the other.[93] Miss Honey rescues Matilda from her parents and from intellectual stultification and Matilda plays the heroic role of rescuing Miss Honey from her aunt, Miss Trunchbull, the Ugly Sister character, 'a gigantic holy terror'.[94] When Matilda first visits Miss Honey's home she finds that her teacher is living in a small, dark cottage in the wood.[95]

Matilda is surprised and slightly frightened by its wild isolation, its decrepit state and lack of furniture and food.[96]

Miss Honey feels no such fears about her cottage and reassures Matilda by reciting lines from a poem. This intertext is the first stanza of Dylan Thomas's 'In Country Sleep'.[97] The dark irony is that the poem's apostrophised addressee is a dead girl, which is why, one assumes, only the first stanza is quoted, but also why Miss Honey, the narrator tells us, is 'embarrassed at having revealed such a secret part of herself'.[98] Here the character reveals more of her despair than even the empathetic Matilda will fathom. During this visit Matilda decides that, 'There was a mystery in this house, a great mystery'.[99] Matilda discovers that the cottage is Miss Honey's sanctuary from her aunt. The fairy tale cottage is thus resignified as a place of safety, symbolising Miss Honey's agency in escaping her aunt's domination. Matilda devises a ruse that exposes Miss Trunchbull's murder of Miss Honey's father and the theft of Miss Honey's inheritance. Matilda employs her psychokinetic 'eye-power'[100] to have a piece of chalk scribe Miss Trunchbull's crimes on the blackboard. No doubt this is the reason that West argues that Matilda 'is one of the few child characters from Dahl's writing to care enough about an adult's problems to try to do something about them'.[101]

The female characters represented in the comic mode, Matilda's mother and Miss Trunchbull, serve different functions in the storylines and so have different impacts on the novel's feminism. Matilda's mother undermines the ideal of patriarchal marriage and motherhood even though she is complicit in patriarchy, as a beneficiary of its provision for all her needs. The mother takes advantage of the freedom and money provided by a male breadwinner and contributes nothing to childcare or to domestic labour and yet is disloyal to her husband. Mrs Wormwood is a parody of the social norms that interpellate the ideal mother as selfless, generous, wise, a domestic slave and an omnipresent caregiver. Traditional 'mothering' virtues are absent in Matilda's mother. Mrs Wormwood is so unappealing that her disapproval of 'bluestocking girls' and her opinion that a girl should concentrate on making herself attractive in order to get a husband are immediately suspect. Her comic *bon mot* is that 'Looks is more important than books'[102] but readers understand its irony. Miss Trunchbull functions as one of Dahl's comic grotesque characters and is to be understood as an outrageous monster, but one that is incredible. As such, Miss Trunchbull is a diabolical adult rather than a diabolical female character. She provides a balance in the novel to the representation of Matilda's father, the cruel male adult character; both characters exemplify Dahl's tendency to 'satirize authoritarian adults'.[103]

Matilda makes femininity visible, particularly in the chapters employing the school story genre, by including a broad range of agential and often transgressive female characters, both girls and women who resist domination. The schoolgirl characters possess reconfigured female character attributes that allow them to lead feisty attacks against Miss Trunchbull's unjust provocations. Hortensia is a student from a higher grade than Matilda who warns of Miss Trunchbull's horrific (slapstick) violence to children. Hortensia sets a brave example, as a master 'in the art of skulduggery', having defied Miss Trunchbull many times and suffered awful punishments, including solitary confinement in 'The Chokey', a narrow cupboard whose sides are covered in protruding 'sharp spikey nails'.[104] Matilda's friend is the ironically named Lavender who 'longed to do something truly heroic',[105] like Hortensia and Matilda, to punish the hideous headmistress. Lavender, as focaliser, thinks that it is now 'her turn' to act heroically as she plans her prank. The narrator employs a lexical set of warfare terms: 'plot', 'exploit', 'secret weapon', 'bomb', 'blow someone to bits' to represent Lavender's thinking about her heroic intentions.[106] In *Matilda* the adult–child, or specifically, the girl–woman barrier, is overturned by Mrs Phelps, the village librarian, as well as by Miss Honey. Mrs Phelps is the adult who fosters Matilda's reading, first with children's books and then by steering Matilda towards a 'formidable list' of canonical writers.[107] The girls and women in *Matilda* admire one another, value education, are employed in the public sphere and so are economically independent, and support other girls and women to be likewise liberated.

Conclusion

Children's literature scholarship must trace the broad and evolving contribution of children's literary texts to society's gender debates. An examination of Dahl's contribution to the project of second-wave feminism provides insights into the narrative project of degendering patriarchal literary conventions. From our current historical position in a post-second-wave feminist world, critique of the traditional Western dual gender system is alert to the repressive practices of all dominant discourses, even those of second-wave feminism, a discourse formerly self-identified as liberatory. Now gender scholarship goes beyond the examination of the gendered discourses embedded in both patriarchal and feminist literary texts.[108] Nevertheless, it is undeniable that the literary reconfigurations of female subjectivity, the alterations of female metanarratives and shifts in narrative conventions are significant second-wave feminist strategies that rupture the patriarchal literary tradition. These strategies make femininity visible in literary texts, reconfigure interpersonal gendered character relations, and offer new understandings of 'family'. One unfortunate outcome of such narratives is the perpetuation of a rent in male–female gender relations: the process of pluralising and resignifying female subjectivities has often meant a concomitant pejoration of male subjectivities,[109] as is evident in the resolution of *Matilda*. This study demonstrates the extent of Dahl's reconceptualisation of 'girlhood' across the decades from the publication of *The Magic Finger* (1966) to the publication of *Matilda* (1988). While *The Magic Finger* and *The BFG* undermine aspects of patriarchal metanarratives, they do not offer patterns of degendered society to the extent that *Matilda* does. Dahl's novels certainly establish female subjects, like the girl in *The Magic Finger*, Sophie in the *BFG*, and Matilda, as sites of enunciation and thus recuperate some negative female stereotypes. *Matilda* asserts the heterogeneity of female experience and problematises the matrices of social power that continue to position girls and women as subordinate to men, a process in which women like Matilda's mother are complicit. In *Matilda*, Dahl succeeds in representing democratic adult–child intersubjectivity and subverts patriarchal literary idealisations of 'girl', 'woman' and 'family'.

Notes

1. Mark I. West, *Roald Dahl* (New York: Twayne, 1992); Anne-Marie Bird, 'Women Behaving Badly: Dahl's Witches Meet the Women of the Eighties', *Children's Literature in Education* 29(3) (1998): 119–29.
2. Roald Dahl, *The Magic Finger* [1966] (London: Puffin, 2008); *The BFG* [1982] (London: Puffin, 2007); *Matilda* [1988] (London: Puffin, 1989).
3. Pierre Bourdieu, *Masculine Domination*, trans. Richard Nice (Cambridge: Polity Press, 2001); Deborah Chambers, *Representing the Family* (London: Sage, 2001): 23.
4. R. W. Connell employs the term 'degendering' in *Masculinities* (St Leonards: Allen & Unwin, 1995) and *The Men and the Boys* (St Leonards: Allen & Unwin, 2000). Connell's argument in his ethnographic studies of masculinity align with those of second-wave feminists that, as 'a strong cultural opposition between masculine and feminine is characteristic of patriarchal gender orders, commonly expressed in culture as dichotomies and negations' (Connell 2000: 31), society's goal should be 'recomposing the elements of gender; making the full range of gender attributes available to all people (205). The goal then, 'is not to abolish gender but to reshape it' (225) so that the 'symbolism of difference' is not implicitly the 'symbolism of dominance' (208). The degendering process with regard to literary narratives started with attempts to overcome patriarchal

stereotyping of female character attributes, but it soon became clear that the process must extend to include the alteration of male character attributes and most significantly to the representations of male–female relationships. This move requires modifications to genres and to story-lines; John Stephens, 'Gender, Genre and Children's Literature', *Signal 79* (1996): 17–29; Beverley Pennell, 'Redeeming Masculinity at the End of the Second Millennium: Narrative Reconfigurations of Masculinity in Children's Fictions', in John Stephens (ed.), *Ways of Being Male* (London: Routledge, 2002).

5. Bourdieu (2001); Chambers.
6. Catherine Itzin, 'Bewitching the Boys', *Times Educational Supplement*, 27 December 1985: 13; David Rees, 'Dahl's Chickens: Roald Dahl', *Children's Literature in Education* 19(3) (1988): 143–55; Michele Landsberg, *World of Children's Books: A Guide to Choosing the Best* (New York: Simon and Schuster, 1988).
7. West: 130.
8. Bird; Roald Dahl, *The Witches* [1983] (London: Puffin, 2007); *The Witches* [1989] directed by Nicolas Roeg (Warner Bros., Warner Home Video (UK) Ltd, 1994).
9. Bird: 121. Dahl, *The Witches*: 39.
10. *The Witches*: 24.
11. Andrew Stott, *Comedy* (New York: Routledge, 2005): 63; Eric Weitz, *The Cambridge Introduction to Comedy* (Cambridge: CUP, 2009); Marina Warner, *From the Beast to the Blonde: On Fairy Tales and Their Tellers* (London: Vintage, 1994).
12. Jeremy Treglown, 'The Height of Fancy', *Guardian*, 9 September 2006. At: www.guardian.co.uk/books/2006/sep/09/roalddahl.fiction? INTCMP=SRCH (accessed 26 April 2012); West: 61.
13. Frances Gray, *Women and Laughter* (Charlottesville: Macmillan, 1994): 15.
14. Pennell (2002): 55–77.
15. *The Magic Finger*: 18, 24.
16. *Ibid.*: 24–9.
17. West: 66.
18. *Ibid.*: 81.
19. Stephens (1996): 17–29; Pennell; 'Ozzie Kids Flee the Garden of Delight: Reconfigurations of Childhood in Australian Children's Fictions', *Papers: Explorations into Children's Literature* 13(2) (2003): 5–14.
20. Weitz: 23.
21. Warner: 127.
22. *Ibid.*: 202.
23. *Ibid.*: 186, 208.
24. *Ibid.*: 193. Some of the verse narratives from *Revolting Rhymes* (1982) are of interest to an assessment of Dahl's feminist contributions but space precludes a full examination of them here, except to note that these are an indication of Dahl's interest in feminism, or, at the very least, in the humorous possibilities provided by fairy tale reversions. Such fairy tale

parodies only require the inversion of traditional gender attributes in order to achieve a humorous effect from the resulting incongruity. In *Revolting Rhymes* female characters transgress the traditional femininity schema of goodness, vulnerability, dependence and non-violence. For instance, in the last two verse narratives, 'Little Red Riding Hood and the Wolf' and 'The Three Little Pigs', the Red Riding Hood character is acquisitive and murderous and, the reader is told, ends up with not one, but '*two* wolfskin coats' as well as a pigskin travelling case. Roald Dahl, *Revolting Rhymes* [1982] (London: Puffin, 2001): 47 (emphasis in original). The volume also includes an anti-classist as well as a somewhat feminist 'Cinderella' who decides against the bloodthirsty prince and sees wealth as having an undesirable effect (11). However, in the storyline's closure, the patriarchal gender order is maintained because even though Cinderella wants 'No more princes, no more money', she is still in search of 'a decent man' and 'lovely feller' (12) to thereby ensure 'they were happy ever after' (12). The reversioned verse fairy tales and the focus novels demonstrate Dahl's interest in offering feminist shifts in the literary representations of female characters' attributes and their participation in primary storylines.

25. West: 61.
26. Bourdieu (2001): 1.
27. *The Magic Finger*: 1.
28. *Ibid.*: 7.
29. John Stephens and Robyn McCallum, *Retelling Stories, Framing Culture: Traditional Story and Metanarratives in Children's Literature* (New York: Routledge, 1998): 122.
30. *The Magic Finger*: 8
31. Bronwyn Davies, *Frogs and Snails and Feminist Tales: Pre-school Children and Gender* (Sydney: Allen & Unwin, 1989): 4 (emphasis in original).
32. Philippe Ariès, *Centuries of Childhood* (London: Jonathan Cape, 1962): 61.
33. *The Magic Finger*: 2.
34. *Ibid.*: 5.
35. *Ibid.*: 4.
36. *Ibid.*: 4.
37. Pierre Bourdieu, 'The Family Spirit', in *Practical Reason: On the Theory of Action* (Cambridge: Polity Press, 1998): 64–74.
38. *The Magic Finger*: 54.
39. *Ibid.*: 2.
40. *Ibid.*: 19.
41. *Ibid.*: 56–7.
42. *Ibid.*: 57.
43. Weitz: 192.
44. West: 83.
45. Bourdieu (2001): 56–7; Chambers: 23.
46. Chambers: 50.

47. Peter Hollindale, *Ideology and the Children's Book* (Stroud: Thimble Press, 1988); Stephens (1996); Pennell (2002).
48. Stephens (1996); Pennell (2002).
49. *The BFG*: 3.
50. *Ibid.*: 9.
51. *Ibid.*: 23.
52. *Ibid.*: 11, 15.
53. *Ibid.*: 7–18.
54. *Ibid.*: 22, 33, 80.
55. *Ibid.*: 178.
56. *Ibid.*: 13–14.
57. *Ibid.*: 40.
58. *Ibid.*: 17.
59. *Ibid.*: 43.
60. *Ibid.*: 42 (emphasis in original).
61. *Ibid.*: 94.
62. *Ibid.*: 70.
63. *Ibid.*: 108.
64. *Ibid.*: 37.
65. *Ibid.*: 55.
66. *Ibid.*: 28.
67. *Ibid.*: 184.
68. *Ibid.*: 47.
69. *Ibid.*: 149.
70. Bourdieu (2001): 9.
71. *The BFG*: 198.
72. *Ibid.*: 199.
73. Bourdieu (2001): 94; Pennell (2002).
74. Aries: 7.
75. Stephens: 26.
76. Chambers: 143.
77. *Ibid.*: 142.
78. Bird: 128.
79. West: 129.
80. Weitz.
81. Hollindale; Stephens (1996); Pennell (2002): 76–7.
82. *Matilda*: 180.
83. *Ibid.*: 231.
84. Hollindale.
85. *Matilda*: 29.
86. *Ibid.*: 24–5.
87. Treglown.
88. *Matilda*: 41.
89. *Ibid.*: 238.
90. *Ibid.*: 239, 240.
91. Chambers: 130.

92. *Matilda*: 240.
93. The representation of cooperation between women is an important feminist representational strategy (see Warner).
94. *Matilda*: 67.
95. *Ibid.*: 183–5.
96. *Ibid.*: 187–90.
97. Dylan Thomas, 'In Country Sleep', in *Collected Poems 1934–1953*, ed. Walford Davies and Ralph Maud (London: Phoenix, 2003).
98. *Matilda*: 186.
99. *Ibid.*: 191.
100. *Ibid.*: 210.
101. West: 93.
102. *Matilda*: 97.
103. West: 128.
104. *Matilda*: 108, 104.
105. *Ibid.*: 136.
106. *Ibid.*: 136, 137, 139, 151.
107. *Ibid.*: 18.
108. Pennell (2002).
109. Hollindale: 19.

7

An Unsuitable Read for a Child? Reconsidering Crime and Violence in Roald Dahl's Fiction for Children[1]

Heather Worthington

'Vulgar, violent, sexist, racist, criminal': children's literature?

In the oft-quoted words of Arthur Ransome, 'You write not for children but for yourself, and if, by good fortune, children enjoy what you enjoy, why then you are a writer of children's books.'[2] These words could have been written with Roald Dahl in mind; he wrote about what he knew and enjoyed, and although in his writing for children he generally adopted a different narrative voice from that of his fiction for adults, the themes of and the humour in the two formats are uncannily similar.[3] But, as Peter Hunt has noted, Dahl had a worldwide reputation as a writer of sinister short stories 'that dealt with the very dark corners of human nature before he became a writer for children'.[4] Hunt goes on to query whether Dahl's 'zestful exploitation of childish instincts for hate and revenge, prejudice and violence, [can] be as innocent as it appears'.[5] In the developed world, societies tend to define the child precisely as that which is not adult, endeavouring thus to set up clear demarcations between the two states of being, a position evident in children's literature. In this context, given the thematic similarities in his writing for children and for adults, particularly the pervasive presence of violence and the frequent representation of crime, can Dahl's juvenile fiction be considered to constitute a 'suitable' read for a child?

Of course, the very concept of 'suitability' is problematic; decisions as to what is 'suitable' or indeed 'unsuitable' for children are inescapably subjective and temporally and culturally contingent, as critical analyses of Dahl's fiction demonstrate. In 1991, Jonathon Culley offered a defence of Dahl's fiction, noting that while his texts had 'been heavily criticised for … vulgarity, fascism, violence, sexism, racism, … promotion of criminal behaviour', because they are located in the folklore and fairy tale tradition they escape these charges. The child reader, Culley suggests, implicitly already familiar with the conservative patterns of such narratives (good triumphing over evil, virtuous characters rewarded and wicked ones punished, the triumph of the underdog), understands the imaginary status of the stories and so is unaffected by their content.[6] In his 2010 biography of Dahl, Donald Sturrock devotes five pages to the adverse critical reception of Dahl's fiction for children.[7] And yes, Dahl's juvenile texts wrap their violence and other potentially controversial aspects in a tissue of fantasy and they make the representation of crime acceptable either by moral justification or by ensuring its containment and punishment. Twenty years after Dahl's death and Culley's defence, in a world that in its reliance on television and electronic media would undoubtedly have horrified Dahl and which exposes children to actual violence and crime in unprecedented ways, his children's fiction seems less controversial and, I suggest, might now have more positive functions that outweigh the often negative adult perceptions of its suitability in moral terms of its content for their imagined child reader.

My contention here is that for the child of the twenty-first century and in the context of the contemporary emphasis on representing the 'real' in literature for children, Dahl's juvenile canon affords escapist reading par excellence. As in crime fiction, Dahl's writing for adults offers its readers a variety of potentially cathartic reading positions – protagonist, antagonist, victim – and this is equally true, I suggest, of his stories for children.[8] These allow child readers a safe space in which to explore their personal and social anxieties and to vent, in their imagination and/or unconsciously, their own feelings of anger and resentment towards the adults who control their world. In many ways, modern children are given unprecedented and often unmediated access to the trappings of the adult world, particularly in terms of clothing and popular culture: they are less imitation adults than simulacra, having the appearance of – but without the substance or properties of – adulthood. More visibly perhaps than ever before, adult power is revealed to but denied the child. In Dahl's narratives, adult and juvenile, a constant theme is the reversal or circumvention of normative power relations and the revenge taken by the disempowered upon the empowered, but where in the adult stories the social and narrative status quo is, disturbingly, not necessarily restored, the children's fiction mostly adheres to the normative conservatism of happy, if quirky, endings.

The stories which Dahl produced specifically for children are, for the most part, clearly marked out as fantasy. They accord with Rosemary Jackson's concept of narratives, which 'assert that what they are telling is real – relying upon all the conventions of realist fiction to do so – and then they proceed to break the assumption of realism by introducing what – within those terms – is manifestly unreal'.[9] Jackson is speaking of adult fiction, but Dahl's writing for a juvenile audience conforms to her description, presenting to the child reader a recognisable and often familiar world, peopled with everyday figures and events, and then introducing the patently unreal – animals and insects that can speak, children with magic fingers and kinetic powers, witches, giants.[10] In Jackson's model, fantasy literature is precisely a literature of subversion, and the empowerment of the child and the (temporary) reversal of normative social structures in children's literature are subversive. In Dahl's texts the representation of adults is equally subversive; frequently they are depicted as at best thoughtless and at worst actively and intentionally cruel. Furthermore, this cruelty is always punished by a means that is directly or indirectly orchestrated by the child – or animal – victim. Once this has occurred, however, the subversion of the narrative is curtailed and conservative values and the proper status quo are restored, if in unconventional or reconfigured forms.

This containment of temporary subversion within conservatism, the veiling of violence in fantasy and the essentially restorative closures of the narratives are, in part, what make the majority of Dahl's fiction for children unthreatening and construct it as acceptable and morally appropriate, so making it 'suitable' reading for a child. They are also what make it escapist literature: for the space of their reading, child readers can live in their imagination and can possess the control over their lives and circumstances that reality does not afford. This is a space in which the child can be naughty, scatological, empowered and, perhaps most importantly, be metaphorically revenged on the adults who control children's lives. From the child's perspective, the methods of control are not always pleasant and the rationale behind them unclear; from the adult perspective this control is conventionally seen to be part of the process of civilising the child. For Dahl and perhaps for other adults, 'children … are only semi-civilised'[11] and need training to become good (conformist) adult subjects. What Dahl's writing for children recognises is the child's perspective, particularly when adult behaviour is inconsistent or evidently unfair. Consequently, justice is often implicit in the revenge that is at the centre of much of Dahl's fiction. In *Matilda* the eponymous heroine decides to revenge herself on her parents every time they mistreat her: 'A small victory or two would help her tolerate their idiocies and stop her from going crazy.'[12]

Fantasies of vengeance, natural justice and empowerment

Vengeance and a sense of natural justice are evident from the very beginning of Dahl's writing for children. *James and the Giant Peach* (1961), Dahl's first successful story for children, features orphaned James's distinctly unpleasant guardians, Aunts Sponge and Spiker.[13] Their cruelty to their ward is punished when the giant peach, now containing James and his new friends the Centipede, the Grasshopper, the Ladybird, the Earthworm, the Glow-worm and the Spider, accidentally rolls over the Aunts and crushes them to death. The world outside the peach is relatively realistically portrayed, as is the admittedly exaggerated treatment meted out to James by his aunts; the world of the peach is decidedly fantastic, with creatures the same size as James that initially – and understandably – terrify him. But it is in the 'real' world outside the peach that the Aunts are subjected to a process of 'natural' justice and punished, while James's fantasy life continues into a fairy tale 'happy ever after' with his friends, who in various ways also function as his (idealised) family. Revenge in *James and the Giant Peach* is not actively carried out by James; rather it is the narrative, and implicitly its author, that ensures the Aunts receive their just deserts, suggesting that in reality cruel adults should – and will – be punished.

   Charlie and the Chocolate Factory (1964) is less overt in terms of violence and vengeance; the objectionable children there seem to bring their own punishments – which are clearly marked as fantastic – upon themselves, but it is their parents, and perhaps implicitly real-life parents, who are being castigated for their improper parenting skills. *The Magic Finger* (1966) allows its unnamed female child protagonist-narrator to ensure that the punishment fits the crime when her supernatural digit turns her gun-happy neighbours into human birds and their duck victims into quasi-humans.[14] In *Fantastic Mr Fox* (1970) the fox of the title, in part representing the child, defeats the adult human farmers who seek to kill him; *The Twits* (1980) sees the unpleasant Mr and Mrs Twit's performing (child) monkeys literally turn the tables – and chairs – on their (adult) trainers.[15] Crime and violence, accidental in *James and the Giant Peach* and implicit in

Fantastic Mr Fox, where Mr Fox's theft from the farmers is excused both by the fantasy and by the natural eating habits of the fox, is rather more troubling in *George's Marvellous Medicine* (1981).[16] George's purpose in creating the magic medicine is to make better his 'horrid old witchy' grandmother, famously described as having 'a small puckered-up mouth like a dog's bottom'.[17] But his father's motive in giving his mother-in-law a later version of the medicine has definite criminal aspects. He knows that it will, at the very least, shrink the old lady down to a minute size; in the event, she disappears entirely in what might be read as an act of deliberate murder. The narrative is obviously fantastical, but the revenge here is not of the child upon the adult but of one adult upon another, aligning the text with much of Dahl's short fiction for adults.

This slippage in Dahl's writing, between his adult and child registers, is a major contributor to adult anxieties about the suitability of his texts for child readers, as issues more often found in texts for adults find their way into his juvenile fiction. While children will enjoy the humour of *George's Marvellous Medicine*, the potentially realistic depiction of family dynamics in which an elderly relative is seen as intrusive and unwanted – indeed, the entirely negative representation of old age – is relatively unusual in children's literature, which tends to support rather than criticise the ideology of family. *The Witches* (1983), by contrast, offers a positive depiction of the elderly in the figure of the grandmother.[18] If the word 'marvellous' in the title of *George's Marvellous Medicine* suggests its fantastical status, *The Witches* is even more clearly labelled and the events of the narrative confirm it as fantasy; apparently-ordinary women are revealed to be witches intending to carry out by magical means the mass murder of children. While the criminal aspects of the text seem to have escaped criticism, *The Witches* has been castigated for its negative representation of the feminine.[19] Dahl's witches are truly frightening creations made doubly unnatural through their deformed non-human appearance once unmasked and by their clear rejection of the nurturing child-centred traditional ideology of the feminine maternal.[20] Violence is implicit in the desire to dispose of children by turning them into mice which will then be killed in mousetraps; the crime is self-evident. The very excess of the plot in part locates it as pure fantasy, as does the boy-turned-mouse protagonist and narrator. Thus far, thus fantastic, and so escapist and acceptable – the child reader can enjoy the frisson of fright safely contained in the fiction.

But the reality suggested by the frame narrative of the orphaned child protagonist is perhaps less enjoyable, despite the loving relationship between boy and grandmother. When she becomes ill, the unnamed boy faces the very real possibility of being orphaned for a second time by her death – she is after all, 80 years old (and a smoker of cigars). His subsequent fate – being turned permanently into a mouse by the Witches, using a magic spell which would more usually in children's fiction later be reversed – has the effect of shortening his life dramatically, ensuring that he and his grandmother will have a better chance of dying at the same time and so removing the threat of his being abandoned.[21] The avenging fantasy in the concluding pages of the narrative, where the boy/mouse and his grandmother plan to track down all the Witches, use their own potion to turn them into mice and then release cats to kill them, perhaps to some extent ameliorates the bleak message of finite life and the certainty of death implicit in the text. As in many of Dahl's texts intended for children, fantasy permits what might otherwise seem an inappropriate preoccupation with death. And for a child reader exposed to or anxious about family loss or abandonment, the promise of boy and grandmother being together until both their deaths provides a consolatory and comforting conclusion. Surprisingly, then, despite its gruesome and violent aspects, *The Witches* can perhaps be seen, certainly in bibliotherapeutic terms, to be an eminently 'suitable' read for some children.

This is perhaps because, as in much of his writing, Dahl's own life inflects the fiction; although set in England, *The Witches* begins and ends in Norway, the home of Dahl's parents and grandparents: in the fiction, the boy and his grandmother have to move to England in order for the boy to continue his English education, while in Dahl's own life his family move from Wales to England for the same reason.[22] The idealised intergenerational relationship also has its origins in Dahl's own childhood holidays with his grandparents in Norway, related in the autobiographical *Boy* (1984).[23] The self-referential frame narrative of *The Witches* is less a story for children than the story of a child directly drawn from the memory of the adult, both making it appropriate for the child reader but equally aligning it with Dahl's writing for adults and therefore making it problematic in terms of its suitability. *Matilda*, perhaps the last of Dahl's children's texts to engage closely with justice and revenge, adult–child power relations, violence and crime, was, in its original incarnation, also in adult rather than child mode. Dahl's original version features the compulsive gambler Miss Hayes, transformed in the published version into the adorable Miss Honey, while the delinquent Matilda's magical powers are used to fix the outcome of a race on which they have laid a large bet. The plot resonates with that of the adult 'Claud's Dog' story sequence, where in 'Mr Feasey' (1953)[24] there is also an attempt to fix a race, although by rational rather than supernatural means.

Fracturing fantasy

Careful editing and some of the tactful suggestions for revising the story made by Stephen Roxburgh resulted in the published edition of *Matilda*.[25] While this version is, despite the intrusive voice of the adult narrator, firmly within the bounds of children's literature, with the narrative focalised through the child heroine, the demarcation between fantasy and realism is less clearly marked than in the texts discussed earlier.[26] Matilda's family may be composed of carica-tures, but it is not fantastic. Her intellectual abilities suggest she is a child prodigy, but again are kept within the bounds of reality – the isolated child's recourse to books and reading as a solace for loneli-ness is not uncommon, and neither is the child's feeling that he or she has been placed in the wrong family.[27] Matilda's revenge on her parents – superglue in her father's hat, bleach in his hair tonic, the parrot up the chimney – are all (just) within the bounds of the real. Even in the episodes at school, where headmistress Miss Trunchbull abuses the children and Miss Honey physically and verbally, the violence is less fantasy than exaggerated reality. In Dahl's representa-tion of Miss Trunchbull there is a sadism which, taken out of the context of humour, is truly unpleasant. As Hunt observes, '*Matilda* is a book fractured between the farcical grotesque and the sinisterly realistic'.[28] While the violence inflicted on Miss Trunchbull's pupils is sometimes marked as unreal, as when she swings Amanda Thripp around by her pigtails and sends her flying into the sky, the episode in which Bruce Bogtrotter is forced to eat a whole cake until he is on the verge of vomiting is all too believable.

Matilda's acquisition of seemingly supernatural kinetic powers is generated by her sense of injustice when she faces a false accusation.[29] Another pupil has placed a newt in Miss Trunchbull's water glass; Matilda's rage at being wrongly accused and her desire for revenge release her telekinetic power,[30] allowing her to make the glass tip over and spill water and newt onto Miss Trunchbull. Her newfound power is subsequently used not for revenge but in the interests of justice and restitution. Crime and violence in *Matilda* are located in the reality of the text and are not fantastic or magical but realistically represent child abuse and murder. Miss Honey tells Matilda how as an orphaned child she had been ill treated by her aunt/guardian, revealed to be Miss Trunchbull. No details of the abuse are given, but

Miss Honey's statement suggests the horror perhaps more vividly than could graphic description: 'I don't want to talk about it … But in the end I was so frightened of her I used to shake when she came into the room'.[31] Not only is Miss Trunchbull revealed to be abusive, but to be a murderer, having, the text implies, killed Miss Honey's father and made it look like suicide in order to cheat Miss Honey out of her inheritance.

Matilda uses her 'magical' powers to frighten Miss Trunchbull into restoring Miss Honey's property and fortune; the issue of the murder is left unresolved, but Miss Trunchbull is excised from the narrative. The restoration of Miss Honey to her rightful place allows Matilda to return to her proper position as a child. Her magical power is no longer needed and circumstances are manipulated in order to allow her to form a new family with Miss Honey. This is where the true fantasy lies in *Matilda*. It is one of the most popular of Dahl's books for children, perhaps in part precisely because of its realism, which makes the child protagonist's empowerment more believable. However, the criminal content of this sometimes uneven narrative seems suited to an adult rather than a child audience – a consequence of Dahl's original imagining of the story, which was more aligned with what Hunt calls Dahl's 'sinister short stories' for adults.[32] Published in collected editions such as *Someone Like You* (1953), *Kiss Kiss* (1960) and *Switch Bitch* (1974), much of Dahl's macabre, sometimes criminal, and often violent adult fiction appeared before he began writing for children, though latterly he produced stories for both audiences simultaneously. Dahl continued to produce children's fiction up to his death in 1990, but he also carried on writing short stories for adults until 1986.[33]

The relationship between Dahl's writing for an adult audience and his books for children is not simply one of tone and theme. As Jeremy Treglown observes, when the vengeful animals glue the eponymous protagonists' furniture to the ceiling in *The Twits* (1980), Dahl is reusing the main plot element of the adult tale 'Smoked Cheese' (which appeared in *Atlantic Monthly*, November 1945).[34] 'The Sound Machine' (*The New Yorker*, May 1949) introduces a man who believes he can hear the noises made by plants when they are damaged or cut down, an idea that resurfaces in *The BFG* (1982), and there are many other examples of Dahl's recycling of material in what might almost be considered his self-plagiarism.[35] In *Danny, the Champion of the World* (1975), Dahl unapologetically took the plot of an adult story, 'The Champion of the World' (*New Yorker*, 1959; *Kiss Kiss*, 1960), and transformed a narrative about two adult poachers into a tale for children mainly by substituting a father–son relationship for that of the two men.[36] In the juvenile version, while retaining much of the original plot, Dahl drew on the memory of his actual and his imagined and idealised childhood to reconfigure it as a child's story.

Set against a realist background, *Danny* is a fantasy of an ideal father–son relationship in which the child and parent are completely self-sufficient; the mother has conveniently died and Danny has been brought up solely by his father. Such is their contentment with each other, at least from Danny's perspective, that Danny has no desire to bring his school friends home, feeling that this would simply reduce the time spent with his father.[37] The idealisation of the relationship stems from Dahl's own childhood; his father died when Dahl was only four, and subsequently he was the only boy in a female-dominated household.[38] Within the fantasised childhood of *Danny*, elements of the reality of Dahl's early years find a place; for example, Danny is falsely accused of cheating at school by his teacher, who is clearly based on Captain Hardcastle, a master from Dahl's preparatory school, here transformed into 'Captain Lancaster'. Where in his autobiographical account of Dahl's own childhood, *Boy* (1984), the punishment is carried out by the headmaster and a yellow cane is used, in *Danny* the cane is white, the punishment is inflicted by Captain Lancaster, and the injury done to Danny's hand rather than his buttocks.[39] Nonetheless, the fictional episode resonates with the factual event and the description of the pain is remarkably similar. Unprotected in *Boy*, Dahl's fictional alter ego in *Danny* has a father, who immediately threatens to return violence with violence: "'I'll kill him!" he softly whispered … "I'm going to beat the living daylights out of him!"', a threat which his son persuades him not to carry out.[40]

But violence is peripheral to *Danny*, although the gamekeepers who patrol the land on which Danny's father carries out his poaching activities have the potential to be violent. As in *Matilda*, it is crime that is central to the text: poaching pheasants is illegal, whatever the motives of the poacher. Danny's discovery that his father's night-time absences are caused by his poaching activities fills him with horror: 'I was shocked. My own father a thief!'[41] Prior to this discovery, father and son have, despite their extreme closeness, largely maintained the normative parent–child power relationship, with Danny the recipient of his father's superior knowledge and in possession of skills more usually acquired later in life – he is a competent mechanic by the age of seven – but nonetheless very clearly the dependent child. However, in the chapters following the discovery of his father's night-time activities, the power balance subtly changes. In the wake of the confession, father and son have a conversation in which the parent justifies his poaching – stealing – to the son. He draws on history, suggesting that originally it was necessity that drew men to poaching, but falling quickly into the admission that it also exciting.

Part of the excitement is the element of danger – gamekeepers who carry guns, the possibility of capture – and Danny is sensibly anxious about this. As he points out to his father, unlike their poaching predecessors, neither he nor his father is starving, and surely the risks of poaching outweigh the pleasure. Undeterred, his father moves on to a socialist defence of poaching: 'Only the very rich can afford to rear pheasants just for the fun of shooting them'[42]; he establishes the family tradition of poaching and then turns the act of theft into a work of art by describing the different methods he uses to trap the birds. After this episode, father and son seem more like equals than adult and child, and the representation of negative adulthood is realigned instead with a negative representation of wealth, figured in Mr Hazell.[43] The pheasants that Danny's father steals belong to Hazell, as do the woods in which the birds live and roost. Wealth is here conflated with power; Hazell as landowner and Danny's father as lowly garage mechanic represent, metaphorically, adult and child. Hazell, 'a roaring snob' with a 'great glistening beery face … pink as a ham, all soft and inflamed from drinking too much',[44] is a loud, arrogant bully who at one point threatens Danny with a riding crop. He owns all the land locally except the small plot on which Danny's father's filling-station stands. The usual conflict between child and adult in Dahl's children's fiction is transposed onto the conflict between Hazell and Danny's father, between rich and poor. The theft of pheasants is thus justified as the oppressed taking revenge on the oppressor.

Danny now takes on the dominant role: he rescues his father after he falls into a pit in the woods that is intended to catch poachers and breaks his leg, an incident that makes father dependent on son. In the process, Danny breaks the law by driving a car – he is by this point in the narrative nine years old. In classic children's literature tradition, the child is literally the saviour of the man – his father. The episode of the trap is the trigger for the plan of revenge that Danny and his father devise: they will steal all the pheasants from Hazell's wood just before the landowner's pheasant shoot, to which all the local dignitaries are invited, thus making him look a fool. But while his father conceives the idea, it is Danny who comes up with a way of carrying it off. Eventually, the local community becomes involved in the plot in various ways, including the local policeman: the plan works, Hazell is satisfactorily defeated and his pheasant shoot ruined. Pheasants as well as peasants have their revenge, as they scratch Hazell's prized Rolls Royce, landing on it when he tries to shoo them back to the woods to be slaughtered. In the concluding pages of the narrative, Danny and his father return to the proper parent–child relationship, but with the promise of excitements to come, implicitly including poaching.

Although the idealised relationship between father and son perhaps pushes the bounds of possibility, *Danny* is not fantastical in the way of much of Dahl's other writing for children. There is no magic here, no talking animals; only humour alleviates the fact that the narrative makes crime seem not merely acceptable but justifiable. Mark West suggests that the text 'introduces children to situational ethics', implicitly excusing its criminal content, and he goes on to say how the majority of critics who reviewed the book ignored the crime and focused on the loving parent–child relationship.[45] The single critic who considered that the glorification of poaching might encourage the child reader into other kinds of theft finally concluded that the text was sufficiently 'make-believe' to avoid such a charge.[46] Yet this adult-inspired text might, in the context not of a rural and interdependent small community but of the alienated consumer-commodity culture of the modern city, seem to make crime acceptable to the child reader and so function as a negative influence, making it improper or unsuitable reading for a child. *Danny* makes stealing from the rich appear to be a justifiable act of (political) defiance in an inequitable society. This perhaps unintended effect is the inevitable result of Dahl converting – with minimal alterations – his adult story into children's fiction; in 'The Champion of the World', the poaching is described as 'a crusade, a sort of private war that Claud was waging single-handedly against an invisible and hated enemy',[47] a Marxist message that may be understood by the adult reader but not by the child.

Registering reality

Despite its often violent and sometimes adult content, the generally conservative if eccentric conclusions and the largely positive if anarchically delivered values of Dahl's fiction written specifically for children generally outweigh the potential effects of any negative elements. Dahl rightly claimed that 'Children know that the violence in my stories is only make-believe … when violence is tied to fantasy and humour, children find it … amusing'.[48] Even when the violence – or the crime – is realistically presented, it is still contained in the fiction and coloured by the fantasy elsewhere in the narrative. But in Dahl's single foray into teenage fiction, *The Wonderful Story of Henry Sugar and Six More* (1977), a text that has received little if any critical attention, the lack of thematic differentiation between his adult and juvenile narratives results in a very different mode of writing and one which it is at times hard to claim as being intended for, and so 'suitable' for, young readers.[49] Of the seven stories that comprise *The Wonderful Story of Henry Sugar* (1977), only two, 'The Swan' and 'The Boy Who Talked with Animals', both written in 1976, possibly with a juvenile audience in mind, feature children.

The remaining five narratives are adult focused, intended originally for adult audiences and criminally inflected: 'The Hitchhiker' implicitly champions criminality, dealing as it does with the skills of a pickpocket and how they enable a speeding driver to avoid a possible conviction for the offence (it also appeared in *Atlantic Monthly*, August 1977, and later in *Tales of the Unexpected*, 1979); 'The Wonderful Story of Henry Sugar' incorporates elements of another adult story, 'The Amazing Eyes of Kuda Bux' (1948) and features a man who in essence cheats at cards by learning to use the powers of his mind to read them through their backs, enabling him to amass a great fortune which he spends benevolently on opening orphanages, thus justifying his fraudulent behaviour. 'The Mildenhall Treasure' (*Saturday Evening Post*, 20 September 1947) is a fictionalised version of the actual discovery of Roman artefacts in a farmer's field. In the fiction, the owner of the field endeavours fraudulently to assert his claim to the treasure over the genuine claim of its finder. The remaining two tales are autobiographical: 'A Piece of Cake' is a reprint of Dahl's first foray into writing for adults and describes the plane crash that eventually took him out of the war; and 'Lucky Break' purports to recount how Dahl became a writer, but in fact dwells on his childhood, his time in Africa and his early experiences as a pilot, and is a very much abbreviated version of his later autobiographical works, *Boy* (1984) and *Going Solo* (1986).

While the tales above were presumably selected because their subject matter might reasonably be of interest to young (and probably male) adolescents, and their content is essentially innocuous, it is the two stories in *Henry Sugar* which have child protagonists that are most disturbing and least 'suited' to or appropriate for the juvenile reader, occupying rather an unsettling territory between adult and child audiences. Dahl's assertion (mentioned above) that young readers 'know that the violence in my stories is only make-believe' is brought into question in 'The Boy Who Talked with Animals' and especially in 'The Swan', where the fantasy elements are minimal and the humour non-existent. Admittedly, 'The Boy' is premised on the fantasy that the child of the title can speak, like Dr Doolittle, to animals. But the tale, set in Jamaica, is macabre rather than fantastic: the narrator creates an atmosphere of danger and violence with references to voodoo and suggests that 'there was something malignant crouching underneath the surface of this island'.[50] The reader is led to expect a sinister story, but the expectation is fulfilled in an unexpected way. The narrator and the other hotel guests witness fishermen landing a live giant turtle, intended, via the hotel kitchen, for dinner. There is much excitement among the onlookers, with a subtext of competitive masculine aggression and a concomitant arousal of female sexual desire that seems to locate the narrative as one of Dahl's adult fictions.[51] The sexual tension of the scene is broken by the arrival of a small boy and his parents; the intrusion of a child into the narrative and the subsequent slippage into fantasy reconfigure the story as juvenile fiction.

The boy accuses the adults present of cruelty; his words and perhaps his child presence silence the grown-ups, who take on 'the slightly hangdog air of people who had been caught doing something that was not entirely honourable'.[52] Despite the fishermen's warnings of danger, the boy approaches and apparently speaks with the turtle. Subsequently, with financial encouragement, the venal hotel manager and the fishermen are persuaded to release the turtle back into the sea. The following morning, the boy has disappeared; the fishermen later report seeing him riding on the back of the great turtle, far out at sea. A year later a party of Americans sailing a yacht over 500 miles away from Jamaica also see the boy and the turtle, and then the two vanish, never to be seen again. Despite the attempt to invoke an atmosphere of magic in the boy's relationship with the turtle, the text in actuality contrasts the innate nobility of the animal and the 'natural' innocence of the child with the greed and implicit savagery of the adults. As demonstrated earlier, the negative representation of adulthood is a recurring theme in Dahl's writing for children, as is the triumph of the child over the grown-ups, but the story's status as children's literature is subverted because in 'The Boy' the narrative is focalised through the adult narrator; while the child reader might identify with the boy in the text, the central reading position is occupied by an adult.

To some extent the intrusive adult narrator is also the focaliser in 'The Swan'; the teenage characters are respectively too negatively and too passively represented for the child reader to identify with either. The narrative opens with 15-year-old Ernie, who has been given a .22 rifle for his birthday, being ordered by his father to use the gift to kill a rabbit for supper. Father and son's social status and attitude are made immediately, if stereotypically, clear: class and character are signified by the father's inability to raise his eyes from the television while speaking to his son, by his demand for a bottle of brown ale, and by his threat of physical punishment should the boy pinch the change from the pound note he is given to buy the beer. Ernie's predilection for violence is evident in the enthusiasm with which he shoots at songbirds on his way to hunt for rabbits. As in many of Dahl's stories for children and adults, physical appearance corresponds to character: Ernie is 'a big lout of a boy [with] small slitty eyes set very close together … Brought up in a household where physical violence was an everyday occurrence, he was himself an extremely violent person'.[53] The violence in part finds expression in hooliganism, but more often in tormenting smaller boys. His accomplice in bullying is his friend, Raymond. Together, the two boys shoot 14 small birds before they find an alternative source of amusement in 13-year-old small, studious, polite, bespectacled, frail and middle-class Peter Watson. Peter is watching, rather than shooting, birds, and the remainder of the story is an unpleasant account of an episode of bullying which, though extreme – even exaggerated – in its violence, is not fantasy and which exceeds rather than resonates with the associated experiences or anxieties of a teenage reader.

After some general abuse and manhandling, the two bigger boys tie Peter lengthways between the nearby railway lines and wait for a train to come; the description of the experience, both the waiting and the terror as the train passes over his bound body, serves to demonstrate Peter's intelligence, bravery and strength of mind but is frightening in its emotional intensity and potential violence. He survives, but is subjected to further torment when Ernie first shoots a nesting swan, then, 'using the knife, … proceeded to sever the great white wing … There is a joint in the bone where the wing meets the side of the bird, and Ernie located this and slid the knife into the joint and cut through the tendon'.[54] The severed wings are tied onto Peter's arms and he is forced to climb a tree and told he must try to fly over the lake below or Ernie will shoot him. Peter refuses and is shot in the leg; in a kind of out-of-body experience he sees a light of 'brilliance and beauty … beckoning him' and launches himself into flight towards it.[55] This is the only moment of fantasy in the story, as Peter flies over the village to land, injured but safe, in his own garden, where he is discovered by his mother. The narrative implicitly criticises violence and bullying in its negative representation of Ernie and Raymond and equally suggests the power of resistance and the triumph of moral courage in its depiction of Peter.

There is, then, some element of the empowerment of the underdog commonly seen in children's literature; there is also a distorted version of the home–away–home pattern that is one of the defining features of the form. Significantly, though, the cruelty and violence of the older boys against both Peter and the birds they shoot are not shown to be punished, although this is implicit in Peter's survival and the intervention of his mother – clearly the authorities will become involved since Peter has lived to tell his tale. The revenge motif that is so often either the cause or the consequence of violence in Dahl's fiction, for children and adults, seems oddly absent.[56] Equally, the restoration of conservative values and the justice that is usually meted out to the wicked, particularly in Dahl's stories for children, is not in evidence. This lack of closure accords with the narrative's liminal status between adult and juvenile fiction, but ultimately results in the reader remembering the violence done to boy and birds. Retrospectively, the story resonates unpleasantly with the case of toddler James Bulger, kidnapped and murdered in 1993 by two older boys who subsequently dumped his body by a railway track. Seen in the context of that and of more recent cases of violence done to children by children, 'The Swan' makes for uncomfortable reading for adults and is evidently considered by them to be unsuitable reading for children: the Heinemann Education edition of *The Wonderful Story of Henry Sugar*, in their New Windmill Series for juvenile readers (1979), omitted it from the collection. This implicit censorship suggests that just two years after its original publication 'The Swan' was seen to be inappropriate for a young audience, possibly because its realism might frighten young readers or even because of its potential appeal to an already-disturbed child.[57]

The realism of 'The Swan' resonates with Dahl's non-fictional writing for children in the autobiographical *Boy*. Dahl's early life experiences, his memory of his child self's lack of autonomy, and the often unjust or excessive physical punishment inflicted upon him by adults fed into his self-declared empathy with children: 'I have a great affinity with children. I see their problems … all these bloody giants around you who are always telling you what to do and what not to do … subconsciously in the child's mind these giants become the enemy.'[58] In *Boy* there are several references to episodes in which he or other boys in the various schools he attended are caned for minor or presumed offences.[59] It is not simply the violence of the punishment that he records, however, but the apparent pleasure some of those involved – schoolmasters, prefects – took in inflicting pain, either directly or vicariously in condemning a child to be beaten. The sense of the child's powerlessness in such situations is vividly described: sent to the headmaster at St Peter's Preparatory School to be punished for a mistaken misdemeanour, Dahl recounts how he was frightened of the cane. 'It wasn't,' he observes, 'simply an instrument for beating you. It was a weapon for wounding. It lacerated the skin. It caused severe black and scarlet bruising that took three weeks to disappear'.[60] Faced with this weapon, the child Dahl pleads innocence; disbelieved, he is instructed to '"Be quiet and bend over" … Very slowly, I bent over. Then I shut my eyes and braced myself.'[61] The fantastical physical violence seen in his children's fiction, which can seem shocking to a modern (adult) audience, has its roots in the reality of an earlier time when the physical punishment of children was considered to be a normal part of the childhood experience, although Dahl was then and later a critic of such practices.

Significantly, while children now may be shocked by it, the very real violence depicted in *Boy* seems to have attracted little adult criticism or comment, despite the fact that the book was written for and marketed at a juvenile audience. This is possibly because the temporal distance between modern modes of childhood education and discipline and those experienced by Dahl relegates the violence to history and so makes it unreal, or perhaps it is simply consequent upon the text's non-fictional status. Dahl's early experiences of unjust treatment and physical punishment find their way into his fiction for children in various ways, as demonstrated earlier, but the violence is generally contained in fantasy and made safe by the fictional status of the narratives. Central to his children's stories are issues of justice and fairness, concepts close to Dahl's own heart and which inflect his fiction for adults as well as for children. Perhaps, after all, what makes Dahl's juvenile stories a suitable read for a child is not only the escape they offer from the not always pleasant reality imposed upon children in the twenty-first century, not simply the cathartic release of repressed emotions, not the (temporary) empowerment, not even at a basic level their humour and fun. Perhaps it is that, always, child readers can hear Dahl's child voice speaking to and for them, making the stories literature that really is suited to children, in the sense that it is 'tailored' to their needs.

Notes

1. The title pays homage to P. D. James's *An Unsuitable Job for a Woman* (1972), which features a female detective who faces criticism for her choice of employment, as the crime and violence associated with detective work is considered by contemporary society to be unsuitable for women. Lissa Paul in *Reading Otherways* makes a general case for the similarities

between women and children as groups within patriarchy and it seems to me that this issue of what is or is not suitable for the contemporary cultural perceptions of femininity can be mapped onto the issue of what constitutes appropriate reading material for the child. Lissa Paul, *Reading Otherways* (Stroud: Thimble Press, 1998).

2. M. Crouch and A. Ellis, *Chosen for Children*, 3rd edn (London: The Library Association, 1977): 6.

3. Julia Round discusses the relationship between Dahl's autobiographical writing and his fiction, drawing attention to how one feeds into the other and vice versa. See Julia Round, 'Roald Dahl and the Creative Process: Writing from Experience', unpublished MA essay, Cardiff University, 2000. Available at: www.roalddahlfans.com/articles/crea.php (accessed 9 September 2010).

4. Peter Hunt, *Children's Literature* (Oxford: Blackwell, 2001): 57.

5. Hunt: 57.

6. Jonathon Culley, 'Roald Dahl – "It's About Children and It's for Children" – But Is It Suitable?' *Children's Literature in Education* 22(1) (1991): 59–73, at 59.

7. Donald Sturrock, *Storyteller: The Life of Roald Dahl* (London: HarperPress, 2010): 492–7.

8. Richard Raskin discusses the social and psychological functions of crime fiction in 'The Pleasure and Politics of Detective Fiction, *Clues* 13(2) (1992): 71–113.

9. Rosemary Jackson, *Fantasy: The Literature of Subversion* (London: Routledge, 1981): 13.

10. Eileen Donaldson analyses the functions of fantasy in Dahl's fiction for children in 'Spell-Binding Dahl: Considering Roald Dahl's Fantasy', in Thomas Van der Walt (ed.), *Change and Renewal in Children's Literature* (Westport: Praeger, 2004): 131–40.

11. Cited in Mark West, 'The Grotesque and the Taboo in Roald Dahl's Humorous Writings for Children', *Children's Literature Association Quarterly* 15(3) (Fall 1990): 115–16, at 116.

12. Roald Dahl, *Matilda* [1988] (London: Puffin, 1989): 29. In Dahl's first, unpublished draft of *Matilda*, as Treglown notes, Matilda is '"born wicked" … and spends the first part of the book inflicting various tortures on her harmless and baffled parents'. Jeremy Treglown, *Roald Dahl: A Biography* (London: Faber, 1994): 242.

13. Roald Dahl, *James and the Giant Peach* [1961] (London: Allen & Unwin, 1967). An early attempt at children's fiction, *The Gremlins*, had been published as a cartoon book by Disney in 1943.

14. Road Dahl, *The Magic Finger* [1966] (London: Puffin, 2008).

15. Road Dahl, *Fantastic Mr Fox* (London: Puffin, 1974); *The Twits* [1980] (London: Puffin, 2007).

16. Roald Dahl, *George's Marvellous Medicine* [1981] (London: Puffin, 1982).

17. *George's Marvellous Medicine*: 12, 2.

18. Roald Dahl, *The Witches* (London: Puffin, 1983).

19. See David Rees, 'Dahl's Chickens: Roald Dahl', *Children's Literature in Education* 19(3) (1988): 143–55.

20. For example, Anne-Marie Bird's 'Women Behaving Badly: Dahl's Witches Meet the Women of the Eighties', *Children's Literature in Education* 29(3) (1998): 119–29. Bird's focus is on the film version, but many of her comments can be read against the original text. See also Catherine Itzin, 'Bewitching the Boys', *Times Educational Supplement*, 27 December 1985: 13; Michele Landsberg, *World of Children's Books: Choosing the Best* (London: Simon and Schuster, 1988): 89. These accusations of misogyny must be seen in the context of the feminist climate of the 1980s.

21. The film version of *The Witches* (1990), directed by Nicholas Roeg, adheres to convention and the child protagonist is returned to his human form.

22. The Dahl family originated in Norway but was based in Wales at the time of Dahl's early childhood; when his father died, Dahl's mother was constrained by her husband's wishes to ensure that, rather than return to her native country, she should remain in Britain so that their children could have an English education.

23. Roald Dahl, *Boy* and *Going Solo* [1984, 1986] (London: Puffin, 2008).

24. 'Mr Feasy', in *Roald Dahl: Collected Stories*, ed. Jeremy Treglown (New York and London: Random House, 2006): 343–69.

25. Treglown: 242–5.

26. Dahl incorporated some of Roxburgh's suggestions but fell out with the editor after writing a second draft. Hunt has described the published version as a self-indulgent 'work in progress'. Hunt: 59.

27. Freud discusses the child's imagined substitution of a preferred family for the reality in 'Family Romances', *On Sexuality* [Standard Edition, vol. 9], Penguin Freud Library vol. 7 [1977] (Harmondsworth: Penguin, 1991).

28. Hunt: 60.

29. *Matilda*: 162.

30. *Ibid.*: 168.

31. *Ibid.*: 198.

32. Hunt: 57.

33. Two further children's stories, *The Vicar of Nibbleswick* and *The Minpins*, were published posthumously in 1991.

34. Treglown: 81.

35. Roald Dahl, *The BFG* (London: Puffin, 1982).

36. Roald Dahl, *Danny, the Champion of the World* [1975] (London: Puffin, 1994).

37. While Danny is content, the narrative makes several references to his father feeling the loss of his wife, both as partner and as parent to their child.

38. Dahl's only close male relative was Louis, his considerably older half-brother by his father's first wife.

39. In an earlier episode in *Boy*, based on events that occurred when Dahl was at a local primary school in Llandaff, his mother confronts the headmaster who has beaten her son. This later episode takes place when Dahl is at boarding school and so lacks even a female protector.

40. *Danny, the Champion of the World*: 122.
41. *Ibid.*: 30.
42. *Ibid.*: 3.
43. This 'equality' is perhaps the result of Dahl's minimal alteration of his adult story, 'The Champion of the World'; in rewriting it for children, he lifted whole sections unaltered from the original.
44. *Danny, the Champion of the World*: 44–5.
45. Mark West, *Roald Dahl* (New York: Twayne, 1992): 79.
46. *Ibid.*: 80.
47. Roald Dahl, *Collected Stories*: 583.
48. Mark West (ed.), *Trust Your Children: Voices Against Censorship in Children's Literature* (New York: Neal-Schuman 1988): 75.
49. Roald Dahl, *The Wonderful Story of Henry Sugar and Six More* [1977] (London: Puffin, 2001).
50. *The Wonderful Story of Henry Sugar and Six More*: 2.
51. While teenage readers may want and expect some representation of sexual desire in literature intended specifically for them, it is more usually sexual desire between members of their own age group rather than between adults who may be of the same peer group as their parents.
52. *The Wonderful Story of Henry Sugar and Six More*: 10.
53. *Ibid.*: 70.
54. *Ibid.*: 87.
55. *Ibid.*: 93. Donald Sturrock observes that Dahl frequently alluded to the experience of flying in his writing, drawing on his own experiences as a fighter pilot. Sturrock suggests that 'Dahl viscerally understood …]the dazzling bright aviator's light, the fine thread that separates life from death.' Sturrock also notes that Dahl was asked to 'write a movie adaptation of Paul Gallico's novella *The Snow Goose*', and that its 'depiction of the relationship … between the man and the bird affected Dahl deeply … he would evoke its mood and subject matter in his own short story "The Swan"'. Sturrock: 137, 197.
56. This element is also absent from 'The Boy Who Talked with Animals'.
57. More recent editions retain 'The Swan', but are clearly marketed as teenage or adult fiction. An exchange of emails with the publisher in November 2010 reveals that while they have no records concerning the decision, their guidelines for appropriate material in publications intended for children would still consider 'The Swan' unsuitable.
58. Christopher S. Sykes, 'In the Lair of the BFG', *Harpers and Queen* October (1991): 80–5, at 82.
59. In writing *Boy*, Dahl was able to revisit his child self in the letters he had written to his mother while at school and after. There were over 600 of them, 'each one in its original envelope with the old stamps still on them'. *Boy and Going Solo*: 82.
60. *Boy and Going Solo*: 120.
61. *Ibid.* According to Jeremy Treglown, approximately one-tenth of *Boy* is taken up with accounts of 'beatings and other forms of physical punishment' (Treglown: 24).

8

All Grown Up: Filmic Interpretations of Roald Dahl's Novels

June Pulliam

To date, seven of Roald Dahl's 17 children's stories have been adapted into live action and animated films. In each adaptation, the director has expanded the implications of Dahl's narratives by introducing new themes and concerns, and placing the stories in broader political contexts which can be particularly appreciated by adult viewers. Many adult viewers are familiar with the original Dahl stories, having read them as children, so watching these adaptations is part of an 'ongoing dialogic process' in which they compare the work they already know with the one on the screen.[1] As a result, the viewing experience creates a sense of metatextuality, simultaneously adding texture and context to the tales, making them more relevant, more timely and more mature. In other words, these film versions are Dahl's children's stories, all grown up.

By its very definition, adaptation is not a literal translation. Rather, as Linda Hutcheon explains, adaptation is 'a process of making the adapted material one's own'.[2] Directors make Dahl's stories their own by complicating his narratives and widening their implications. Some adaptations of Dahl's works transform his child protagonists into characters who might have the power to reshape the world as adults, while others reflect on wider social forces and individual limitations that potentially deprive his protagonists of agency. In this essay, I consider how film-makers have interpreted Dahl's work beyond the typical themes of empowerment that characterise children's fiction. Some directors consider how forces such as feminism and capitalism affect individuals. Others build upon themes about morality and the power of imagination that are already present in Dahl's work. Many of these films challenge the conservative themes in Dahl's work.

Sexual politics and children's agency

Nicholas Roeg, Danny DeVito and Brian Cosgrove reconsider Dahl's sexual politics in their versions of *The Witches* (1990), *Matilda* (1996) and *The BFG* (1989) (officially released under the title *Roald Dahl's The BFG*). Dahl's novels frequently reinforce sexist gender norms in that he only valorises female characters who are selfless nurturers. This is the case in *The Witches* and *Matilda*. Roeg's *The Witches* magnifies Dahl's anti-feminist elements, whereas DeVito's *Matilda* and even Cosgrove's *The BFG* add feminist nuances that were not articulated in the novels.[3]

Dahl's *The Witches* is arguably the most openly sexist of his *oeuvre*: his witches are parodies of second-wave feminists, who have been caricatured by conservatives as women dabbling in the occult and who violently hate children.[4] Dahl's boy-turned-mouse narrator tells us that though witches look like 'ordinary women', they differ from them in their ambition 'to rid the world of children'.[5] Dahl's witches are devouring mothers who only pretend to love children in order to do them harm. The author describes his witches in terms implying that they would like to consume his child narrator rather than nurture him by offering him sustenance. The unnamed witch who tries to coax Dahl's narrator from his tree house has a toothy smile and gums 'like raw meat',[6] suggesting that she might like to eat him. The Grand High Witch's visage also hints at her desire to consume others. Beneath her mask is the face of a corpse whose rotting skin is 'cankered and worm-eaten'[7] like that of a zombie, suggesting that she is both being devoured and might devour the narrator.

Anne-Marie Bird argues that Roeg's film *The Witches* broadens the emphasis of Dahl's narrative to address male fears about the implications of second-wave feminism. The director changes Dahl's witches from devouring mothers into femme fatales whose sexuality is as threatening to patriarchy as their hatred of children. Roeg's film, made at the end of the 1980s when second-wave feminism enabled women to assume more assertive and active public roles, reflects the resulting male crisis of identity. In this context, Roeg's Grand High Witch, with her power suit, brief case and mobile-phone-wielding assistant, is the 'castrating bitch' of the 1980s who is a threat not just to children, but to an entire social order that is rooted in feminine subordination.[8] Roeg's depiction of witches follows how women are typically defined in film in terms of their sexuality. Good women are 'young, blonde, and attired in white', like the Grand High Witch's personal assistant Miss Irvine, who will eventually see her error, renounce witchcraft and embrace her conventional gender role.[9] Bad women are 'usually dark-haired and dressed entirely in black', like the Grand High Witch, who is 'a predatory vamp in her stiletto heels, tight, low-cut black dress, severe black hair, and blazing red lipstick'.[10]

Roeg's witches are ultimately more sinister than Dahl's because they elect to become witches. Dahl's witches are born with their loathing for children, making them inherently incapable of assuming the traditional role of mother. Early in Dahl's novel, we learn that, while witches are always female,[11] not all women are witches. Roeg's witches, on the other hand, choose this role, as demonstrated through the character of Miss Irvine. At the end of the film, when Miss Irvine resigns her position as the Grand High Witch's assistant, she also stops being a witch and embraces 'her "natural" role as a woman (maternal, procreative, nurturing)' by allowing the narrator 'to be reborn as a human child'.[12] Dahl's narrator remains a mouse. Miss Irvine's choice, however, has sinister implications for other women: if she can stop being a witch, other women can reject their subordinate positions by electing to *become* witches. So when the narrator in Roeg's film opines that witches are 'everywhere', he is also commenting on the potential of all women to rebel.

Finally, Roeg's film has greatly increased the boy narrator's ability to change the world. In both Roeg's and Dahl's endings, the narrator and his grandmother, now in possession of the Grand High Witch's mouse-making formula, plan to hunt down the world's remaining witches and turn them into vermin. However, since in Roeg's version all women can choose to become witches, the scope of the narrator's mission is greater – he is thwarting rebellious women everywhere instead of ferreting out a small, but dangerous minority.

While Roeg's *The Witches* expands Dahl's sexist representations of women, DeVito's *Matilda* and Cosgrove's *The BFG* introduce feminist elements to the author's stories that enable viewers to imagine the films' girl protagonists becoming modern young women with the ability to shape their destinies. DeVito greatly enhances Matilda's telekinetic abilities. In his analysis of the film *Matilda*, Peter Cumming concludes that neither Dahl nor DeVito creates a feminist children's text because Matilda is not permanently empowered in either version. However, Cumming does not consider how DeVito's Matilda's telekinesis is connected to her emerging feminist consciousness, a perspective which gives her more agency than her paranormal abilities do.[13] In the novel, Matilda's telekinetic abilities surface only briefly, allowing her to defend herself and others against Miss Trunchbull, the bullying headmistress of Crunchem Hall. After Matilda makes Miss Trunchbull leave town, her powers desert her, and she is once again merely a little girl who is so modest that her intellectual precociousness does not disqualify her as conventionally feminine.

DeVito's Matilda's powers are expanded, and she retains them after Miss Trunchbull is chased from Crunchem Hall. In the film's final scene, Matilda uses her telekinesis to lift from a bookshelf a copy of *Moby Dick* for Miss Honey to read to her before bedtime. Cumming claims that this scene represents Matilda as deprived of agency, as she has only 'the modest and child- and female-appropriate power of reading books by and about men'.[14] However, Cumming does not consider how Matilda's supernatural abilities are intricately tied to her developing feminist consciousness. At the film's closing, Matilda is fully aware of her own agency, which she can use to resist subordination and remake the world.

In both versions, Matilda's telekinesis is born of her resulting anger[15] after adults misuse their power to bully and silence others. In Dahl's novel, Matilda's powers do not emerge until the last third of the text, when she tips a glass of water on Miss Trunchbull after the headmistress has falsely accused her of putting a newt in the water pitcher.[16] Matilda's powers momentarily become stronger after she learns that Miss Trunchbull probably killed Miss Honey's father and stole her patrimony. Matilda's indignant reaction to this injustice strengthens her telekinesis, which she uses to redress the wrong done to Miss Honey. In DeVito's film, Matilda's telekinesis appears much earlier, but is still linked to her indignant response to injustice. Matilda makes the family television set explode after her father tears up her book and forces her to watch an inane programme with the rest of the family. Later, when Miss Trunchbull hurls a student over a fence, she uses her budding powers to save the child from being impaled on its spikes. However, Matilda's paranormal abilities are not confirmed for the viewer until the scene with Miss Trunchbull and the water pitcher.

The link between Matilda's telekinesis and her anger is appropriate given the film's feminist bent. Lyn Mikel Brown examines how girls are taught to disassociate themselves from their anger as part of a more general cultural silencing of their sex in preparation for the subordinate feminine subject positions they are coerced into occupying as adult women. Anger in this context is a political emotion whose expression is 'intimately tied to self-respect, to the capacity to realize and author one's life fully'.[17] For this reason, women's anger is often considered by those in power to be an 'act of insubordination' because it signals that women 'take themselves seriously' and 'believe they have the capacity as well as the right to be judges of those around them, even of those who are said to be their "superiors"'.[18] Matilda's anger is similarly connected to her self-respect and increasing capacity to fully author her life, and her desire that others have the same ability.

However, in both versions, Matilda's supernatural abilities are not the basis of her strength. Rather, they are the magical manifestation of an indomitable spirit that detests injustice. In DeVito's film, this spirit exemplifies Matilda's feminist consciousness, which allows her to transcend gender roles in order to be empowered. Her telekinesis enables her to thwart others such as her parents and Miss Trunchbull who would silence her because she is female. In both versions, Matilda's parents refuse to foster her intellectual growth because it will hinder her chances of finding a husband, which both parents view as the only appropriate goal for a girl. And while Miss Trunchbull bullies both male and female students, she punishes boys such as Bruce Bogtrotter for their misdeeds, while she punishes many female students, Matilda included, for merely talking back to her. In this context, Matilda's expanded magical response exemplifies her feminist consciousness in that she is always responding to others' attempts to silence her because she is a *female* child.

Roberta Seelinger Trites would view Matilda's use of power as feminist because it is 'more about being aware of one's agency than it is about controlling other people'.[19] Matilda uses her paranormal abilities to enable herself and others to be empowered regardless of gender through becoming aware of their own strengths to resist domination. Matilda later helps her classmates see their own strengths when she chases Miss Trunchbull from the school by making the headmistress believe that she is being pursued by the ghost of Miss Honey's father. In Dahl's novel, Matilda acts alone to banish the principal, whereas in DeVito's film, she encourages her classmates to participate in their tormentor's banishment. As a terrified Miss Trunchbull escapes through the hall, Matilda uses her telekinesis to place food in her classmates' hands so they can pelt the retreating principal. The students, who know nothing of Matilda's paranormal abilities, are empowered through collectively scourging the headmistress, which allows them to realise that they can stand up to a bully.

However, while children's anger in both versions of *Matilda* is tied to self-respect, women's anger is represented as illegitimate and incompatible with normative femininity. Miss Trunchbull becomes angry when she is thwarted in her attempts to bully others. Unlike Matilda, Miss Trunchbull has no feminist consciousness: she uses her prodigious physical strength and her authority as principal of

Crunchem Hall to have power over other people rather than resist domination.[20]

While DeVito's film does endow Matilda with a feminist conscious-ness, it is not free of sexism. Instead, the film reproduces Dahl's repre-sentations of women according to a sexist dichotomy between good and evil. Miss Trunchbull is unsympathetic in part because her size and athletic prowess are qualities associated with hegemonic masculinity. Miss Honey, on the other hand, is a sympathetic character because she is appropriately feminine – she is nurturing, sweetly pretty, passive to the point of being easily victimised,[21] and never angry. DeVito visu-ally represents all of his characters in a way that telegraphs their moral status. The evil characters, including Matilda's parents and brother, appear cartoonish – they are unattractive, are larger or shorter than average (as is the case with DeVito and Rhea Pearlman, who play Matilda's parents), wear outlandish clothing, and live in tastelessly decorated homes. Good characters such as Matilda, Miss Honey and the students at Crunchem Hall, on the other hand, appear normal because they are of average size and attractiveness.

Nevertheless, the conclusion of DeVito's film leaves the viewer with a vision of feminist empowerment that is not present in Dahl's novel. At the close of Dahl's novel, a male teacher becomes the new principal. Meanwhile, Matilda's telekinetic powers disappear, she comes to live with Miss Honey, and the two spend their days having tea parties. In DeVito's film, Miss Honey becomes the new princi-pal of Crunchem Hall, and she and Matilda reclaim Miss Honey's childhood home as their own space. Moreover, Miss Honey and Matilda's relationship is one of equals rather than one involving a nearly omniscient parent and relatively powerless child. Matilda is still in full possession of her powers when Miss Honey tucks her in to read to her. True, Matilda uses these abilities to pull from the shelf a book by a male author, but her choice of reading material does not automatically signify that she is disempowered. Rather, both Matilda and Miss Honey have similar intellectual abilities, including a love of literature, that many children (and adults) would find daunting. But most importantly, Matilda's telekinesis and her feminist conscious-ness have *not* disappeared. Rather, Matilda's predilection for using her power to transcend the limitations of gender lets us imagine that, as an adult, she will be able to make momentous changes in the world.

Cosgrove's *The BFG* also introduces feminist elements to Dahl's narrative: viewers can imagine how Sophie, Dahl's protagonist, is similarly situated to change the world as an adult. Like Henry Selick's *James and the Giant Peach* (1996), Cosgrove's *The BFG* emphasises the importance of fantasy to agency.[22] The director changes Sophie from a girl who retreats to a passive domesticity at the end of her adventure (as in the novel) to a character who will use her empowerment through fantasy to better understand and control the world around her.

Dreams in Dahl's *The BFG* and Cosgrove's film are a type of non-realistic fiction that allow children to imagine situations in which they have agency, providing them with a model for becoming autonomous adults. As Ursula K. Le Guin points out, non-realistic fiction is a valuable tool that 'opens alternatives to reality',[23] permitting the reader to make sense of her world and act upon it. In this way, non-realistic fiction is potentially subversive because it allows individuals to imagine ways to resist domination. Dahl's Big Friendly Giant (the BFG) gives children dreams that are empowerment narratives in which they imagine themselves having agency in situations with more powerful adults. In one dream, a boy saves his teacher from drowning; in another, the President of the United States asks a boy for advice.[24]

Cosgrove puts greater emphasis on Sophie's empowerment through fantasy than does Dahl. In Cosgrove's version, the orphanage where Sophie lives is a place of exacting discipline: according to a sign next to Sophie's bed, the institution's strict rules include the prohibition of games. Games are a type of fantasy or imaginative play that can be subversive, enabling players to contemplate alternatives to subordination. So when Sophie is snatched from her room by the BFG, she does more than have a marvellous adventure – she has her consciousness expanded through her encounter with the fantastic, something demonstrated in Cosgrove's ending. Dahl's Sophie follows the typical trajectory for female protagonists whose maturity is marked by a retreat into the domestic sphere and an acceptance of a subordinate feminine subjectivity. Dahl's Sophie's transition to young adulthood comes after she helps imprison the child-eating giants. The Queen recognises Sophie's maturity by awarding her a house near the royal palace, indicating that Sophie's progress towards adulthood necessitates that she exchange the Land of Dreams for feminine domesticity. Cosgrove's Sophie rejects the Queen's offer, opting to return to the Land of Dreams with the BFG. There she will presumably continue to assist him in giving empowerment dreams to children. In this position, Sophie, too, will be more empowered.

The relatively simple animation of Cosgrove's *The BFG* calls attention to the power of imagination. *The BFG* was made in the 1980s, when viewers had experience of more sophisticated animation

techniques such as the elaborately drawn and more realistic full animation produced by Disney studios which allows viewers to temporarily
believe that they are watching a reasonable facsimile of reality. *The
BFG*'s animation is more typical of cartoons: stylised forms and shapes
are outlined in pen and simply coloured. As a consequence, the viewer
is always aware of the artist's hand whose own powers of imagination
have created the film. Also, Cosgrove's animated giants closely resem-
ble Quentin Blake's illustrations of them in Dahl's novel. Notably, both
Blake's and Cosgrove's BFG bear a striking resemblance to Roald
Dahl, the creator of this and many other imaginative worlds.

Henry Selick's film *James and the Giant Peach* also emphasises the
importance of fantasy to individual empowerment, allowing viewers
to imagine how they too have had their consciousness expanded
through this medium. Selick's film is a combination of highly stylised
live action and stop-motion animation, the latter used to contrast
James's fantastical adventures inside the peach with his mundane
existence. The denouement of both Selick's film and Dahl's novel
reveals James to be both narrator and protagonist of the story. Selick's
film, however, is similar to Cosgrove's in how it emphasises the ability
of fantasy to empower children. In Selick's film, Aunts Sponge and
Spiker are not killed by the escaping peach as they are in Dahl's novel.
Instead, they survive and travel to New York to reclaim the colossal
fruit, which they value because it generates income as a curiosity.
In order to take possession of the peach, the aunts must undermine
James's claim of ownership by impugning his story about his arrival
in New York with an enormous piece of fruit. They dismiss as the
ramblings of a pathological liar James's improbable narrative about
harnessing a hundred seagulls to fly the peach across the ocean. James,
however, undercuts his aunts' claims with an impassioned speech
about the value of dreams. While James admits that he first imagined
the story of the giant peach, he asserts that his dreaming made it
real, a situation he likens to the creation of New York City, which
he reasons must also have begun as someone's dream. James's speech
prompts his talking giant insect friends to materialise in front of the
incredulous on-lookers, their presence on the screen blending the
film's stop-motion animation with the live action. Now that fantasy
has merged with reality, the city authorities must believe James's story
and permit him and his peach to remain in New York. While both
versions conclude with James as an autonomous adult who creates
fantastic narratives, Selick's James is in a better position to change the
world because he can articulate the connection between fantasy and
momentous accomplishment.

The evils of greed and consumer capitalism

While the film versions of *The Witches*, *Matilda*, *The BFG* and *James and the Giant Peach* emphasise the power of the individual to change the world, Mel Stuart's *Willy Wonka and the Chocolate Factory* (1971), Wes Anderson's *Fantastic Mr. Fox* (2009) and Gavin Millar's *Roald Dahl's Danny, the Champion of the World* (1989) build upon Dahl's critique in these novels on the evils of greed.[25] Tim Burton's *Charlie and the Chocolate Factory* (2005), Anderson's *Fantastic Mr. Fox* and Gavin Millar's *Danny, the Champion of the World* expand Dahl's narrative to explore how the individual is shaped by larger social forces.

Dahl's *Charlie and the Chocolate Factory* and Stuart's musical version of it, *Willy Wonka and the Chocolate Factory*, are morality tales where the wicked are punished and the good rewarded by Wonka, confectioner and trickster god. Robert M. Kachur examines the Christian themes in Dahl's *Charlie* and the two film adaptations of it, noting that Wonka is similar to both the Old and New Testament God. Wonka's mixing room is described in Edenic terms: like Adam and Eve, Wonka's guests are permitted by the sweet-maker to 'eat anything, from the tops of the trees to the grass beneath their feet, with the biblically analogous exception of one important item' – the chocolate river.[26] In Stuart's version, Wonka is a deity who is similar to Milton's trickster God of *Paradise Lost*, actively setting up for failure those he has invited into his universe. On the eve of the tour, one of Wonka's employees masquerades as rival confectioner Slugworth, tempting each contestant with a large monetary reward to steal one of Wonka's unreleased products. Before the children can take the tour, Wonka further sets them up for failure by forcing them to sign a lengthy and obfuscating liability waiver that they cannot read beforehand, which is full of caveats that make it difficult for any to win the secret grand prize, ownership of Wonka's factory.

Four of the five contestants in Dahl's novel are already so morally flawed, however, that they cannot win the grand prize available only to those who complete the tour: Augustus Gloop's and Veruca Salt's greed cause them to be physically ejected from the factory, whereas Violet Beauregarde and Mike Teavee must drop out after they become injured due to their lack of self-control. Charlie alone is perfect, so he wins the grand prize by default. Stuart's Charlie, however, is as morally flawed as the other contestants: Kachur describes Charlie in this version as an Everyman figure who, like the other children, 'sins in relation to food and must be redeemed'.[27] After Mike's disobedience of Wonka's instructions leaves him unable to complete the tour, Charlie should be the default winner of the grand prize. Yet earlier, supposedly out of sight of the sweet-maker and his Oompa-Loompas, Charlie and his grandfather helped themselves to Wonka's fizzylifting drinks, narrowly escaping injury in an exhaust fan. This transgression puts them on par with the other contestants who have either consumed food that Wonka forbade them or otherwise disobeyed his directions. Wonka, however, sees all, so Charlie and his grandfather are dismissed from the tour for their misbehaviour. Yet 'Charlie's response is unique among transgressors … he implicitly acknowledges his sin against Wonka by returning the Everlasting Gobstopper he has been given as a gift' rather than profiting by it as his grandfather urges him to do.[28] Charlie's gesture of penitence redeems him in Wonka's eyes, and he is declared the winner of the contest and heir to Wonka's factory.

Burton's *Charlie* is, like all of the director's films, a sort of grown-up children's story for adults who appreciate his surreal visual compositions and complicated interpretations of literature they read in their youth. Burton's *Charlie* 'diminishes the story's relationship to the biblical metanarrative'.[29] Instead, Burton humanises the sweet-maker with a plot thread about his childhood and broadens the narrative's scope to consider how Wonka the capitalist has affected others. Moreover, the audience can easily imagine Burton's Charlie as an adult since he is more grown up in comparison to Wonka, whose lack of maturity is demonstrated through his bursts of childish behaviour and his unresolved relationship with his father. In Burton's *Charlie*, Wonka is the son of a prominent dentist who denies him sweets in order to preserve his teeth. Wonka rebels by running away from home to become a confectioner. Although the adult Wonka declares that family ties just hold people back, he is clearly bothered by his estrangement from his father, as evidenced through flashbacks precipitated by his contact with Charlie. Charlie's bond with his grandfather contrasts with the strained relationships the other children have with the parents accompanying them on the tour. Moreover, Charlie demonstrates his maturity at the end of the film by rejecting the grand prize after learning that he must abandon his family as a condition of acceptance. Charlie recognises the value of family, something that marks him as more mature than Wonka, who has yet to have a close relationship with anyone who is not his subordinate. Burton's film concludes with Wonka learning how to cultivate familial ties: Charlie helps the sweet-maker reconcile with his father and gets him to participate in family life with the Buckets.

Burton's *Charlie* also fleetingly considers how capitalism affects social relations. In Dahl's novel, no explanation is given for the

Buckets' poverty. In Burton's film, however, the family's Dickensian poverty is a consequence of Wonka's business practices. Charlie's father loses his job in the toothpaste factory after the frenzy incited by the golden ticket contest causes sweet consumption to soar, and with it, a rise in cavities and a subsequent increase in toothpaste sales. To keep up with demand, the toothpaste factory employing Mr Bucket mechanises the plant and fires the slower (and more expensive) human workers. Burton also hints that Wonka might have affected the Buckets' fortunes a generation earlier, when he shut down his factory upon discovering that some of his workers were stealing his trade secrets – Grandpa Joe was among the laid-off employees. However, this critique of capitalism is somewhat weakened by the Buckets' affectionate relationship with one another in the face of starvation.

Stuart's and Burton's versions of *Charlie* also radically re-vision Dahl's Oompa-Loompa workforce, who were originally represented as African pygmies so 'incompetent in jungle living' that they must be rescued by Wonka, 'the great white father'.[30] In a journey reminiscent of the Middle Passage,[31] the sweet-maker smuggles the Oompas into his country 'in large packing cases with holes in them'.[32] In this context, the Oompas' place of origin and habit of breaking into song as they labour liken them to a happy slave workforce of the sort represented in minstrel shows and in early twentieth-century films about the antebellum South. In order to be sensitive to a racially diverse audience in 1971, Stuart changed the Oompas' appearance and titled his film *Willy Wonka and the Chocolate Factory*, since, at the time, 'Charlie' was African-American slang for a white man.[33] Stuart's Oompas, with their green page-boy haircuts and orange faces, are similar to the Munchkins in *The Wizard of Oz* rather than any class of exploited labourers.[34] Burton's Oompas revisit Dahl's representation of them as a class of workers: they are from the Amazon rather than Africa, hinting at another sort of exploited labour – undocumented illegals from across the border. Burton's Oompas are all played by one person, the Indian actor Deep Roy, whose dark skin gives him a Latin appearance. Roy's image was multiplied through CGI technology, creating the illusion of an entire workforce while giving the Oompas a uniform appearance, indicating that they are as interchangeable as the cogs in the numerous machines throughout the factory.

Dahl's *Fantastic Mr Fox* also examines the consequences of greed. The farmers Boggis, Bunce and Bean are defeated by their avarice, which drives them to embark on a scorched earth campaign to eradicate Fox and his animal friends, who have been raiding the farmers' storehouses in order to feed their families. Though Dahl's animals are as intelligent as humans, the author does not anthropomorphise them: instead, these characters behave as wild animals who are motivated by the need to survive.

Anderson's stop-motion animated film *Fantastic Mr. Fox* anthropomorphises Dahl's animal characters, complicating the author's relatively simple story of animals versus humans into one representing Mr Fox as in the throes of a midlife crisis. Anderson's animals are upwardly mobile bourgeois consumers who wear clothing, attend school and have careers: their lives are just shorter versions of those lived by humans. As a result, Anderson's film is very 'grown up' in its preoccupation with the problems of adulthood. Anderson's depiction of the three farmers, however, remains true to Dahl's cartoonish conception of them. Dahl is one of Anderson's heroes, so in a tongue-in-cheek homage to the author, Bean, the smartest and meanest of the farmers, looks like Dahl.[35] Also, Anderson's animals speak with American accents, while his human characters have British accents.

Like Burton's *Charlie*, Anderson's *Fox* considers how capitalism transforms social relations. Because Anderson's animals are bourgeois consumers, they steal from the farmers not to feed their families, but to satisfy an ineffable longing. Anderson's Fox is sufficiently prosperous to support his wife and son. Instead, his midlife crisis prompts him to seek thrills by what the film describes as 'poaching' from the farmers. This description of Fox's raids is a metatextual reference connecting the film to Dahl's *Danny, the Champion of the World*, whose protagonist also poaches.[36] In the film's first few minutes, we learn that Young Fox engaged in this activity as an expression of his anti-establishment attitude. In this scene, Young Fox and his wife Felicity (the name given to her by Anderson) are dressed in hippie attire, indicating their link to a rebellious counter-culture and desire to transgress social boundaries. But Fox must renounce his poaching to become a mature adult. When Fox and Felicity are caught in one of Bunce's traps, Felicity reveals that she is pregnant and makes her husband promise to stop raiding farms if they escape their predicament. Seven non-fox years later, Fox leads a quiet bourgeois life as a newspaper columnist residing in a modestly appointed den with his wife and son. Fox's midlife crisis begins after he grows discontented with what he describes as 'being an animal and living in a hole in the ground', a condition that, while natural for members of his species, 'makes him feel poor'. To combat feeling impoverished, Fox purchases a tree house, against the advice of his lawyer, who reminds him that foxes are not meant to live above ground. Yet Fox's lavish new digs, in sight of Boggis, Bunce and Bean's industrial farms, only intensify his ineffable longing, which he concludes can only be satisfied by 'the feel of a chicken in his teeth'. This need both confirms Fox's animal nature and is a departure from it in that bourgeois consumerism is represented as normal for all creatures in the anthropomorphised universe of Anderson's film. When Fox brings home a chicken from a raid, he conceals his illicit activity from Felicity by packaging it as a store-bought item, indicating that animals in this narrative normally satisfy their dietary needs through shopping, not hunting.

While killing chickens is normal behaviour for foxes, in Anderson's film it is also a deviant activity that leads to trouble because 'poaching' defies the established social structure whereby goods are distributed through an orderly capitalist system. So when Fox and his friends are cowering and starving underground, their dire predicament is the fault *both* of Fox and the farmers who want to destroy them. If Fox had been content with his life, then the farmers would have left them alone and all of the animals could have lived in peace and plenty.

Anderson's animals can survive only after they resolve to live as animals, which in the film means becoming bourgeois consumers. Fox and his friends dig a collective home so deep underground that the farmers can never get them, sustaining themselves by raiding the farmers' storehouses in Dahl's novel, and the farmers' collectively owned supermarket in Anderson's film. Unlike the farmers' storehouses, the supermarket is full of processed products: in the movie's final scene, Fox and family toast one another with juice boxes taken from this store. As a consequence, Fox is both reconciled to his animal nature in that he lives in a den once more, but he also becomes an allegorical representation of the bourgeois consumer whose needs are met only through industrial production.

Danny, the Champion of the World, one of Dahl's few non-fantasy works for children, is also about the evils of greed and the value of family. Gavin Millar, however, reworks Dahl's narrative to examine the wider social forces that undermine the modern family unit. In Dahl's novel, Danny's poaching is framed as his way of protecting his small family from the cupidity of Mr Hazell, the snobbish brewery owner who holds shooting parties on his estate to gain acceptance with affluent and titled people. Millar's adaptation, however, goes beyond condemning the greed of an individual to considering how modern capitalism transforms human relationships. Millar's Hazell is a greedy real-estate developer who has bought nearly all the land in Danny's village, which he intends to turn into a housing estate (or in American English, a subdivision of homogeneous dwellings). Hazell's business plan is typical of the process by which many small communities whose inhabitants looked after one another were replaced after the Second World War with a hollow facsimile of this way of life in the name of progress and modernity.

In Dahl's novel, Danny and his father William poach from Hazell in response to his personal threat to their small family unit. A year before the action of the novel occurs, Hazell brings his Rolls Royce to William's filling-station, threatening to beat Danny with his riding crop if the boy does not keep his 'filthy little hands' off the car while fuelling the vehicle.[37] An enraged William throws Hazell out of his filling-station. Soon after the incident, social workers, presumably sent by Hazell, arrive to investigate William's fitness as a parent: father and son live behind the filling-station in an old gypsy caravan without electricity and indoor plumbing, and William has kept his son out of school. The social workers quickly learn, however, that William is an exemplary father: Danny is always clean and well fed and has been schooled at home by William, who has made sure that his son is both literate and mechanically precocious. In this context, poaching allows William an outlet to take surreptitious revenge against an individual who wantonly threatened his family.

In Millar's film, poaching is a defence against Hazell's economic violence, which threatens to destroy the community. Millar represents the 1955 England of Danny's childhood as a Europeanised version of small-town America, a saccharine and idyllic world that never really existed.[38] Millar's English village is a Frank Capra-esque small town. The inhabitants are humble, everyday people who are part of a tightly knit community whose members tolerate each other's foibles, such as headmaster Snoddy's alcoholism, represented in both novel and film as a harmless vice, although he drinks on the job. But the most anachronous facet of Millar's narrative is that the corporal punishment of children is not tolerated. Headmaster Snoddy threatens to fire Captain Lancaster, Danny's sadistic and pompous teacher, for beating the boy's hands as a punishment for cheating. In reality, corporal punishment was widely practised by parents and educators in the 1950s, who saw it as a sound disciplinary technique.

Hazell threatens this idyllic way of life in Millar's film. During the Second World War, while most men of the village were away fighting, Hazell stayed at home and took advantage of others' poverty by purchasing their land cheaply. Ten years later, Hazell owns most of the village, which he hopes to replace with a housing estate after he attracts investors. Only William stands in Hazell's way by refusing to sell his property, which is in the middle of the proposed development.

In Millar's version, William's refusal is the source of the festering grudge between him and Hazell.

In both versions, Danny takes up poaching to defend his family. Danny initially objects to his father's poaching, which he sees as stealing. However, Danny revises his opinion after his father is nearly killed while on a poaching expedition when he falls into one of Hazell's traps. William breaks his leg in the fall, narrowly escaping with his life since the developer fully intends to shoot all trespassers whether or not they pose a threat to his safety. Enraged that Hazell would shoot his father to protect a few pheasants, Danny masterminds the poaching of all of the developer's birds on the eve of his 'shooting party'. Danny's scheme publically discredits Hazell in front of his guests when he cannot deliver on his promise of plentiful and easily killed game, thereby depriving the developer of some of his power.

Dahl's novel concludes with the preservation of Danny's family unit, whereas Millar's film concludes with the preservation of an entire community – albeit one that nurtures Danny and William's familial relationship. In Millar's film, both William's refusal to sell his land to Hazell and Danny's poaching of the developer's pheasants effectively kills the proposed housing estate. Hazell's inability to secure all the land for the project and his failure as a host raises questions for potential investors about his ability to deliver on any bigger project. In this way, Millar's film is also more 'grown up' in its consideration of how complex social forces shape family and community dynamics.

While each of these films is relatively faithful to Dahl's work, the directors also complicate the original narrative in ways that are better understood by adults. Some of these reworkings are subtle, such as Cosgrove's and Selik's consideration of how fantasy empowers individuals in *The BFG* and *James and the Giant Peach*. Other films update Dahl's narratives to incorporate more timely perspectives about power relations. DeVito's *Matilda* and Roeg's *The Witches*, for example, respond to second-wave feminism in different ways, whereas Millar's *Danny, the Champion of the World* puts Dahl's novel into a broader historical context to make poaching less objectionable to adult viewers. Still other adaptations such as Burton's *Charlie and the Chocolate Factory* and Anderson's *Fantastic Mr. Fox* could be described as children's films for adults in that the directors appeal to their adult audiences through expanding the scope of the original narratives and using elaborate visual storytelling techniques whose artistry is more fully appreciated by adults. In this way, these film versions of Dahl's novels are all grown up.

Notes

1. Linda Hutcheon, *Theory of Adaptation* (New York: Routledge, 2006): 21.
2. Hutcheon: 20.
3. Roald Dahl, *The BFG* (New York: Puffin, 1982); *The Witches* (New York: Puffin, 1983); *Matilda* (New York: Puffin, 1988). Films: *Roald Dahl's The BFG (Big Friendly Giant)*, directed by Brian Cosgrove (Cosgrove Hall Films, 1989); *The Witches*, directed by Nicholas Roeg (The Jim Henson Company, 1990); *Matilda*, directed by Danny DeVito (TriStar Pictures, 1996).
4. This characterisation of second-wave feminists can be traced back to Pat Robertson in a 1992 fundraising letter opposing an Iowa state equal rights amendment. In this letter, Robertson famously described feminism as 'a socialist, anti-family political movement that encourages women to leave their husbands, kill their children, practice witchcraft, destroy capitalism and become lesbians'; Maralee Schwartz and Kenneth J. Cooper, 'Equal Rights Initiative in Iowa Attacked', *The Washington Post*, 23 August 1992. This quotation is often erroneously attributed to Robertson's Republican convention speech in the same year.
5. *The Witches*: 30.
6. *Ibid.*: 43.
7. *Ibid.*: 66.
8. Anne-Marie Bird, 'Women Behaving Badly: Dahl's Witches Meet the Women of the Eighties', *Children's Literature in Education* 29(3) (1998): 119–29, at 126.
9. Bird: 121.
10. *Ibid.*: 121–2.
11. *The Witches*: 9.
12. Bird: 128.
13. Peter E. Cumming, 'The Cigar Was Essential: Contestations of Power in Roald Dahl's *Matilda*', in Laurie Ousley (ed.), *To See the Wizard: Politics and the Literature of Childhood* (Newcastle: Cambridge Scholars Publishing, 2007).
14. Cumming: 104.
15. In his earlier book *The Magic Finger* (New York: Harper and Row, 1966), Dahl similarly connects a girl's magical abilities to her anger, which she uses to dispense justice rather than for her own material gain.
16. *Matilda*: 164–5.
17. Lyn Mikel Brown, *Raising Their Voices: The Politics of Girls' Anger* (Cambridge, MA: Harvard University Press, 1998): 10.
18. Brown: 10–11.
19. Roberta Seelinger Trites, *Waking Sleeping Beauty: Feminist Voices in Children's Novels* (Iowa City: University of Iowa Press, 1997): 8.
20. In fact, women's anger is represented as pathological in most of Dahl's works, as it is connected to their rejection of conventional femininity:

Dahl's angry women hate children and refuse the maternal role. Miss Trunchbull characterises children as insects who 'should be got rid of as early as possible' (*Matilda*: 159). The Grand High Witch (*The Witches*) and James's Aunts Sponge and Spiker (*James and the Giant Peach*) are also angry and 'unfeminine' women whose wrath is directed towards children. Roald Dahl, *James and the Giant Peach* (New York: Puffin, 1964).

21. Cumming: 92–3.
22. *James and the Giant Peach*, directed by Henry Selick (Allied Filmmakers, 1996).
23. Ursula K. Le Guin, 'Why Kids Want Fantasy', *Cheek by Jowl: Talks and Essays on How and Why Fantasy Matters* (Seattle: Aqueduct Press, 2009): 131–5, at 133.
24. *The BFG*: 99, 105–6.
25. Roald Dahl, *Charlie and the Chocolate Factory* (New York: Puffin, 1964); *Fantastic Mr. Fox* (New York: Puffin, 1970); *Danny, the Champion of the World* (New York, 1975). *Willy Wonka and the Chocolate Factory*, directed by Mel Stuart (David L. Wolper Productions, 1971); *Roald Dahl's Danny, the Champion of the World*, directed by Gavin Millar (Children's Film and Television Foundation, 1989); *Charlie and the Chocolate Factory*, directed by Tim Burton (Warner Brothers Pictures, 2005); *Fantastic Mr. Fox*, directed by Wes Anderson (Twentieth Century Fox Film Corporation, 2009).
26. Robert M. Kachur, 'A Consuming Tradition: Candy and Socio-religious Identity Formation in Roald Dahl's *Charlie and the Chocolate Factory*', in Kara K. Keeling and Scott T. Pollard (eds), *Critical Approaches to Food in Children's Literature* (New York: Routledge, 2009): 221–34, at 225.
27. Kachur: 229.
28. *Ibid.*: 229.
29. *Ibid.*: 230.
30. Lois Kalb Bouchard, 'A New Look at Old Favorites: *Charlie and the Chocolate Factory*', in Donnarae MacCann and Gloria Woodard (eds), *The Black American in Books for Children: Readings in Racism* (Metuchen, NJ: Scarecrow Press, 1972): 112–15, at 112.
31. The Middle Passage was the arduous journey undertaken by millions of Africans who had been sold into slavery. These Africans, who were considered as cargo rather than humans by their captors, were crammed in the holds of ships to be transported to the New World.
32. *Charlie and the Chocolate Factory*: 71.
33. Jeremy Treglown, *Roald Dahl: A Biography* (New York: Farrar, Straus and Giroux, 1994): 189.
34. June Pulliam, 'Charlie's Evolving Moral Universe: Filmic Interpretations of Roald Dahl's *Charlie and the Chocolate Factory*', in Leslie Stratyner and James R. Keller (eds), *Fantasy Fiction into Film*. (Jefferson, NC: McFarland, 2007): 103–14, at 110.
35. 'Trivia for Fantastic Mr. Fox', *The Internet Movie Database*. n.p., n.d.: www.imdb.com/title/tt0432283/trivia (accessed 2 August 2010).

36. A further connection to *Danny, the Champion of the World* is found in a scene where Fox puts sleeping powder into blueberries to get past one of the farmer's guard dogs. This ploy is similar to Danny's putting sleeping pills into raisins in *Danny, the Champion of the World* in order to poach Mr Hazell's pheasants. When Dahl's lawyers learned that the film-maker had used part of *Danny, Champion of the World* in *Fantastic Mr. Fox*, they wanted the director to remove the material. However, because the scene had already been filmed, Anderson was able to convince the lawyers to permit him to keep it in the film ('Trivia for Fantastic Mr. Fox').

37. *Danny, the Champion of the World*: 43.

38. For a more thorough discussion about how popular cultural representations of life in the 1950s and 1960s have come to be substituted for reality at the close of the twentieth century, see Stephanie Coontz, *The Way We Never Were: American Families and the Nostalgia Trap* (New York: Basic Books, 1992).

9

Roald Dahl and Quentin Blake

Carole Scott

Author–illustrator collaboration

When Roald Dahl agreed with his publisher, Tom Maschler, that Quentin Blake should be his collaborator for *The Enormous Crocodile* (1978),[1] he found an artist who shared his vision that the author and illustrator could work together as a team to reflect and augment each other's contribution, so that the ultimate work of art would embody a combination of the two. Prior to this time, his publishers had selected a variety of different illustrators,[2] even using (and not always acknowledging) different artists for the UK and US editions. Dahl 'wanted the drawings to do part of the work',[3] vociferously demanding more pictures when he thought there were not enough. And Blake's approach to illustrating another's text was to 'bathe yourself in it, be immersed in it before you start to draw' in order to 'match the spirit of the book itself', 'the whole atmosphere'.[4] The extent of Dahl's repertoire, which covers an impressively wide range of styles and genres – from carnivalesque exaggeration, to vulgar and cruel misogyny, comic fantasy and relative realism – is a challenge to the illustrator. Blake adapted his graphics to respond to the style of the verbal text and further interpret the particular world that Dahl had created, visualising his role as a kind of 'illustrator-as-theatre-director',[5] one who is presented with someone else's words and not much in the way of stage directions.

They were different in many ways: Dahl's love of adventure and danger, and his daredevil and sometimes subversive exploits – including rebellious teenage shenanigans, brushes with death as a wartime pilot and spying activities – proclaimed a character who grew increasingly irascible as he matured. Blake, who gently describes their differences by noting that Dahl was very practical and a sportsman while he was not,[6] made it his business to respond to and expand Dahl's work, believing that it was their shared love of 'comedy, exaggeration and activity'[7] that made their partnership a success. This gave Blake the confidence to re-illustrate the earlier works even after the author's death, sensing that he knew what Dahl would have liked. As they became increasingly engaged with each other, Dahl became more and more aware of what would be fun or challenging for Blake to draw, while Blake tells us that, 'What I always did with Roald was to draw [the characters] and then consult him to see whether he felt they looked like that, and we made adjustments.'[8] For example, in the case of *The BFG*, after much discussion the Giant's clothing was modified, abandoning the 'black hat, apron and large black boots' that Dahl had originally described, making the Giant 'softer and more lovable' and replacing the boots with sandals actually modelled on Dahl's own Norwegian footwear.[9]

Their personal bonding reflects the nature of the verbal–graphic interaction of the books. As developed in *How Picturebooks Work* and more specifically in 'From Symmetry to Counterpoint: An Aesthetic Study of Picturebooks', the spectrum of the dynamic between word and picture ranges from the replicative and complementary through harmonious expansion and enhancement, to counterpoint and dissonance.[10] The Dahl–Blake dynamic is clearly in the centre of the spectrum, as Blake both enhances and expands Dahl's text, believing that 'The text is the guide to the illustrator. It is perfectly possible to draw in your own way, to have a characteristic way of working, but be guided in everything you do by the words of the text …'[11] Not only does he give graphic definition to Dahl's often grotesque descriptions and quirky language, he also develops details of actions that Dahl simply hints at. His illustrations develop and define character and interpersonal relationships, sustain and reinforce tone and mood, and support Dahl's distinctive narrative voice that weaves a complex range of emotions both dark and light with a wry, whimsical and sometimes raw humour. In addition, Blake matches the affect of his illustration to the genre of the piece, exaggerating the bizarre and mediating the violent as he judges appropriate. On occasion, he even moves beyond enhancement by commenting, through his images, on the modality of the piece where Dahl's boundary between fact and fiction is blurred.

Before turning to a detailed analysis of the Dahl–Blake dynamic, it is instructive to compare Blake's work with that of earlier illustrators. Nancy Ekholm Burkert illustrated *James and the Giant Peach* some 30 years before Blake.[12] Differences in format are obvious: Blake's version has slightly more than twice as many pictures as Burkert's; Blake's illustrations (excepting the cover) are all black-and-white while Burkert includes four full-plate multicolour pictures and ten peach-coloured wash illustrations. More significant are the general approach and style.

Burkert introduces us to James on the first page with a realistic picture of a happy small boy sitting with his cat beside an open window, his toys nearby; she contrasts this five pages later with a melancholy, dark picture of him enclosed by a prison-like barred window. Blake gives us no 'before and after' scenario, and his presentation of the boy is suggestive rather than carefully delineated. His single-line sketch is closer to the flat effect of a cartoon than it is to Burkert's careful, subtle shading of light and dark that gives a three-dimensional appearance.[13] Blake's illustration distances the boy's emotions, enhancing the fantasy element of the story rather than engaging the reader's emotions as Burkert's more intimate presentation does. The images of the aunts follow suit: Burkert's Aunt Sponge and Aunt Spiker make one squirm, while Blake's are just weirdly grotesque. Burkert has some beautiful, carefully formed pictures of horses and sheep and the Giant Peach in the sky, pulled by the birds,[14] but in comparison with Blake's more impressionistic images, they seem static, set pieces. Blake acknowledges the influence of abstract impressionism on his style, which he characterises as 'informal', 'spontaneous' and 'fluent'.[15] He affirms, 'I only add the details that I think are necessary'.[16] Blake's drawings are filled with action; they titillate rather than satisfy the reader's eye and add excitement and speed to the narrative rather than capturing specific moments to expand with realistic detail.

For the great parade of the peach through New York City,[17] Burkert creates a clear, colourful picture carefully worked, and, though not really photographic, her illustration has some feeling of a happy moment, a delightful scenario, captured. Presented from the perspective of a bystander, the crowd of children in short dresses and trousers are climbing on the peach and waving to James and his travelling companions. Blake's illustration is depicted from above, looking down on the parade. The scene encompasses a much larger area than the focus of Burkert's and is filled with movement. The drawing highlights a number of actions: for example, a policeman keeping order has been outsmarted by a little girl whose enthusiasm has led her to break through the line and rush toward the limo. The crowds are portrayed by moving parts: flags waving, faces peering, arms pointing with suggestions of many people, but pictured as a mass rather than being individualised. Wild squiggles cover a large part of the page, suggesting the swirling of ticker tape tossed from the buildings. The scene feels wild and somehow chaotic, prompting the imagination to recall the experience of a parade rather than how it looks.

Another early illustrator, Donald Chaffin, creates anthropomorphic animals in *Fantastic Mr Fox* (1970), resembling toys rather than real animals, and dressed in period clothes reminiscent of Beatrix Potter's Sawrey.[18] The images are decorous and formal, even when presenting action. For example, Mr Fox escaping with two captured chickens looks more as though he is dancing with the chickens than running away with them, and the picture is framed with an oval border of leaves like a Victorian vignette.[19] In another image, the farmers hunting the fox stand posed as though in an early photograph.[20] In contrast, Blake's Mr Fox is a funny, cartoon-like figure full of energy and always in motion: leaping, climbing ladders, digging tunnels, and expressing intense emotion whether it be at the sight of the mechanical diggers penetrating the ceiling, or having the stump of his tail soothed when the farmer shoots it off.[21] Unlike the Chaffin pictures that are usually separated from the text, sometimes by a shaded area and often by 'frames' of leaves, branches, ribbons or flowers, Blake's images are informally placed on various levels of the page and even across the gutter, giving the impression that they are truly part of the action. They emphasise the exuberance of the animal's subversive acts against the stodgy establishment represented by the farmers, supporting Dahl's inversion of the natural and civilised worlds in which the human beings are stupid and beastly, and the animals clever, sophisticated, witty and endowed with strong family values.

Moderating violence in *The Enormous Crocodile*

The extensive range of Dahl's *oeuvre* is well exemplified in his initial collaborations with Blake: *The Enormous Crocodile*, *The Twits* and *George's Marvellous Medicine*. The first, for younger children, is gently ridiculous with hints of peril carefully mitigated, while the other two reveal Dahl's delight in violence, the grotesque, the disgusting and the subversive. *The Enormous Crocodile* is decidedly a picture book rather than an illustrated text. Large, colourful pictures appear on every page, some extending into double spreads which may serve as frames or backgrounds to the verbal text, and, as the book continues, the images dominate the page as the verbal text becomes sparser. Dahl's text describes the Crocodile as 'enormous' with 'hundreds of sharp white teeth' that 'sparkled like knives in the sun'.[22] The Crocodile is greedy, with the desire for one 'fat juicy little child' increasing to a yen for six.[23] He creates rapturous poems about the quality, taste and consistency of his intended meal (sound bites included), reminding the reader of flesh-eating witches and giants in fairy tales: 'The sort of things I am going to eat / Have fingers, toe-nails, arms and feet' and 'You mash it and munch it, / You chew it and crunch it! / It's lovely to hear it go squish!'[24] Blake, determining immediately that 'the main thing is the character of the crocodile', made many 'experimental drawings' of it, coming to realise that 'this evil person, this Richard III person was someone you loved to hate'.[25]

In this book for younger children, Dahl does not venture into the realm of some of his earlier books that, prior to the 1980s, 'were often condemned by adult critics who found them vulgar, excessively violent, and disrespectful toward adults'.[26] No adults are present, but the elephant, hippo and other animals protect the children and provide security for them in the face of danger. Furthermore, the dangerous Crocodile, though wily, is bumptious and derided from the beginning, even by his fellow croc, for his ineptitude: 'You've only [hunted children] once ... They all saw you coming and ran away'.[27] The rude names he is called are comical; unlike the other animals he has no proper name (it is only generic), and he is defined primarily by his greedy appetite. Dahl adopts a stance similar to that of Lewis Carroll, whose Alice books frequently tease children by alluding to death by being eaten.[28] His Crocodile spends the story licking his lips, dribbling with excitement, and going 'yum, yum, yum', 'squish crunch gobble', but he ends up himself as a morsel of food as he is 'sizzled up like a sausage!' by the hot sun, suggesting that the intended eater becomes the eaten.[29]

Dahl undermines the violence of his Crocodile by making fun of him. Blake responds to and echoes Dahl's taming of the beast's cruelty, telling us that 'he reminds me of the crocodile in the Punch and Judy shows [with] wooden teeth. His teeth are nothing like crocodile's real teeth. They are teeth for eating children with'.[30] So he depicts a kind of puppet crocodile with jagged teeth formed with a single up-and-down line, frequently revealed in a sort of toothy smile. He shows the Crocodile in some hilarious attempts at camouflage, which undermine the seriousness of his evil intent, for example in his masquerade as a coconut palm. Dahl has set up a fantastically ridiculous scene – a croc pretending to be a coconut tree! – and Blake has enhanced the fun. The Crocodile is pictured gingerly balancing on his tail, clutching armfuls of coconuts to his breast, with one eye and a few teeth peeking out from a mass of palm leaves, giving the impression of a top-heavy dowager provocatively balancing a huge feather hat, with just a hint of seduction.[31] And when Blake represents the Crocodile biting, the angle of his jaws suggests a clumsy, wooden motion. When 'with one bite of his huge jaws, he bit through the tree that Muggle-Wump was sitting in',[32] the picture shows the Crocodile's jaws opening vertically, on the same plane as the tree, instead of horizontally to encompass it;

and when he snaps off the Roly-Poly Bird's tail feathers,[33] the teeth do not clamp shut. Blake illustrates the Crocodile biting the elephant, again with vertically opening jaws, with teeth that do not penetrate, and with eyes that catch the elephant's eye with a look that is more naughty than cruel. The Crocodile is very much the stage villain who, despite his ardent desire to be wicked, fails to convince the audience that he can be an effective evil figure. Even the fact that he is 'Enormous' is belittled by Blake's representation of how small he is next to the much larger elephant. In all these ways Blake accentuates the Crocodile as a figure of fun rather than being dangerous. In so doing, he adds an element of his own interpretation by accentuating the more playful aspect of Dahl's humorously frightening tale.

Not only does Blake echo the light-hearted affect of the story with colourful, impressionistic washes, he also captures the sense of energetic action that characterises Dahl's narratives. Even though Blake's animal figures are not realistically delineated, he characterises them with movement that expresses their quirky attributes. The image of the hippo vigorously butting the Crocodile disguised as a coconut tree features unexpected visual force fields that match the verbal text's intensity.[34] The hippo's back feet are raised way off the ground, pitting the whole weight of its body against the Crocodile, which, instead of falling away from the hippo's thrust, topples, equilibrium disturbed, onto the hippo's back, coconuts tumbling in all directions. A visual image, by its nature, reflects spatial but not temporal relationships and events. By depicting the disequilibrium of the scene, Blake's illustration not only expresses the disharmony of the action, but also takes on elements of a temporal narrative, explicitly signalling the inevitable outcome of the action and underscoring the vitality of Dahl's plot.

Blake pictures another narrative sequence when Trunky spins the Crocodile in a circle round his head with ever-increasing speed, and then tosses him like a sausage into the sun for final disposal. Dahl's description of 'a blurry circle going round and round Trunky's head'[35] is transformed by Blake into a visual synecdoche of elephant: a small patch of grey featuring two elephant eyes and a little piece of trunk within a green circle, with four legs below it. Dahl's 'blurry circle' is represented as thick and green, formed of countless overlapping images of the whirling crocodile in simultaneous succession. Only the first half of these images has eyes, so that the Crocodile's point of view disappears as they do. Action filled, the comic scene most significantly accentuates Dahl's fantasy genre by depersonalising the Crocodile as he is progressively dissolved into a design feature.

Picturing the grotesque in *The Twits* and *George's Marvellous Medicine*

The next two collaborations, *The Twits* (1980) and *George's Marvellous Medicine* (1981)[36] are for children a little older than the audience targeted in *The Enormous Crocodile*. Both books are well balanced between verbal and visual text – almost every page and certainly every double spread offers at least one drawing – and reveal Blake's ability to complement and expand Dahl's expression at its more acerbic and grotesque. To begin with, Dahl mocks adults as insensitive, immoral and physically disgusting, using vulgar and repulsive language to describe them. George's Grandma, for example, is described as a person with 'pale brown teeth and a small puckered-up mouth like a dog's bottom'[37]; she is 'always complaining, grousing, grouching, grumbling' and despises children; she loves to eat caterpillars, slugs, worms, crunchy beetles and earwigs. In short, she is a 'filthy old woman' who terrifies George with her threats of harming him with her magic power. Needless to say, George 'really *hated* that horrid witchy woman'.[38]

Mr and Mrs Twit spend their time insulting and torturing each other and the creatures that live around them. They are hateful in action and revolting in appearance, and Dahl goes out of his way to connect the two: 'if a person has ugly thoughts ... the face gets uglier and uglier until it gets so ugly you can hardly bear to look at it ... but if you have good thoughts they will shine out of your face like sunbeams and you will always look lovely'.[39] This insistence on each individual's personality determining how he or she appears involves another hint to the illustrator, suggesting that what must be presented is the essence of character 'shin[ing] out of your face' rather than a straightforward presentation of outward appearance. To capture this thought, Blake contrasts the person with good thoughts with four sketches of Mrs Twit, whose straight hair becomes increasingly spiky and sharp, whose mouth becomes increasingly downturned and unpleasant, whose profile turns more crone-like and spotty, and whose head crunches forward into her chest until her neck disappears. The 'lovely' person has indeed 'a wonky nose and a crooked mouth and a double chin and stick-out teeth',[40] but her large body looks comfortably rotund, with her hands clasped contentedly over her bosom. She is not composed of straight prickly lines, but primarily of circular strokes: she has curly hair, a semicircular smile in a roundish head, a simple round dot for an eye. And, though her nose and teeth stick out from the circle, they are simply acceptable idiosyncrasies on a clearly affable person. Many of Dahl's unpleasant characters are physically unattractive, but Blake's effects depend very much on stance, gesture and facial expression, so that a few strokes can communicate the necessary vibrancy of emotion and personality, differentiating between those who are kindly and sympathetic, and those who are unkind, selfish and cruel.

Blake characterises George's Grandma by focusing upon the relationship with her grandson in a series of five images, all unframed, and placed on the top half of page 3 (recto), the bottom third of page 5 (recto), a central third of page 6 (verso) and the bottom third of pages 8 (verso) and 9 (recto). All are line drawings: a single line for George, and Grandma spiky and dark with bristly lines for hair, and her body shaded in with rough, scribbly strokes, what Blake calls his 'soft sort of scratching'.[41] Grandma's mouth is a gash, and her nose a beak. But most telling is the posture of the figures. In the first image Grandma is curled forward, glowering at George who is very upright and a little tense. In the second, Grandma is even further forward, looking increasingly like a bird of prey, while George leans backwards, one arm protectively across his chest. The third image changes point of view as the positions are reversed, George on the left side, while Grandma's hand now echoes her nose, so that two beak-like projections point at George. He has a bubble over his head with a slug in it. Facing this image is a page of text, including the old lady's statement that 'You're trying to get away from me aren't you?'.[42] And over the page, the fourth of the series reveals Grandma (now on the left again) with her whole head poked far forward and a menacing expression on her face, while George leans so far backward and away from her that he almost falls over. In terror, 'George ran into the kitchen, slamming the door behind him'[43] and the image, directly facing the last one, shows George in temporary relief leaning with his back to the closed door, and arms pressed tightly against it.

The first and last images show the figures against a simple backdrop of furniture, windows, curtains and pictures. But the intensity of the central three images is increased by eliminating any background, and featuring just the figures and Grandma's chair, so that the reader focuses upon the power of the passions expressed. In this situation, Blake makes only one reference to the details of the conversation (the slug in the thought bubble, which is more of a humorous aside than anything else) and chooses to characterise, by bodily contortion and facial gesture, Grandma's evil nature and the hatred, disgust and fear which motivate George's future actions. This is a perceptive choice on Blake's part, for it is the reader's empathy with the young boy's terror and revulsion that makes the notion of the magic medicine accept-able. When George thinks of concocting 'one that is so strong and so fierce and so fantastic it will either cure her completely or blow off the top of her head',[44] the reader shares his feelings, as both verbal and visual text complement one another. Certainly the potential violence of the magic medicine, which is described in verse like a spell, sounds very appropriate for a witch uttering threats, incantations and hexes.

The carnivalesque scenes which follow as George frenziedly throws the most extraordinary ingredients into his medicine – ranging from toiletries and house cleaning materials to boot polish and paint, chilli sauce and horseradish, and medications for hens and for pigs – are captured by Blake in a string of action vignettes emphasising George's manic hunt, and the haphazard choices he makes from a plethora of containers in every place imaginable. Blake's black–and–white line drawings give the impression of simple hurried sketches expressing the sense of speed and of time pressure as Grandma roars for her medicine. And he intersperses a few impressionistic sketches involving a back-ground setting – bathroom, kitchen, tool shed – with many purely action images of George pouring, shaking and spilling ingredients. The latter are sometimes quite minimalist suggestions of head, arms and upper torso in vigorous movement. One of them pictures George in a frenetic dance, one arm up, one bent in a grotesque position, one leg kicking high into the air, while he is surrounded by stars, dots and squiggles expressing his bursting, joyful emotion at the sight of his magical brew.[45] Blake has reinforced the genre and the emotional affect of the piece as well as giving visual impact to Dahl's action scenes.

When George's medicine takes effect, first on Grandma and then on the farm animals, Dahl describes the acrobatic gyrations they go through as they erupt into growth – some taller, some fatter, all larger and highly energetic. Then Dahl explicitly hands over to Blake, prompting him with 'it looked like this', 'this is what happened', and Blake responds with multiple sketches that finally drive the words from the page altogether.[46] The line drawings, sometimes tracing the creatures' explosion in size, comically express the astounded facial expressions and increasing physical contortions of the hen, pig, sheep, pony and goat as they leap around or until their legs tangle around each other. Grandma, who has simply become incredibly tall but 'frisky as a ferret'[47] is portrayed as a kind of stick insect stretched out, or bent over, and resembling a paper clip. This is a perfect example of what Blake meant when he said that Dahl 'wanted the drawings to do part of the work' (noted above), again expanding and accentuating the humour and the fantasy of the text.

Blake found plenty of scope for his whimsical depictions in *The Twits*, which fascinated him 'because it is so dark, the humour is so acerbic'.[48] Dahl portrays the couple's vicious, childish attacks on each other – frogs in the bed, worms in the spaghetti – and Mr Twit's intention to dispose of 'the old hag', the 'ugly old cow',[49] by tying her to gas balloons to launch her into the stratosphere, and he describes their unpleasant characters in disgusting detail. Mr Twit's beard full of rotting scraps of food is included in Blake's drawings of the bristly, prickly, revoltingly unkempt pair with their evil expressions and her witch-like look and spiky features. Their appearance is balanced by the fluid grace of the monkeys, the fluttery flocks of birds and the energy of the children who escape Mr Twit's retribution. As the action progresses, Blake's drawings become increasingly inventive. An intense, forceful energy pervades much of Dahl's writing, and it is clear that Blake has the ability to capture and expand this power in his images. Dahl's description of the Twits' attacks on the animals which they catch and eat, or imprison and torture, provokes an escalating sense of anger and dismay, stoking the animals' drive for revenge, while the time pressure of the Twits' brief absence from the house adds tension to the scene.

The genre of the piece moves from exaggerated comedy to hilarious fantasy, as Dahl describes the creatures gluing the carpet, furniture and knick-knacks to the ceiling in their stratagem to deceive the Twits into turning themselves upside down. Blake responds with numerous line drawings of the birds and the monkeys involved in this task, and the scene grows in size, stretching across the double spread, and leaving room for less than two inches of verbal text. Unlike some of the simpler, impressionistic drawings in which he often expresses an emotion or action with just a few lines, Blake here has responded to the significance and the excitement of the comically fantastic scene with complex panoramas in explicit detail. One picture[50] shows 'the great glue-painting'[51] of the ceiling: four monkeys and about 33 birds (or parts of them) are included, and all are busy about the task. Where Dahl lists some specific birds and notes that the birds are 'carrying paintbrushes in their claws and beaks',[52] Blake depicts a plethora of dark birds, spotted birds, grey birds, patchy or mottled birds, and white birds. There are crested birds, birds with toucan-like bills, curlews with long spoon-shaped beaks, owls, ducks, birds with long tails, short tails, stumpy wings and elegantly curved wings, large birds and tiny ones. Some are flying with paint pots clutched in their talons (smaller birds team up); others are holding a glue brush either in their beaks or by their feet. Dahl's off-hand, minimal description that 'Everyone was splashing about like mad'[53] encourages the picture to carry the weight of the scene's description. Certainly Blake has become a full partner in the venture, taking Dahl's few words into another dimension of expression by providing images whose idiosyncratic and humorous postures and gestures mirror and expand Dahl's vision. The birds are flying in every direction in a bustle of activity, while the monkeys clamber up furniture to make themselves high enough, sharing their glue pot with the birds.

The simple 'splashing away like mad' is transformed into a scene of pulsating energy not simply through the actions of the creatures, but also through the design of the illustration, including the vector of movement created by the positioning of each element in it. The picture dominates the pages, pushing the seven lines of verbal text to the bottom edge of the verso leaf. The vitality of the action reaches beyond the page, for this frameless double spread cannot contain it. Parts of the birds are cut off by the edge of the page, one of the monkeys is shown from the waist up with his hands falling off the page; and only the head of the fourth monkey appears, after much searching by the reader, at the bottom of the page almost hidden by the gutter.

Another complex picture that exemplifies the use of pattern and design carrying deeper import[54] is the double spread that depicts the moving of the carpet, preparatory to gluing it to the ceiling.[55] This time the wrapped verbal text is about four inches long on the top right-hand side of the double spread, and describes the size and colour of the carpet, the words and emotions of Muggle-Wump, the monkey directing the event, and the description: 'with the monkeys and the birds all pulling and puffing, the carpet was dragged off the floor and finally hoisted up onto the ceiling'.[56] Again the creatures are in full action, monkeys and birds working together, and the action extends beyond the page. But in this case Blake reveals his ability to create a truly aesthetic design. While the former picture was perfectly balanced, with its vector of activity arising from the bottom right-hand corner and bursting upward in both directions, this picture is strikingly beautiful in its sweeping motion from bottom left to top right. The sense of energy takes on pattern, as the birds at the top of the carpet predominantly use their beaks while the birds pulling on the sides use mainly talons, giving a push/pull dichotomy, directed by the hyperactive monkey at the bottom centre, balanced over the gutter. The furniture at the bottom left provides a counterweight to the upward motion. The design is completed by the pattern of the carpet, which gives depth and dimension to the whole and whose squirls echo the postures of the animals. The humour with which Blake constantly expresses Dahl's quirky perspective on the world has here been raised to a higher level. While the reader laughs at Blake's earlier picture of the Twits' Wednesday Bird Pie with 13 pairs of bird feet poking through the crust, the effect of the Twits' murderous greed shown by this picture of the animals' revenge captures a sense beyond laughter as it presents the pattern of life and of justice which will rebound upon the Twits' unethical behaviour against the natural order.

Fictive reality, order and harmony

This sense of the critical significance of essential balance within the natural order, and of justness, fair play and love in human interaction, is fundamental to Dahl's view of the way the world should be. His autobiographically based work, *Boy*, which evocatively describes the climate of sadistic punishment at his British public school, and of the vicious thrashings he received for boyhood misdemeanours, led him early, Sturrock suggests, to 'construct … a sunnier alternative reality' as his letters home reveal.[57] The letters and telegrams in *Going Solo* similarly reveal a light-hearted and ironic approach to danger and catastrophic injury, reflecting an intrepid attitude to pain and death and a strong and independent adherence to his own moral code rather than to power and authority.[58] In his fictional work, Dahl deals with fear and adversity by making fun of them and mitigates tragedy by downplaying it and considering it simply as a matter-of-fact issue and the opportunity for adventure. For example, when the young protagonist of *The Witches* is irreversibly turned into a mouse, he does not fret and, after considering the pros and cons, decides he 'rather like[s] it' as long as he can live happily with his loving Grandmother.[59]

Dahl's posthumous work *My Year* – part observation, part commentary upon the nature and habits of plants and animals, and part autobiography – reveals a keen, almost spiritual sense of connection with the natural world, and of involvement in the seasonal round which has provided a sense of stability during a lifetime of change and adventure.[60] Blake has responded to this book with representational watercolour drawings that capture the sense of beauty, serenity and joy that Dahl's words evoke. The mellow tone of the drawings echoes that of the text; there is no intrusion in the pictures of quirkiness, passion or comedy. Both the image on the front cover, of a man and his dog walking through the fields, and the frontispiece picture of a snowy path, marked with footsteps, under an archway of trees leading to a yellow door reflect the experience of someone who lives in harmony with nature.

This evidence of being in tune with Dahl's mood is further evinced in Blake's drawings for *Danny, the Champion of the World*, which tends towards a realistic depiction.[61] Despite the frightening (and criminal) situation his father leads him into, Danny's comfort in his father's proximity is repeatedly communicated by Blake in the way the boy reaches for his father's hand,[62] watches his attentiveness with trust,[63] and leans towards him, relying on his protection when confronted by the angry gamekeeper.[64] The pictures contribute to the sense of enjoyment, mitigating the feelings of peril underlying the story, and accentuating the positive, adventurous aspects of the boy's experience. In this way, Blake's interpretation of the scenes in his illustrations emphasises the devil-may-care aspects of Dahl's approach to danger, rendering it more exciting than frightening.

When *More About Boy* was published, the earlier reproductions of actual documents, advertisements and photographs from the original edition of *Boy*, as well as the line drawings and sketches by an unacknowledged artist were all included, as was Dahl's statement in the foreword that 'All is true'.[65] Blake was thoroughly familiar with Dahl's penchant for 'always tak[ing] a story in a direction that made it more interesting than in a way that made it more accurate' and was well aware from his extensive collaboration that Dahl wrote 'hybrids of true autobiography, recollections and his own imagination'.[66] So it is very fitting that *More About Boy* also included a large number of Blake's illustrations, almost entirely taken from the books on which he and Dahl had collaborated. By creating a graphic context in which both realistic and fictional elements are represented, *More About Boy* draws attention to the construction of illustrated texts, adding a strong metafictive element to the work, and commenting on the notion that fiction is an essential part of the author's processing of factual experience.[67] This is evident also in the pictures Blake was asked to provide for one of the *Roald Dahl Treasury* excerpts from *Boy*. For 'A Drive in the Motor-Car', Blake creates a couple of altogether new pictures, in colour, which are appropriate for a well-developed story rather than an unembroidered factual account.

In his illustrations of Dahl's work, Blake chooses what is 'more realistic' and what is 'more like caricature'[68] to harmonise with Dahl's style and to extend each book's impact. He expresses the delight in disorder as well as ugliness and pain, and reflects the humour and word play that Dahl employs to distance adversity and distress. His self-termed 'idiosyncratic' style works in tandem with Dahl's vision, on the one hand creating a sensitive Friendly Giant who, like a writer, catches dreams and slips them into people's minds, and, on the other, assisting Dahl's nastiest characters to disappear without regret: burned up in the sun like a sausage (*The Enormous Crocodile*); shrinking down into nothing (*George's Marvellous Medicine, The Twits*); or, like Aunts Spiker and Sponge, squashed 'flat and thin and lifeless as a couple of paper dolls cut out of a picture book' (*James and the Giant Peach*).[69] In the aesthetically remarkable drawings such as those in *The Twits*, and the serenity of those in *My Year*, Blake has captured Dahl's strong sense of the order and moral direction that lie deep in nature and defy the grotesque actions of wicked people, and has affirmed the energy and power of the human spirit working in harmony to set the world to rights.

Notes

1. Roald Dahl, *The Enormous Crocodile*, illus. Quentin Blake (New York: Alfred A. Knopf, 1978).
2. For example, Michel Simeon, Faith Jaques, Pat Marriott, Joseph Schindelman and Nancy Ekholm Burkert.
3. Quentin Blake, National Theatre Interview: http://media.nt-online.org/audio/Quentin_Blake.mp3 (accessed 9 May 2011).
4. Quentin Blake, YouTube Interview: http://youtu.be/nYeCwqueLpI (accessed 9 May 2011).
5. Quentin Blake, 'The Strange Story of the Unidentical Twins: the Patrick Hardy Lecture', *Signal* 91 (2000): 52–63, at 56.
6. Blake, National Theatre interview.
7. Blake, National Theatre interview.
8. Blake (2000): 58.
9. Roald Dahl, *The BFG*, illus. Quentin Blake (New York: Farrar, Straus and Giroux, 1982). Donald Sturrock, *Storyteller: The Life of Roald Dahl* (London: HarperPress, 2010): 527. For Dahl's delightful description of his collaboration with Blake and Blake's illustration of the two of them, see 'Creating Characters' in *The Roald Dahl Treasury* (New York: Viking, 2003): 62–3.
10. Maria Nikolajeva and Carole Scott, *How Picturebooks Work* (New York: Garland, 2001); 'From Symmetry to Counterpoint: An Aesthetic Study of Picturebooks', in Anne Mørch-Hansen (ed.), *Billedboger & Borns Billeder* (Copenhagen: Høst & Søn, 2001): 135–62.
11. Blake (2000): 58.
12. Roald Dahl, *James and the Giant Peach*, illus. Nancy Ekholm Burkert (New York: Alfred A. Knopf, 1961).
13. Roald Dahl, *James and the Giant Peach*, illus. Quentin Blake (New York: Puffin, 2007).
14. Burkert: 41, 67.
15. Blake, YouTube interview.

16. Blake, National Theatre interview.
17. Burkert: 117.
18. Roald Dahl, *Fantastic Mr Fox*, illus. Donald Chaffin (New York: Alfred A. Knopf, 1970).
19. Chaffin: 33.
20. *Ibid.*: 2, 23.
21. Roald Dahl, *Fantastic Mr. Fox*, illus. Quentin Blake (New York: Puffin, 2007).
22. *Ibid.*: 3, 4.
23. *Ibid.*: 3.
24. *Ibid.*: 7, 9.
25. Blake (2000): 59.
26. Mark I. West, *Roald Dahl* (New York: Twayne, 1992): 19.
27. *The Enormous Crocodile*: 4.
28. Lewis Carroll (Charles Dodgson), *Alice's Adventures in Wonderland & Through the Looking Glass* [1865, 1871] (New York: Signet, 2000). Carroll's continuous theme regarding death by eating is well exemplified by the song 'Turtle Soup', sung by the main ingredient, the Mock Turtle (102), and by the 'fill in the blank' poem (101) of the Owl and the Panther: 'While the Panther received knife and fork with a growl, / And concluded the banquet by -------' [eating the Owl]. And we should not forget, in this context, Carroll's poem about the crocodile who 'welcomes little fishes in / With gently smiling jaws' (28).
29. *The Enormous Crocodile*: 17, 25, 32.
30. Blake (2000): 59.
31. *The Enormous Crocodile*: 13.
32. *Ibid.*: 8.
33. *Ibid.*: 10.
34. *Ibid.*: 15.
35. *Ibid.*: 29.
36. Roald Dahl, *The Twits*, illus. Quentin Blake (New York: Puffin, 1991); *George's Marvellous Medicine*, illus. Quentin Blake (New York: Scholastic, 1997).
37. *George's Marvellous Medicine*: 2.
38. *Ibid.*: 10.
39. *The Twits*: 9.
40. *Ibid.*: 9.
41. Blake, National Theatre Interview.
42. *George's Marvellous Medicine*: 7.
43. *Ibid.*: 9.
44. *Ibid.*: 12.
45. *Ibid.*: 28.
46. *Ibid.*: 52, 53, 57.
47. *Ibid.*: 60.
48. Blake (2000): 58.
49. *The Twits*: 26, 74.

50. *The Twits*: 56–7.

51. *Ibid.*: 56.

52. *Ibid.*: 56.

53. *Ibid.*: 56.

54. For additional understanding of the implications of framing and architectural design, see Carole Scott, 'Frame-making and Frame-Breaking in Picturebooks', in Teresa Colomer, Bettina Kümmerling-Meibauer and Cecilia Silva-Diaz (eds.), *New Directions in Picturebook Research* (New York: Routledge, 2010): 101–12.

55. *The Twits*: 60–1.

56. *Ibid.*: 60.

57. Roald Dahl, *Boy* (London: Jonathan Cape, 1984). Sturrock: 75.

58. Roald Dahl, *Going Solo* (New York: Puffin, 1999).

59. Roald Dahl, *The Witches*, illus. Quentin Blake (New York: Puffin, 2007): 118.

60. Roald Dahl, *My Year*, illus. Quentin Blake (New York: Viking, 1993).

61. Roald Dahl, *Danny, the Champion of the World*, illus. Quentin Blake (New York: Alfred A. Knopf, 2002).

62. *Danny, the Champion of the World*: 330.

63. *Ibid.*: 335.

64. *Ibid.*: 339.

65. Roald Dahl, *More About Boy* (New York: Farrar, Straus and Giroux, 2009).

66. Quoted in Sturrock: 537.

67. This is strongly emphasised by the many comments included in sidebars, such as the one accompanying a picture from *Matilda*: 'This is Matron. Oops, sorry. No. It's actually Miss Trunchbull from *Matilda*. But it's very easy to get them mixed up' (*More About Boy*: 96).

68. Blake, YouTube interview.

69. *James and the Giant Peach*: 49.

10

Roald Dahl and the Commodification of Fantasy

Peter Hunt

It is not inconceivable that in 50 years' time an historian of children's books might call the 1970s and 1980s 'the Dahl moment'. Cometh the hour, cometh the man.

In 1964, when *Charlie and the Chocolate Factory* lurched its way onto the British market, childhood was still generally seen as protected space, and its literature (as always) reflected this. By the time of Dahl's death, in 1990, there had been a radical change in attitudes to childhood, and, symbiotically, its literature, and Dahl's seminal influence is still felt today. Very often, this influence is seen in the visible vulgarisation of children's books – or, at least, in broadening the range of 'acceptable' language – but his role in the commodification of fantasy and its genres is far more significant. His use of the carnivalesque and his apparent collusion with an audience constructed as subversive (in contrast with his innate conservatism) is central to this.

At the beginning of the 1960s, the dominant mode – the dominant post-war mode – was fantasy, and fantasy that took itself seriously. Far from being escapist literature, it meditated nostalgically on the vagaries of the modern world (as in Philippa Pearce's *Tom's Midnight Garden* [1958], heir to Mary Norton's 'Borrowers' sequence [from 1952] and Lucy M. Boston's 'Green Knowe' sequence [from 1954]); it considered the psychology of the fantastic (Catherine Storr, *Marianne Dreams* [1958] and Ursula le Guin, *A Wizard of Earthsea* [1968]); and it paid respectful homage to old traditions (Susan Cooper, *Over Sea, Under Stone* [1965], William Mayne, *Earthfasts* [1966]). It was 'safe', but, paradoxically, it was simultaneously challenging; it was conservative in form and cautiously radical in content; there was a tension between the nostalgic nervousness of the writers and the potential eagerness for the future of their audience. Even the mavericks, like Joan Aiken's para-history, *The Wolves of Willoughby Chase* (1962), with its fiery female hero, were totally traditional in form.

Of course, Dahl was writing for a rather broader market, and his fantasies might be better compared with those of writers like Michael Bond, whose Paddington Bear was on his sixth mildly anarchic outing in 1964 (*Paddington Marches On*), and Enid Blyton, who was approaching her 600th book, and who published the sixtieth Noddy Book (*Noddy and the Aeroplane*) and the twenty-second Mary Mouse book (*Mary Mouse and the Little Donkey*) in that year. She had published the twenty-first and last of the 'Famous Five' novels – a distinctive kind of fantasy – in 1963. Other notable books of 1964 were Jeff Brown's *Flat Stanley*, and Maurice Sendak's *Where the Wild Things Are*; and Disney's anodyne *Mary Poppins* was released.

Blyton and Dahl are often considered together in critical terms, but their approaches to their audiences, and their treatment of fantasy and its forms, were quite different. Dahl, who (some critics suggest) portrayed himself as *The BFG*, presented a persona that identified with children:

> I have a great affinity with children. I see their problems. If you want to remember what it's like to live in a child's world, you've got to get down on your hands and knees and live like that for a week. You find you have to look up at all these bloody giants around you who are always telling you what to do and what not to do ... Children absolutely warm to this. They think, 'Well, Christ! He's one of us'. I don't think you find many chaps ... in their mid-seventies who think like I do and joke and fart around.[1]

This *persona* could hardly be further from Blyton's, although they might initially seem to be similar. As Nicholas Tucker observed, 'In war-damaged Britain, fantasies at least remained off-ration ... In Blyton's books, these daydreams were carefully tended and encouraged by an author who had a unique ability to access the child within herself.'[2] (As with Dahl, this famous ability may be more self-proclaimed than actual.) But Blyton's persona was as the mother of the nation's children, and in 1949 she wrote that her books

> give children a feeling of security as well as pleasure – they know that they will never find anything wrong, hideous, horrible, murderous or vulgar in my books, although there is always plenty of excitement, mystery and fun ... I am not out only to tell stories ... I am out to inculcate decent thinking, loyalty, honesty, kindliness, and all the things that children *should* be taught.[3]

No getting on hands or knees or farting around; and no cavalier adaptations of fantasies – Blyton is the storyteller with the children at her knee, using fantasy so that, as David Rudd puts it, 'the reader is gently comforted'. That is not to say that Blyton is anodyne – as Rudd adds with reference to the 'Noddy' books, 'there is an underlying insecurity, a fear that the celebration of existence is in the face of nothingness ... that consumerism is itself a conveyor-belt that has to keep turning, or its emptiness becomes apparent.'[4] But the thrust of Blyton's work was confirmatory, designed for an audience characterised as innately civilised, whereas Dahl's was iconoclastic, at least in manner, and designed for an audience in need of civilising. Vitally, Dahl, some of whose books, notably *Matilda*, almost achieved the status of 'crossover' books, does not, like Blyton, write for an exclusively child audience.

In this context, it is hardly surprising that Dahl's particularly robust brand of fantasy has been considered rather strong meat by some critics, from Eleanor Cameron's famous attack, to David Rees's disapproval of the 'unnecessary tone of glee and spite' in the descriptions of his villains, to Michele Landsberg, who detected, as well as much else, Holocaust images and a parody of rape, and who concludes that 'hatred is not funny'.[5] Dahl's books were disliked by Judy Taylor at Gollancz, who turned down *James and the Giant Peach*, and Kaye Webb at Puffin, who was 'secretly very glad that I was resigning before they did *George's Marvellous Medicine*'. In general, parents 'were not always happy with this new literary frankness ... Children's books for adults still broadly stood for something different and better than ordinary reality – a reversion to older norms.'[6] That reversion would soon become much more difficult.

Dahl's influence went far beyond gradually extending the acceptable range of language or subject matter in children's books. He was – unlikely as it may seem for a deeply conservative ideologue – part of a postmodernist movement that fostered an ironic self-awareness in even the youngest readers, towards fantasy. He made a major contribution to changing the nature of a generation's response to fantasy, and his true legacy was the commodified and to some extent denatured children's-book fantasies of the twenty-first century.

Dahl's influence was so great partly because he turned to writing for children at a propitious moment: British children's publishing was on the upward curve of an unprecedented growth, with over 50 publishers establishing children's departments since 1945. This coincided with the growth of the science of public relations – Vance Packard's *The Hidden Persuaders* had been published in 1957. It also coincided with a cultural moment: as Carolyn Daniel suggests, the cultural conservatism (not to say implicit anti-Americanism) of *Charlie and the Chocolate Factory* 'marries with [the idea that] populist discourses about culture and taste in Britain in the 1930s–60s tended to focus on the "levelling down" of moral and aesthetic standards and the erosion of fundamentally British values …'[7]

Of course, Dahl was not alone, but his pivotal position is indisputable. For example, the year after *Revolting Rhymes* (1982), which required its readers to already know the 'straight' version of the folk and fairy tales being satirised, Tony Ross published a version of *The Three Pigs*, with the opening line: 'Pig and his two friends, Pig and Pig lived …' The folk tale mode of fantasy was becoming a commodity controlled by the audience, rather than being a mine of suggestion or a link to a wider, shared culture.

By the time Dahl died the 'moral protectionism' of childhood was rapidly being replaced, in media discourse, with the idea that 'children are no longer predominantly seen as innocent and vulnerable to influence. On the contrary, they are increasingly regarded as sophisticated, demanding, "media-wise" consumers. … The broadly "child-centred" ethos that flourished in the UK in the 1960s and 1970s is increasingly losing ground to an essentially consumerist approach.'[8] This was reflected in the change in the books. In the years around Dahl's death, notable books included Anne Fine's political treatise in fantasy form for younger children, *Bill's New Frock* (1989), Gillian Cross's ambiguous study of terrorism, *Wolf* (1990), and Salman Rushdie's *Haroun and the Sea of Stories* (1990). Kimberley Reynolds's description of that book could be a summary of Dahl's work: 'On the one hand it is dependent on and respectful of the education system and the didactic tradition; on the other, it is subversive and liberating, mocking and critiquing the values and practices of these same systems.'[9] In 1992, Jon Scieszka and Lane Smith's postmodern *The Stinky Cheese Man* pushed intertextuality to the limits, but, as Roderick McGillis notes (linking *The Stinky Cheese Man* with *Revolting Rhymes*), 'These ostensibly outrageous works just may serve to satisfy the rebellious spirit rather than activate it.'[10] In both cases the driving force behind the text is the manipulation of the child reader by the adult into a position of supposed superiority to the fantasy materials.

In the next 20 years, the 'Dahl effect' led in two directions. In terms of language use, Dahl had let the genie out of the bottle: his success gave licence to a generation of writers who use Dahl's surface characteristics – violence and vulgarity – without the essentially conservative ballast. This led inexorably to frank and jokey books about potty training, or best-sellers like William Kotzwinkle and Glenn Murray's *Walter the Farting Dog* series (2001–). More importantly, in terms of the commodification of fantasy genres, Dahl's self-conscious and ironic use (and deconstruction) of traditional materials is directly implicated in postmodern metafictions such as Lauren Child's *Who's Afraid of the Big Bad Book?* (2002) or quirky satires such as Louis Sachar's *Holes* (1998), and the adult/child films of, for example, Stephen Spielberg and the *Shrek* franchise.

Carnival and conservatism

The change in children's texts (in whatever media) over the half century since the publication of *James and the Giant Peach* (1961) has been radical, and it might be too much to claim that many of these texts would not have existed without Dahl. However, Dahl's work provided a powerful impetus, both to commercialisation and to commodification, and it is important to distinguish between the two.

The 'packaging' of Dahl in the 1980s[11] and onwards has been efficient, but no more so than that of other best-sellers. Beatrix Potter and Enid Blyton both took a keen personal interest in 'spin-offs' and marketing. But their commercialisation – and Dahl's – has long been eclipsed by the awesome scale of the promotion of Harry Potter and a dozen other worldwide brands.

Commodification underlies this process: it is the reduction of shared cultural phenomena (such as fantasy) to psychologically insignificant, saleable norms; it changes the unmanageable to the manageable; it homogenises the complex, and reduces the numinous to the packaged. It absorbs whole cultural moments into self-conscious, often symbiotic subgenres. A nineteenth-century example might be the way in which the complex matrix of capitalism, racism, and class that was imperialism was normalised through boys' fiction.[12] In the case of fantasy, commodification, as demonstrated by Dahl's cavalier use of his sources, turns the subgenres into predictable, ultimately unexciting, units of exchange.

This is often achieved through *carnival* – the *apparent* freedom given to the deprived or dependent through wild, but ultimately circumscribed, play; and this is the central trick in Dahl's writer's bag, that of *appearing* to be on the side of the child. Dahl's books appear to give children a voice, to give them that street wisdom that later writers have capitalised on. And yet his texts are essentially conservative, the epitome of the essentially repressive carnivalesque, characterised by a stylistic tendency to tell rather than show, to control (while adopting the guise and tone of a friendly confidante) rather than to allow freedom of interpretation. Equally, his views may be subversive, but they are commonly subversive of the modern world: *Charlie and the Chocolate Factory*, apart from its well-known attacks on television and chewing gum, satirises bigger issues. As Rashna Singh suggests, perhaps a little contentiously, 'Dahl's deliberate – in fact, transparent – reiteration of stock images and stereotypes points to satire. The system of "guest" workers and the exploitation of immigrant labour in an industrial, capitalist context is what's being satirised. Although *Charlie and the Chocolate Factory* was published well before the era of rampant globalisation it anticipates and disparages its excess.'[13] When it was pointed out to Dahl that his authoritarian self should disapprove of his own books, he agreed: 'It's a tightrope act.'[14]

Consequently, Dahl's satire co-opts the child reader into a conservative ideology. As Jack Zipes has observed, 'Paradoxically the freedom taken by young people ... to articulate their opposition to homogenization is often ... co-opted by the hegemonic culture industry to represent and rationalize a false freedom of choice.'[15] 'Carnival' again. However, Zipes also places faith in the one thing that Dahl appropriated: fantasy. He feels that fantasy is resistant to this 'criminal' tendency to bring individuality 'into line so that our socio-economic system runs smoothly ... Fantasy matters because it can enable us to resist such criminality, and it can do so with irony, joy, sophistication, seriousness, and cunning.'[16] Similarly, Marina Warner concluded that towards the end of the twentieth century,

> there has been a strongly marked shift towards fantasy as a mode of understanding, as an ingredient in survival, as a lever against the worst aspects of the status quo and the direction it is going.
>
> Many characteristics of fairy tale as a tradition have contributed to this change ... the stories' fallaciousness, the very quality that inspired scorn, makes them potential conduits of another way of seeing the world, of telling an alternative story.[17]

Similarly, T. E. Apter suggests that 'the initial impact of fantasy is its deviation from the norm. [Even more fascinating] is the way in which it highlights the instability, inconsistency or underlying preposterousness of the normal.'[18]

In the hands of Dahl and his successors, it can be argued (despite all this optimism) that the opposite has occurred – fantasy has become normalised, absorbed into the status quo. It colludes with the idea of normalcy, rather than subverting it. Thus, if fantasy has been regarded as inherently liberating and mind-expanding, Dahl simplified and homogenised these tales on the surface, in the service of a satirical and disruptive subtext. Unlike Blyton, who produced a fantasy world based on a fantasy world (the middle-class fantasy) which, with her persona of the morally protective makes her world triply safe, he used the fantasy in a frame of an unsafe modern world: and the only way to cope with that was to commodify fantasy. And Dahl makes his point clearly, at the beginning of *The Witches*:

> In fairy-tales, witches always wear silly black hats and black cloaks, and they ride on broomsticks.
> But this is not a fairy-tale. This is about REAL LIFE.[19]

When, of course, it is not. It is part of a shared game of superior knowledge.

Consequently, while advocates of fantasy may feel that 'Fantasy texts fill a gap left by the contemporary marginalization of religion ... [constructing] alternative realities whose systems of meaning offer spiritual guidance without demanding allegiance', or that 'The continued need for monstrous revelations from the literary fantastic is disturbingly guaranteed',[20] commodification ensures that the engagement with fantasy will be rather different than it was 50 years ago.

One of the difficulties of Dahl criticism is the success with which Dahl has persuaded commentators to accept his stated position at face value, that he is, as Peter Hollindale noted, 'both the conscious inheritor of a tradition and a respectful iconoclast in his dealings with it'.[21] Similarly, Margaret and Michael Rustin in *Narratives of Love and Loss* take it as read that Dahl achieved 'a huge appeal by writing against this polite grain, allowing space for the unsocial and tabooed impulses of childhood, saying out loud what children might say out of the presence of adults'.[22] Dahl encouraged this idea: 'Children know that the violence in my stories is only make-believe. It's much like the violence in the old fairy-tales ... These tales are pretty rough, but the violence is confined to a magical time and place ...'[23] Except – again – of course, that it is not. The real world is always present. Peter Hollindale takes the view that Dahl is best read as a satirist – Swift for the twentieth century – and that 'somewhere behind Dahl's work is an implicit model of adult sanity, coupled with ceaseless misanthropic anger at humankind's perpetual betrayal of it'.[24] Dahl's 'real' world may be not quite real, but it relates in a deeply disturbing way to both reality and the modes of fantasy that it co-opts.

Sources and techniques

Dahl was a literary magpie, making use of both surface and deep structures from the cultural myth-kitty: that is, both genres (folk and fairy tales, evangelical stories) and the larger patterns behind them – love, revenge, resolution and so on. His first books were defended on the grounds that this was a good thing. Anne Merrick saw *Charlie and the Chocolate Factory* as composed of 'fairy tale and nursery rhyme ... [with their] robust, folk-qualities ...' Alasdair Campbell, in reply to Eleanor Cameron, wrote: 'I would see *Charlie* as an amoral fairy tale in a modern idiom, belonging to a tradition in which violence and ruthless punishments are taken for granted, and where deliberate stereotyping is a valid technique.' Similarly, the prestigious *Kirkus Reviews* saw *James and the Giant Peach* as 'broad fantasy with all the gruesome imagery of old-fashioned fairy tales and a good measure of their breathtaking delight'.[25] Dahl played with folk tale conventions (and used their more brutal characteristics), for example, at the end of *The Witches*: the boy remains as mouse, a device which has been seen as 'fulfilling the child protagonist's regressive wishes, as well as preserving adult authority'.[26] What he produced was seen as ambiguous: for example, '*Fantastic Mr Fox* marries the character and satire of Aesop with Dahl's uniquely *grotesque misanthropy* to produce a *playful fable* about a kind of "progress" that has brought little but greed, vindictiveness and natural devastation.'[27]

Charlie and the Chocolate Factory is clearly a nineteenth-century morality tale/satire in the mould of *Struwwelpeter*; in *The Witches*, as Hollindale points out, Dahl is working in the tradition of Sarah Trimmer and Anna Sewell: 'here as in so many ways he is a highly traditional writer working themes afresh for a taboo-breaking age'.[28] Similarly, the description of Mrs Twit in *The Twits* – 'If a person has ugly thoughts, it begins to show on the face. And when that person has ugly thoughts every day, every week, every year, the face gets uglier until it gets so ugly you can hardly bear to look at it'[29] – is very close to another opinionated fantasy, Kingsley's *The Water Babies* (Chapter 6).

Most obviously, Dahl's *Revolting Rhymes* – which he regarded as a *jeu d'esprit* – turn traditional tales into texts that the reader dominates rather than the other way around. Again, there is nothing new in this: the folk and fairy tale had been fair game for satirists for years. Notable examples are Archibald Marshall, whose *Simple Stories*, rich with anachronisms, appeared in *Punch* between 1926 and 1934, and James Thurber's 'The Little Girl and the Wolf' (to which Dahl's 'Little

Red Riding Hood' bears more than a passing resemblance) in *Fables for Our Time* (1940):

> When the little girl opened the door of her grandmother's house she saw that there was somebody in bed with a nightcap and nightgown on. She had approached no nearer than twenty-five feet from the bed when she saw that it was not her grandmother but the wolf, for even in a nightcap a wolf does not look any more like your grandmother than the Metro-Goldwyn lion looks like Calvin Coolidge. So the little girl took an automatic out of her basket and shot the wolf dead.

> (Moral: It is not so easy to fool little girls nowadays as it used to be.)[30]

But Dahl was not a satirist of the literary *forms* that he used, as savage as the satire embedded in them might be. Rather, he consciously took over the larger patterns of fantasy: revenge, the triumph of the underdog, the humiliation of the enemy. Thus the ending of *James and the Giant Peach* is the ending of a thousand nineteenth-century fantasies: 'James Henry Trotter, who once, if you remember, had been the saddest and loneliest little boy you could find, now had all the friends and playmates in the world',[31] but its effect relies on collusion with the audience: the reader recognises the artificiality and, with that, fantasy is tamed – commodified.

Dahl's techniques can be seen at their most transparent in *Matilda*, which, as Treglown points out, was essentially no more than a second draft.[32] Like Dahl's other books, it is an amalgam of tropes from fantasy, folk tale and fairy tale. Dieter Petzold, in 'Wish-fulfilment and Subversion: Roald Dahl's Dickensian Fantasy *Matilda*', thinks that Dahl's 'trick of combining realism and satire with a fairy-tale deep structure ... can be traced back to Dickens'. An early review described it as having 'all the elements of the true fairytale which delight children, but which often worry adults.... magic ... gross violence ... child-inflicted retribution ... no well-rounded, three-dimensional characters'.[33] It is, indeed, a double Cinderella story of – or for – our times.

Matilda herself is clearly a Cinderella figure, but in this version Dahl smoothes out any ambiguities. Matilda, for example, is at no point the uncertain, downtrodden girl of Perrault's tale, who was 'gentle and sweet-natured, taking after her mother' and suffered her ill treatment 'patiently'. When her sisters make fun of her while she is combing their hair to go to the ball, 'anyone else but Cinderella would have tangled their hair, but she was good, and she did it to perfection'. And when all is revealed, she 'forgave them with all her heart, and asked them to love her always'.[34] Matilda she is not: the complexity of the tale, albeit slight, is subordinated, commodified, into a simple and simply motivated character, just as the idea of 'goodness' (previously entangled with self–immolation and repression) is equated with power and success.

The second Cinderella in the book, much more in the traditional mould, is Miss Honey: in her story, Miss Trunchbull is the wicked stepmother, ugly sister and all–purpose ogre rolled into one misogynistically drawn monster. True to the folk tale tradition, there is no subtlety of character – but that does not mean that there is no ambiguity, or no appropriation of these fairy tale elements. Dahl appropriates (and therefore commodifies) the structures of fantasy embedded in *Matilda* through his basic stylistic devices.

Firstly, there is his tendency to tell rather than show: to indicate clearly where his sympathies lie and, consequently, where his audience's should lie; in itself, this contradicts the idea that the reader is empowered. Thus we have phrases such as, 'Dickens the great story teller', or 'Miss Honey, in a rather wonderful slow voice, began reciting the poem.'[35] As Barbara Wall notes, 'The narrator seizes hold of the narratee and demands a response, as if he fears that the narrative itself lacks the power to do so.'[36] Even when he is using 'mind style' (or 'free indirect discourse'), where it is not clear whether we are reading the character's thought or the author's comment, he weights the scales: here are some examples from *Matilda*:

> Miss Honey was astounded by the wisdom of this tiny girl.

> Miss Honey marvelled at the child's lack of conceit and self-consciousness.

> There was a moment of silence, and Matilda, who had never before heard great romantic poetry spoken aloud, was profoundly moved.

> These not–quite–so–innocent questions.[37]

The freedom of the reader is immediately restricted: the author is prescribing (or proscribing) thought, the first step towards the commodification of the underlying materials.

Secondly, Dahl (as always) lets his prejudices and predilections show, notably in Matilda's reading list, and her parents' taste for 'awful fried fish and chips' and eating their evening meals in front of the television – even at the expense of taking his eye off the ostensible audience for an over–their–heads joke: '"Mr Hemingway says a lot of things I don't understand," Matilda said ... "Especially about men and woman"', or

an adult viewpoint, as in Mrs Wormwood's thoughts about her discom-
fited husband: 'Hardly the kind of man a wife dreams about, she told
herself'.[38] The fact that Dahl (for all his child-friendly reputation) is
aiming for what Barbara Wall has called the 'double address' – children
and adults separately within the same text[39] – suggests the degree of
control that he was exercising. The fantasy materials (whether or not
derived directly from fairy tale forms), therefore, are being harnessed to
specific ideologies and these devices are conditions for the appropriation and commodification of tales. This can be made quite explicit: Miss
Honey's house, prefaced by Dylan Thomas's sexually loaded 'In Country
Sleep', is 'like an illustration in Grimm or Hans Andersen. ... It was
straight out of a fairy-tale'.[40]

Fantasy, then, for Dahl, is something we share as *apparent* equals,
although he seems to share J. R. R. Tolkien's memorable view of fairy
stories: 'they have been relegated to the "nursery", as shabby or old-
fashioned furniture is relegated to the play-room, primarily because
the adults do not want it, and do not mind if is misused ... Children as
a class ... neither like fairy-stories more, nor understand them better
than adults do.'[41] And so Dahl takes these forms that are in many ways
alien to children, and makes them part of the world that children
can manipulate, rather than a part of the adult world that manipu-
lates *them*. In doing so, he makes them *manageable* and he makes the
fears and emotions that reside in fantasy manageable as well. Thus, in
apparently colluding with the child, fantasy and its various forms are
commodified and packaged, and its dangerous dynamics defused.

The Dahl effect

This commodification, together with the perfection of the art of
commercialisation, has led from *James and the Giant Peach* to the
double-audience norm of twenty-first-century books and films. The
opening of DreamWorks' *Shrek*, which references not merely a fairy
tale, but the Disney version of the fairy tale, assumes just the kind
of insider knowledge that Dahl assumed: it also implies the impo-
tency of that kind of fantasy. The common assumption now is that
audiences know the limitations of fantasy at more than a generic
level, and therefore it has lost much of its potency. It is not simply,
as Marina Warner put it, that 'the Spielberg type of films ... are ...
built on a kind of duplicitous flattery of the child'. This, she observes,
'is just compensatory fantasy'.[42] While that may be true of Dahl, the
readers that he helped to create are readers for whom stories can be
manipulated by themselves on the computer; readers who can choose

or invent endings; and ultimately, readers who are 'insiders' to fiction and fantasy – readers for whom there are not monsters under the bed, but phobias. At its best, perhaps, this has led to a wry self-awareness, epitomised by Terry Pratchett in *Only You Can Save Mankind* (1993). His hero, Johnny, explains to his friends that he has entered a computer game: the response is post-Dahlian:

> 'Well … your mum and dad are splitting up, right? … So you project your … suppressed emotions on to a computer game. Happens all the time … You can't solve the *real* problems, so you turn them into problems you *can* solve. Like … if this was thirty years ago, you'd probably dream about fighting dragons or something. It's a projected fantasy.'[43]

Such self-awareness could be seen as signalling the beginning of the end of fantasy as it was previously understood – and may well signal the death of more vulnerable genres – just as Sergio Leone's caricatures effectively marked the beginning of the end of the genre of the film western. We are accustomed to a godless universe: can humans cope with a fantasy-less universe?

The importance of Dahl in this seismic shift in fantasy and children's books, where fantasy and its forms have been commodified, seems irrefutable. His writing, his philosophy of writing for children, the marketing of his books (and his personality) were a perfect storm in terms of changing the culture. Cometh the hour, cometh the man.

Notes

1. Christopher Sykes, 'In the Lair of the BFG', *Harpers and Queen* (October 1991): 80–5, at 82.
2. Nicholas Tucker, 'Introduction', in Nicholas Tucker and Kimberley Reynolds (eds), *Enid Blyton: A Celebration and Reappraisal* (London: NCRCL, 1997): vii–xix, xi.
3. Quoted in Barbara Stoney, *Enid Blyton: A Biography*, rev. edn (London: Hodder and Stoughton, 1992): 212.
4. David Rudd, *Enid Blyton and the Mystery of Children's Literature* (Basingstoke: Macmillan Press, 2000): 87.
5. Eleanor Cameron, 'McLuhan Youth and Literature', *The Horn-Book* (October 1972): 433–40; David Rees, *What Do Draculas Do? Essays on Contemporary Writers of Fiction for Children and Young Adults* (Metuchen, NJ: Scarecrow, 1990): 192; Michele Landsberg, *The World of Children's Books* (London: Simon and Schuster, 1998): 90.
6. Kimberley Reynolds and Nicholas Tucker, *Children's Book Publishing in Britain Since 1945* (Aldershot: Scholar Press, 1998): 14, 16.

7. Carolyn Daniel, *Voracious Children. Who Eats Whom in Children's Literature* (London and New York: Routledge, 2006): 191.

8. David Buckingham, 'Multimedia Childhoods', in Mary Jane Kehily and Joan Swann (eds), *Children's Cultural Worlds* (Chichester: John Wiley and the Open University, 2003): 183–228, at 204.

9. Kimberley Reynolds, *Radical Children's Literature* (Basingstoke: Palgrave Macmillan, 2007): 64.

10. Roderick McGillis, 'Humour and the Body in Children's Literature', in M. O. Grenby and Andrea Immel (eds), *The Cambridge Companion to Children's Literature* (Cambridge: Cambridge University Press, 2009): 258–71, at 267.

11. Jeremy Treglown, *Roald Dahl* (London: Faber and Faber, 1994): 230.

12. Ymitri Mathison, 'Maps, Pirates and Treasure: the Commodification of Imperialism in Nineteenth-Century Boys' Adventure Fiction', in Dennis Denisoff (ed.), *The Nineteenth-Century Child and Consumer Culture* (Aldershot: Ashgate, 2008): 173–85.

13. Rashna B. Singh, *Goodly Is Our Heritage. Children's Literature, Empire, and the Certitude of Character* (Lanham, MD: Scarecrow, 2004): 104.

14. Treglown: 249.

15. Jack Zipes, *Sticks and Stones. The Troublesome Success of Children's Literature from Slovenly Peter to Harry Potter* (New York: Routledge, 2001): 4.

16. Jack Zipes, *Relentless Progress. The Reconfiguration of Children's Literature, Fairy Tales, and Storytelling* (New York: Routledge, 2009): 67.

17. Marina Warner, *From the Beast to the Blonde* (London: Chatto and Windus, 1994): 415.

18. T. E. Apter, *Fantasy Literature: an Approach to Reality* (London: Macmillan, 1982): 111.

19. Roald Dahl, *The Witches* (London: Cape, 1983): 7.

20. Melody Briggs and Richard S. Briggs, 'Stepping into the Gap: Contemporary Children's Fantasy Literature as a Doorway to Spirituality', in Justyna Deszcz-Tryhubczak and Marek Oziewicz (eds), *Towards or Back to Human Values? Spiritual and Moral Dimensions of Contemporary Fantasy* (Newcastle: Cambridge Scholars Press, 2006): 30–47, at 43; Neil Cornwall, *The Literary Fantastic. From Gothic to Postmodernism* (Hempstead: Harvester Wheatsheaf, 1990): 218.

21. Peter Hollindale, '"And Children Swarmed to Him Like Settlers. He Became a Land." The Outrageous Success of Roald Dahl', in Julia Briggs, Dennis Butts and M. O. Grenby (eds), *Popular Children's Literature in Britain* (Aldershot: Ashgate, 2008): 271–86, at 274.

22. Margaret Rustin and Michael Rustin, *Narratives of Love and Loss: Studies in Modern Children's Fiction* (London and New York: Verso/Karnac, 1987/2001): 22.

23. Mark West, *Trust Your Children. Voices Against Censorship in Children's Literature* (New York: Neal Schuman, 1988): 75.

24. Peter Hollindale, 'Roald Dahl: the Conservative Anarchist', in Pat Pinsent, *Pop Fiction* (London: NCRCL, 1999): 137–51, at 144.

25. Anne Merrick, '*The Nightwatchmen* and *Charlie and the Chocolate Factory* as Books to be Read to Children', *Children's Literature in Education* 16 (1975): 21–30, at 30; Alasdair Campbell, *School Librarian* (June 1981), quoted in Mark West, *Roald Dahl* (Boston: Twayne, 1992): 72; *Kirkus Reviews* (15 August 1961): 727, quoted in West (1992): 65.

26. Maria Lassén-Seger, 'The Fictive Child in Disguise: Disempowering Transformations of the Child Character', in Jean Webb (ed.), *Text, Culture and National Identity in Children's Literature* (Helsinki: NORDINFO, 2000): 186–96, at 186.

27. M. O. Grenby, *Children's Literature* (Edinburgh: Edinburgh University Press, 2008): 20 (my italics).

28. Hollindale (2008): 46.

29. Roald Dahl, *The Twits* (Harmondsworth: Penguin, 1982): 15.

30. James Thurber, *A Web Collection*: www.bigeye.com/thurber.htm (accessed 2 May 2012).

31. Roald Dahl, *James and the Giant Peach* [1961] (London: George Allen and Unwin, 1967): 111.

32. Treglown: 245.

33. Dieter Petzold, 'Wish-fulfilment and Subversion: Roald Dahl's Dickensian Fantasy *Matilda*', *Children's Literature in Education* 23(4) (1992): 185–93, at 186–7; Stephanie Owen Reeder, 'Review of *Matilda*', *Magpies* 3(3) (1988): 4.

34. Neil Philip, *The Cinderella Story* (London: Penguin, 1989): 10, 11, 14.

35. Roald Dahl, *Matilda* (London: Penguin, 1989): 16, 184.

36. Barbara Wall, *The Narrator's Voice. The Dilemma of Children's Fiction* (London: Macmillan, 1991): 17.

37. *Matilda*: 81, 185, 194.

38. *Ibid.*: 56, 49, 18, 35.

39. Wall: 35.

40. *Matilda*: 186.

41. J. R. R. Tolkien, *Tree and Leaf* (London: Unwin Books, 1964): 34.

42. Quoted in Duncan Petrie (ed.), *Cinema and the Realms of Enchantment* (London: Corgi, 1993): 50, 51.

43. Terry Pratchett, *Only You Can Save Mankind* (London: BFI, 1993): 27–8.

Further Reading

Considering Roald Dahl's popularity and productivity as an author for both children and adults, surprisingly little critical material concerning his work is in circulation. Consequently, this section groups together a diverse range of sources that are useful to consider alongside Dahl's work. Some contain direct references to his books; others discuss more general issues in children's literature or a critical approach which those studying his work have found useful.

Biographical sources

The Roald Dahl Museum and Story Centre in Great Missenden, Dahl's home for over 30 years, provides access to numerous letters, photographs and writings. The website is useful for an initial browse: www.roalddahlmuseum. org/archives/default.aspx. The museum is also happy to accommodate researchers if they make contact beforehand.

Of course, Roald Dahl's own *Boy* and *Going Solo* give some autobiographical insight into the author despite his claim in *Boy* that 'This is not an autobiography. I would never write a history of myself. On the other hand, throughout my young days at school and just afterwards a number of things happened to me that I have never forgotten.' Alongside these two autobiographical accounts rest other well-thumbed biographies and interviews and accounts of Dahl. Michael Rosen's biography of Roald Dahl, *Fantastic Mr Dahl*, is due to appear in 2012.

Biography

Carrick, Robert. 'Roald Dahl'. In *Dictionary of Literary Biography*, ed. Darren Harris-Fain, 37–47. Vol. 255. Detroit: Gale, 2002.

Dahl, Roald. *Boy Tales of Childhood* [1984]. Harmondsworth: Penguin, 1986.

Dahl, Roald. *Going Solo* [1986]. London: Penguin, 1999.

Nicholson, Catriona. 'Dahl, The Marvellous Boy'. In *A Necessary Fantasy? The Heroic Figure in Children's Popular Fiction*, ed. Dudley Jones and Tony Watkins, 309–26. New York and London: Routledge, 2000.

Sturrock, Donald. *Storyteller: The Life of Roald Dahl*. London: Harper Press, 2010.

Treglown, Jeremy. 'The Height of Fancy'. *The Guardian*, 9 September 2006: www.guardian.co.uk/books/2006/sep/09/roalddahl.fiction (accessed 2 October 2010).

Treglown, Jeremy. *Roald Dahl: A Biography*. London: Faber, 1994.

West, Mark I. 'Interview with Roald Dahl'. *Children's Literature in Education* 21(2) (1990): 61–6.
West, Mark I. *Roald Dahl*. New York: Twayne, 1992.

The relationship between Dahl and Quentin Blake

Blake, Quentin. National Theatre Interview. Podcast: http://media.nt-online. org/audio/Quentin_Blake.mp3
Blake, Quentin. "The Strange Story of the Unidentical Twins: the Patrick Hardy Lecture." *Signal* 91 (2000): 52–63.
Blake, Quentin. YouTube Interview: http://youtu.be/nYeCwqueLpI

Suitability

Much ink has been spilt over the suitability of Dahl's work for a child reader-ship. There has been a violent debate concerning whether his work is right-wing, misogynist and racist, and whether its violence and carnivalesque tone are what make it at once appealing to and 'unsuitable' for children – therein lies much of the dilemma of both Dahl and children's fiction more gener-ally. While Mark West has been quick to defend Dahl, David Rees, Dieter Petzold and Eleanor Cameron have been scathing.

Appleyard, J. A. *Becoming a Reader: The Experience of Fiction from Childhood to Adulthood*. Cambridge: Cambridge University Press, 1990.
Bergson-Shilcock, Amanda. 'The Subversive Quality of Respect: In Defense of *The Witches*'. In *Censored Books II: Critical Viewpoints, 1985–2000*, ed. Nicholas Karolides, 446–51. Lanham, MD: Scarecrow Press, 2002.
Bouchard, Lois Kalb. 'Charlie and the Chocolate Factory: A New Look at an Old Favourite'. In *Racism and Sexism in Children's Books*, ed. Judith Stinton, 41–4. London: Writers and Readers, 1979.
Cameron, Eleanor. 'McLuhan, Youth, and Literature'. In *Crosscurrents of Criticism, Horn Book Essays 1968–1977*, ed. Paul Heins. Boston: Horn Book, 1977.
Cameron, Eleanor. 'A Question of Taste,' *The School Librarian* 29(2) (1981): 108–14.
Crouch, Marcus and Alec Ellis. *Chosen for Children*. London: The Library Association, 1977.
Culley, Jonathon. 'Roald Dahl – "It's About Children and It's for Children" – But Is It Suitable?' *Children's Literature in Education* 22(1) (1991): 59–73.
Cullingford, Cedric. 'The Exuberant Incorrectness of Dahl'. In *Children's Literature and Its Effects: The Formative Years*, 153–66. London: Cassell, 1998.
Donaldson, Eileen. 'Spell-Binding Dahl: Considering Roald Dahl's Fantasy'. In *Change and Renewal in Children's Literature*, ed. Thomas Van der Walt, 131–40. Westport: Praeger, 2004.

Hall, Christine and Martin Coles. *Children's Reading Choices*. London and New York: Routledge, 1999.

Hollindale, Peter. 'Roald Dahl: the Conservative Anarchist'. In *Pop Fiction*, ed. Pat Pinsent, 137–51. London: NCRCL, 1999.

Hollindale, Peter. '"And Children Swarmed to Him Like Settlers. He Became a Land": The Outrageous Success of Roald Dahl'. In *Popular Children's Literature in Britain*, ed. Julia Briggs, Dennis Butts and M. O. Grenby, 271–86. London: Ashgate, 2008.

Krull, Kathleen. 'Revisiting Eleanor, Marshall, and Roald; or, Having a Sense of Humor in the Millennium'. *Horn Book Magazine* 75(5) (1999): 564–71.

Landsberg, Michele. *The World of Children's Books: A Guide to Choosing the Best*. New York: Simon & Schuster, 1988.

Maynard, Sally and Cliff McKnight. 'Author Popularity: An Exploratory Study Based on Roald Dahl'. *New Review of Children's Literature and Librarianship* 8(1) (2002): 153–75.

Merrick, Anne. '*The Nightwatchmen* and *Charlie and the Chocolate Factory* as Books to be Read to Children'. *Children's Literature in Education* 16 (1975): 21–30.

Petzold, Dieter. 'Wish Fulfilment and Subversion in Roald Dahl's Dickensian Fantasy *Matilda*'. *Children's Literature in Education* 23(4) (1992): 185–93.

Rees, David. 'Dahl's Chickens: Roald Dahl'. *Children's Literature in Education* 19(3) (1988): 143–55.

Royer, Sharon E. 'Roald Dahl and Sociology 101'. *The ALAN Review* 26(1) (Fall 1998).

Sarland, Charles. '*The Secret Seven* versus *The Twits*: Cultural Clash or Cosy Combination?' *Signal* 42 (1983): 155–71.

Talbot, Margaret. 'The Candy Man: Why Children Love Roald Dahl's Stories and Many Adults Don't'. *New Yorker*, 11 July 2005: 92.

Viñas Valle, Laura. 'The Narrative Voice in Roald Dahl's Children's and Adult Books'. *Didáctica. Lengua y Literatura* 20 (2008): 291–308.

West, Mark. 'The Grotesque and the Taboo in Roald Dahl's Humorous Writings for Children'. *Children's Literature Association Quarterly* 15(3) (1990): 115–16.

West, Mark, ed. *Trust Your Children: Voices Against Censorship in Children's Literature*. New York: Neal-Schuman, 1988.

Yu, Chen-Wei. 'Power and Its Mechanics in Children's Fiction: the Case of Roald Dahl'. *International Research in Children's Literature* 1 (2008): 155–67.

Gender

While Kristen Guest, Anne-Marie Bird, Peter E. Cummings and Catherine Itzin's texts are specifically focused on Dahl and gender, the other texts in this section give a brief insight into the topic generally in children's fiction. It is worth noting that Cummings' and Bird's texts could equally be classified under film as both make considerable use of the adaptations.

Bird, Anne-Marie. 'Women Behaving Badly: Dahl's Witches Meet the Women of the Eighties'. *Children's Literature in Education* 29(3) (1998): 119–29.

Cumming, Peter E. '"The Cigar Was Essential": Contestations of Power in Roald Dahl's *Matilda*'. In *To See the Wizard: Politics and the Literature of Childhood*, ed. Laurie Ousley, 87–108. Newcastle: Cambridge Scholars Publishing, 2007.

Davies, Bronwyn. *Frogs and Snails and Feminist Tales: Pre-school Children and Gender*. Sydney: Allen and Unwin, 1989.

Guest, Kristen. 'The Good, the Bad and the Ugly: Resistance and Complicity in *Matilda*'. *Children's Literature Association Quarterly* 33(3) (2008): 246–58.

Itzin, Catherine. 'Bewitching the Boys'. *Times Educational Supplement*, 27 December 1985: 13.

Paul, Lisa. *Reading Otherways*. Stroud: Thimble, 1998.

Pennell, Beverley. 'Redeeming Masculinity at the End of the Second Millennium: Narrative Reconfigurations of Masculinity in Children's Fictions'. In *Ways of Being Male*, ed. John Stephens, 55–77. London: Routledge, 2002.

Fairy tale tradition

While Dahl is often viewed as a modern author, he also owes a considerable debt to the fairy tale tradition and the nineteenth-century cautionary tale. The following list again offers a few articles that are specific to Dahl's work in this area and a more general introduction to the fairy tale genre. Linked with the fairy tale and cautionary tale is the Gothic, hence the inclusion of Julie Cross's work here. Hope Hodgkins' work in particular draws interesting links between Dahl and Oscar Wilde, as both authors and men, and gives a fascinating critical insight into how they both play with language and tradition. While Robert Kachur's article is not specifically related to fairy tales it is included here because of the insightful way in which it draws parallels between *Charlie and the Chocolate Factory* and the Bible, arguing that it is a conservative text based largely on the Fall.

Cross, Julie. 'Frightening and Funny: Humour in Children's Gothic Fiction'. In *The Gothic in Children's Literature: Haunting the Borders*, ed. Anna Jackson, Karen Coats and Roderick McGillis, 57–76. New York: Routledge, 2008.

David, Furniss. 'Keeping Their Parents Happy: Roald Dahl's *Revolting Rhymes*'. In *Censored Books II: Critical Viewpoints, 1985–2000*, ed. Nicholas Karolides, 351–6. Lanham, MD: Scarecrow Press, 2002.

Hodgkins, Hope Howell. 'White Blossoms and Snozzcumbers: Alternative Sentiments in the Giants of Oscar Wilde and Roald Dahl'. *Critic* 65(1) (2002): 41–9.

Kachur, Robert M. 'A Consuming Tradition: Candy and Socio-religious Identity Formation in Roald Dahl's *Charlie and the Chocolate Factory*'. In *Critical Approaches to Food in Children's Literature*, ed. Kara K. Keeling and Scott T. Pollard, 221–34. New York: Routledge, 2009.

Stephens, John and Robyn McCallum. *Retelling Stories, Framing Culture: Traditional Story and Metanarratives in Children's Literature*. New York and London: Routledge, 1998.

Tatar, Maria. *Off With Their Heads: Fairy Tale and the Culture of Childhood*. Princeton: Princeton University Press, 1992.

Tatar, Maria. '"Violent Delights" in Children's Literature'. In *Why We Watch: The Attractions of Violent Entertainment*, ed. Jeffrey H. Goldstein, 69–87. Oxford: Oxford University Press, 1998.

Warner, Marina. *From the Beast to the Blonde*. London: Chatto and Windus, 1994.

Zipes, Jack. *Fairy Tales and the Art of Subversion*. New York: Routledge, 1991.

Zipes, Jack. *Breaking the Magic Spell*. Lexington: University Press of Kentucky, 2002.

Film adaptations

With seven of Dahl's most famous texts having been adapted for film there has been some critical attention directed towards this medium. It is worth noting that Anne-Marie Bird's and Peter E. Cummings' insightful essays, categorised above under gender, could equally be placed in this section.

Cartmell, Deborah. 'Screen Classics'. In *Children's Literature. Approaches and Territories*, ed. Janet Maydin and Nicola J. Watson, 281–95. Basingstoke: Palgrave Macmillan, 2010.

Kertzer, Adrienne. 'Fidelity, Felicity, and Playing Around in Wes Anderson's *Fantastic Mr. Fox*'. In *Children's Literature Association Quarterly* 36(1) (2011): 4–24.

Parsons, Elizabeth. 'Buckets of Money: Tim Burton's New *Charlie and the Chocolate Factory*'. In *Fantasy Fiction into Film: Essays*, ed. Leslie Stratyner and James R. Keller, 93–102. Jefferson, NC: McFarland, 2007.

Pulliam, June. 'Charlie's Evolving Moral Universe: Filmic Interpretations of Roald Dahl's *Charlie and the Chocolate Factory*'. In *Fantasy Fiction into Film: Essays*, ed. Leslie Stratyner and James R. Keller, 103–14. Jefferson, NC: McFarland, 2007.

Psychoanalytical readings

Dahl, with his interest in bodies and the grotesque, lends his work to Freudian and other psychoanalytical readings. With these texts we see a specific focus on power, the body and the child's move towards adulthood.

Hamida, Bosmajian. '*Charlie and the Chocolate Factory* and Other Excremental Visions'. *The Lion and the Unicorn* 9 (1985): 36–49.

West, Mark I. 'Regression and the Fragmentation of the Self in *James and the Giant Peach*'. In *Psychoanalytical Responses to Children's Literature*, ed. Lucy Rollin and Mark I. West, 17–29. Jefferson, NC: McFarland, 1999.

Index